US Politics and
Generation Y

US Politics and Generation Y

Engaging the Millennials

David Rankin

LYNNE
RIENNER
PUBLISHERS

BOULDER
LONDON

Published in the United States of America in 2013 by
Lynne Rienner Publishers, Inc.
1800 30th Street, Boulder, Colorado 80301
www.rienner.com

and in the United Kingdom by
Lynne Rienner Publishers, Inc.
3 Henrietta Street, Covent Garden, London WC2E 8LU

Library of Congress Cataloging-in-Publication Data
Rankin, David M.
  US politics and generation Y : engaging the millennials / David Rankin.
    p. cm.
  Includes bibliographical references and index.
  ISBN 978-1-58826-879-2 (alk. paper)
  1. Generation Y—United States. 2. College students—Political activity—
United States. I. Title. II. Title: United States politics and generation Y.
  HQ799.7.R36 2012
  305.2—dc23

                                                    2012031436

British Cataloguing in Publication Data
A Cataloguing in Publication record for this book
is available from the British Library.

Printed and bound in the United States of America

       The paper used in this publication meets the requirements
  ∞   of the American National Standard for Permanence of
       Paper for Printed Library Materials Z39.48-1992.

  5 4 3 2 1

Contents

Illustrations

Tables

Figures

1

The Millennial Generation
and US Politics

Politics is only as good as the people willing to participate.
—*Presidential candidate George W. Bush, 2000*

Yes we can. —*Presidential candidate Barack Obama, 2008*

"I've been looking [forward to this inaugural] ball for quite some time because when you look at the history of this campaign, what started out as an improbable journey, when no one gave us a chance, was carried forward, was inspired by, was driven by, young people all across America." These were the words of the nation's newly inaugurated president, Barack Obama, as he spoke to a beaming young crowd gathered at the MTV inaugural ball. It was a historic night for the United States, but a particularly profound night for the youth vote that had turned out in droves to support Obama's candidacy.

The 44th US president's words were punctuated by joyous cheers and chants of "yes we can," a central slogan of the Obama campaign. President Obama chuckled along with the boisterous enthusiasm of the memorable scene and continued his thoughts. "I can't tell you how many people have come up to Michelle and myself about how their daughter, she wouldn't budge, she just told me I need to vote for Obama. Or suddenly I saw my son, he was out volunteering and traveling and knocking on doors and getting involved like never before. And so a new generation inspired a previous generation and that's how change happens in America."

As the nation's 47-year-old president and the first lady danced to Etta James's "At Last," in a style he referred to as old school, a glowing sea of cell phone cameras captured this new millennial moment. It was the culmination of a pathbreaking campaign in which the emergence of

1

the so-called Millennial Generation played a critical role in shaping the future of US politics.

It would have been hard to conceive of this moment as we entered the new millennium. After the Y2K scare had worn off and with the Clinton-Lewinsky scandal a fading memory, a new generation of students entered college campuses facing the first election of the twenty-first century or perhaps the last election of the twentieth century. Either way, it was a significant moment in US political history. And college students were generally uninspired and disengaged. Perhaps best exemplifying the mood during most of the 2000 election was a joke frequently posed that seemed to sum up the general sentiment about both candidates: "What do you get when you combine Bush with Gore? Bore."

Then something happened on Election Night 2000, on the way to choosing a president, and we have had little time since to catch our collective civic breath. In the new millennium, we have had a historic election, 9/11, a war on terrorism, war in Iraq, another historic election, Hurricane Katrina, continued war, and yet another historic election contest, not to mention economic crisis and other concerns. By 2004, whatever one thought at that point about George W. Bush and the election facing America, it was unlikely that "Bore" would elicit anywhere near the same meaning. And by 2008, the widespread enthusiasm of young voters seemed a millennium away from the apathy sweeping college campuses at the turn of the new century.

This book considers a relatively recent yet already historic period in US politics, one filled with sudden change as well as developing trends in political behavior, attitudes, and knowledge. In it, I examine how an emerging generation of citizens has contemplated the political world over time and at these critical moments. The book focuses particular attention on the college population nationwide while also contributing a unique survey of undergraduates enrolled in introduction to US politics courses over the first decade of this new millennium. From "freedom fries" to *The Daily Show*, the war in Iraq and YouTube, the Bush era and the age of Obama, we explore how a new generation is learning, thinking, and acting concerning US government and politics as the world swirls and unfolds inside and outside of the educational experience.

Students are refining and solidifying an emerging political consciousness in light of critical moments, the political context, related information resources, and learning. Inherent possibilities and challenges are always present as a younger generation finds its political place and civic footing. A succession of highly salient current events and political realities in this new century arguably heightened students' interest in and attention to aspects of US politics and government. Within this context,

I explore the role of higher education and, in particular, the introduction to US politics course in facilitating the connection between heightened political awareness and related knowledge. In a political environment often rife with emotion-laden symbolism, the book examines how political knowledge and learning can mitigate the influence of emotion while facilitating reasoned judgment as these young minds contend with all of the related information swirling around them.

Understanding how media and new media sources are utilized by this emerging generation is critical to understanding how information is accessed and related to learning. This book explores how the college introduction to US politics can work with media consumption trends and tendencies in order to facilitate knowledgeable media consumption within and beyond the classroom. Internet media is just one of many emerging resources that translate Millennial thought into action. How students are introduced to and learn about US politics also stimulates related interest and engagement.

This book looks at how a developing framework was already in place that would serve as a springboard for the widespread youth mobilization on behalf of the historic Obama candidacy. Yet the Millennial Generation also exhibits traits that raise questions about long-term civic commitments beyond a recent surge in their political interest and electoral engagement. Introductory lessons and experiences in US politics as our students make their way out of college campuses and into the work and civic space are not only a relevant consideration for our nation's institutions of higher education, but also an age-old concern for the health of American democracy.

First and foremost, we need to understand what stimulates political learning and engagement among Millennials as they are introduced to US politics. This book explores how an introduction to US politics course can facilitate new Millennial connections through the integration of contemporary issues of concern. This process includes recognizing the most salient of events for our students, identifying relevant points of political interest, building on surveillance knowledge, enhancing capacity for related policy judgments, and understanding more accessible channels for political participation. Students' attentiveness to salient new millennial political events can be connected to related political learning, interest, policy reasoning and preferences, traditional and new media sources, and familiar as well as emerging forms of political engagement. I examine how successful and sustained political learning and engagement derives from how Millennial cohorts come to connect their understanding of US politics with the unique events of their time.

Talking About a New Generation in US Politics

Each US generation has its defining and enduring attributes (Lancaster and Stillman 2002; Strauss and Howe 1991). There is the World War II generation, Baby Boomers, and Generation X. They each have their identities and their slogans. And each generation can also experience critical moments that suddenly change complacency into concern and apathy into action (Delli Carpini 1989; Jennings and Niemi 1981; Meredith and Shewe 1994).

In this book, I explore how salient Millennial generational experiences facilitate political learning connected to related interest, relevant concerns, resources, and engagement. However, the younger generation often is or at least feels misunderstood as it secures its own identity, related concerns, and actions. In 1965, Baby Boomer Roger Daltrey of The Who sang in "My Generation" about how "people try to put us down." In 2000 the rock rap outfit Limp Biskit took on the angst of Generation X and its perceived disrespect, screaming out, "Go ahead and talk s*** about my generation."

Generations seem to be stuck with the labels and impressions formed through the most visible youthful "time-bound" moments and experiences. Madison Avenue and pop historians seem to like it that way. Boomers are the "peace and love" and/or "protest" generation associated with Vietnam, civil rights, Woodstock, and challenge of authority. Gen Xers have their time-bound stereotypes like Grunge and Nirvana, *Slacker*, and MTV (when it was still considered a relatively new medium for music videos), but are not necessarily recognized for the high-tech jobs they shaped and manage or a booming economy steered by new skills and innovation (see, e.g., Gordiner 2008).

Unlike Xers, Boomers are also associated with more active engagement in politics, coming of age as they did during the JFK administration and grappling with such issues as the Kent State shootings, from service to the country to challenging the government. Generation X carries the more negative mantle of lower interest and engagement in politics, an expectation that they won't necessarily take on government but prefer that it leave them to their own devices (Craig and Bennett 1997). Yet as Robert Putnam (2000) observed in the national bestseller *Bowling Alone*, each successive age group since the World War II generation has fallen increasingly short in terms of participating in their civic duties and governmental expectations. According to some observers, the World War II was the "Greatest Generation" (Brokaw 1998; Mettler 2005), in large part because of general perceptions about their handling of historic events and crises as they came of age.

As we entered the twenty-first century, Generation X passed on the younger generation torch and, with it, future hopes and concerns for American democracy. Those born at the tail end of Generation X—in 1976 or 1977—would have been approaching their mid-twenties in 2000 and moving out of the 18–24 or 15–25 demographic by the early part of the new century. But for those born between 1980 and 1990, many were entering and exiting the college experience amidst the multiple, sudden, and transformative events of the early twenty-first century. Although the beginning point of what is called Generation Y, as the successor to X, has been debated, ranging from the late 1970s to early 1980s, one statistic is widely accepted: Students entering colleges in the twenty-first century are members of the largest generation in absolute numbers since the Baby Boomers born within the period 1946–1964. Members of Gen X have also been referred to as "Baby Busters" because of their small demographic impact, while the successor Generation Y has been called an "Echo Boom," more in the mold of another baby boom. With many of this latest group entering young adulthood and college around the turn of the new century, they were thus dubbed "Millennials."

In *Millennials Rising: The Next Great Generation,* Neil Howe and William Strauss (2000) describe a generation born during the twentieth century's final decades, starting in 1982. Rather than growing up in the 1980s and 1990s, this generation was largely born in those decades. By 2000, this cohort numbered close to 80 million compared with about 78 million Boomers and about 40 million Xers. In *Generation We,* Eric Greenberg and Karl Weber (2008, 13) describe a Millennial cohort as those born between 1978 and 2000, comprising 95 million young people up to 30 years of age, the biggest generation in the history of the nation.

The sheer volume of this age group is beginning to make an impact on the democratic process and political life. By 2006, there were approximately 32 million 18- to 25-year-olds and 42 million in the age range of 18–29 years old. In 2008, 18- to 31-year-olds reached nearly 50 million strong, with about 40 percent of Millennials eligible to vote by Election Day. Based upon where one draws the starting and ending birth points for this generation, anywhere from 80 to 100 million Millennials will be of voting age by the 2016 election. Two presidential election cycles from now, this group we are just beginning to understand and that is still in the process of learning about and shaping its unique role in American democracy will be the most significant generational presence in US politics.

Recognizing Millennial Differences

Entering the new millennium, there was increasing concern about the democratic prospects of the younger generation. Based on decades of accumulated findings, Putnam (2000) suggested that the younger generation was less knowledgeable about politics and less interested and involved in it than were earlier generations at the same age. He warned that the under-30s were paying less attention and thus knew less about current events than not only their elders but their same age groups in earlier decades. In *The Vanishing Voter*, Thomas Patterson (2002) argued young adults were less politically interested and informed than any cohort of young people on record, with 1960–2000 as the longest period of decline in US history. Other studies demonstrated that a younger age cohort was decreasingly likely to care about, know about, and engage in US politics and democracy (Macedo et al. 2005; Wattenberg 2008).

However, a number of trends started to reverse as we moved into the new millennium (CIRCLE 2002; Harvard IOP 2004). While the annual survey of our nation's college freshmen revealed a three-decade trend of declining political interest, hitting a record low in 2000, by 2006 more entering freshmen had expressed interest in discussing politics than at any point in the history of the forty-year survey, including the 1960s (HERI 2007). Studies concluded not only that the emerging generation was more politically engaged, but that we needed to recognize new forms of such democratic participation (Bennett 2007a; Dalton 2008; Zukin et al. 2006).

The nature of this generation's engagement (or lack thereof) has continued to be a matter of debate as Millennials find their way into or away from democratic life, depending on their individual perspectives. For example, Mark Bauerlein's (2008) book *The Dumbest Generation: How the Digital Age Stupefies Young Americans and Jeopardizes Our Future* and Jean Twenge's (2006) *Generation Me: Why Today's Young Americans Are More Confident, Assertive, Entitled—and More Miserable Than Ever Before* describe troubling and self-absorbed, civically disengaged aspects of this age group. On the other side, Greenberg and Weber's (2008) *Generation We: How Millennial Youth Are Taking Over America and Changing Our World Forever* and Winograd and Hais's (2008) *Millennial Makeover: MySpace, YouTube, and the Future of American Politics* paint a much more optimistic, politically savvy, and civically engaged picture of early Millennial impact.

There are clearly differing perspectives on how this emerging generation will or will not contribute to democratic life in the United States. However, there is agreement that the Millennial experience is unique and the opportunities and challenges for this generation are very much associated with the times. In addition to technology, Winograd and Hais point to triggering events such as 9/11, war, and environmental disasters as critical moments that have shifted Millennials toward civic realignment. And Greenberg and Weber argue that such critical events and issues have spurred this generation to engage more in communities and in politics, armed with the promising possibilities of new technology, related skills, and understanding. On the other hand, Bauerlein (2008, 201) argues that today's pervasive technology allows Millennials to "steer competitive instincts toward peer triumphs and not civic duty . . . preferring the company of peers to great books and powerful ideas and momentous happenings" (234). But, in essence, he agrees with Twenge's (2006, 8) assertion that the "accelerated pace of recent technological and cultural change makes it more important than ever to keep up with generation trends. A profound shift in generational dynamics is occurring right now in the 2000s."

New Millennial Impact

Interest in and perceived relevance of significant events can contribute to a lasting worldview (Jennings and Niemi 1981; Zukin et al. 2006) and provide a critical pathway for a generation. It is all about why and when Millennials are paying attention to politics and what political events grab their attention. I contend that recognizable salient events emerging in these young lives contribute to their political knowledge, interest, policy reasoning, and engagement.

In generational terms, the swirl of events occurring in a short time frame brings to mind the cascade of crises from the Great Depression into World War II, an era forever linked with its generation of the same name. Although new millennial events are hardly of the magnitude of the 1930s–1940s, outside of the Vietnam War/Watergate nexus it is hard to imagine in the post–World War II era a period in which so many significant political events were visited upon one particular US generation.

Reflecting on the 2005 survey of US college freshmen, Director Sylvia Hurtado of the Higher Education Research Institute (HERI) noted the impact of "period effects, societal or world events that impact students during an impressionable time of their lives," and the lasting impact on the affected group (HERI 2005a). The Harvard Institute of Politics (IOP) concluded after a review of its 2007 national survey findings that, like the generation schooled by Vietnam and civil rights in the 1960s and 1970s, today's college students also have come together in a time of significant political events of historical importance (IOP 2007). And Cliff Zukin and his coauthors (2006, 209) pondered, "Perhaps the chain of events beginning on 9/11 and including the 2004 election will yet mark a watershed, drawing more Americans more consistently into political life, and even serving as a 'defining moment' for the political identity of Nets [the authors' name for the Millennial Generation]. Only time will tell."

Such reports and related studies have acknowledged the importance of such events to a generation's perspective and engagement. However, they have not examined how critical new millennial events trigger related knowledge and connect to related interests, policy choices, media sources, and aspects of engagement. In short, they do not examine how new Millennial connections can translate their attentiveness to these significant events into connected learning and engagement, and particularly how introduction to US politics courses can strengthen these vital connections.

Salient Connections

As Niemi and Junn (1998, 51) note about the pre-collegiate level, "If high school classes do little to generate political learning and interest it may be because they are dealing sparsely with contemporary events, problems or controversies. Students retained knowledge on aspects of civic information that were already familiar to them from other contexts or somehow meaningful in a more direct way." Niemi and Junn's findings are not bound to the high school environment and are just as relevant to the collegiate experience, particularly for students in introduction to US politics courses making that initial transition. Introducing current events and issues that are relevant to students' lives has been found to boost civic learning (Hess 2009; Lopez and Kirby 2007). While studies connect current events with student learning (Beaumont et al. 2006; Galston 2007; Youniss and Levine 2009), none have examined the course integration of new millennial salient events over a decade.

As Bauerlein laments (2008, 156), "Young people have too much choice, too much discretion for educators and mentors to guide their usage. . . . Inside the classroom, they learn a little about the historical past and civic affairs, but once the lesson ends they swerve back to the youth-full, peer bound present" (200). If one accepts such a perspective, it would seem more important than ever to connect significant and visible political events with the learning process. Working with Millennials' identified areas of interest in politics is critical. There is the need to integrate the political events that our Millennial-age students find to be most relevant.

Events are more likely to resonate when they are highly visible and accessible to the group because they are paying a great deal of attention to an event, crisis, process, and/or issue for some length of time. In other words, there is salience. We would typically associate salience with the most high-profile events, but it can also be matters of particular significance and thus attentiveness by a particular group, in this case Millennials. To introduce a salient event is to introduce relevance, which arguably enhances related learning, interest, and engagement. Thus, I argue that the integration of salient political events as part of an introduction to US politics can generate, reinforce, and/or help to illuminate related learning and interest.

The (Surveillance) Learning Equation

Scholars do question whether citizens need a large store of information to fulfill basic roles as citizens in American democracy (Lupia and McCubbins 1998). What may be most essential to functioning in the contemporary political environment is more of a monitorial obligation (Schudson 1998; Zaller 2003). In this view, citizens should be knowledgeable about acute and pressing problems in the news, perhaps only intermittently surveying political news (Graber 2001; Jerit, Barabas, and Bolsen 2006). When exposed to them, people appear to handle certain surveillance facts more readily than they do textbook facts, and surveillance facts tend to be those that are picked up from and reinforced by the media (Delli Carpini and Keeter 1991).

Because awareness of contemporary political figures and facts presumably depends on a relative surveillance or at least basic grasp of related current events, such understanding is often referred to as surveillance knowledge (e.g., identifying a US senator). On the other hand, there are facts, processes, and institutions in US politics and government that are unchanging, unaffected by political changes and events (e.g., identifying the length of a US Senate term). Commonly referred to as textbook knowledge, such understanding is a foundation of civics curricula in the pre-college experience, and is addressed in the introductory textbooks in a college course on US politics.

We have ongoing debates about what our youth should know when it comes to US politics (e.g., Bauerlein 2008; Wattenberg 2008), with reports continuing to filter in about the dismal state of the younger generation's civic knowledge (e.g., Galston 2004, 2007; NAEP 1998, 2006). But what exactly are Millennial-age college students likely to know and why, and how can we build on the type of knowledge most significantly connected to political attentiveness, interest, policy reasoning, and engagement?

We hope that our students are gaining some basic foundation of textbook knowledge in an introductory US politics course. While these figures can certainly improve, Millennials tend to fare no worse than their older age cohorts on textbook knowledge items, such as the veto override procedure (Zukin et al. 2006, 83). Where Millennials fall increasingly behind their elders is in surveillance knowledge, such as identification of political leaders and partisan control of Congress (Wattenberg 2008, 77–79). Yet despite identifying such gaps, little scholarly attention has been paid to what stimulates surveillance knowledge and learning, particularly in the classroom, and how it connects to political interest and engagement. This book explores how attentiveness to salient political events is particularly connected with our students' surveillance political knowledge, which I contend provides a critical connection to interest, policy reasoning, and engagement.

This book shows how Millennials absorb and utilize political knowledge, particularly surveillance knowledge, gained through the salient events of the times. It explores the influence of introductory levels of political learning on new Millennial interest and engagement. What elements of political learning are important? And how does political knowledge facilitate reasoned policy choices and political participation for our Millennial-age college students?

Informing Millennial Judgment

This book provides access into the minds of Millennials, what type of political information they retain, reinforce, and utilize in reasoning about important policy decisions. What our Millennial students know and learn also impacts how they understand the policy choices in front of them, namely on the most salient political events and processes that capture their interest. In a mediated political environment, our students are often bombarded with emotive political cues and images that trigger their own long-standing affective attitudes and predispositions to reach judgment in lieu of related political information. Political reasoning and sound policy judgments depend on access to and coherent processing of related information (Downs 1957; Lupia, McCubbins, and Popkin 2000). Without related information, there is greater reliance on emotions, political cues, broad images, and what are called symbolic predispositions (Kuklinski 2001; Sniderman, Brody, and Tetlock 1991; Westen 2007). While such cognitive shortcuts provide predictable and even stable responses in an oft-changing political environment (Marcus, Neuman, and MacKuen 2000), they also raise concern as to the basis of such attitudinal formation and the prospects for misguidance or even manipulation through misunderstanding (Redlawsk 2006).

Most books on Millennials examine their level and trends in knowledge and behavior, but pay little attention to the interplay between emotion and cognition that is particularly pronounced when information is introduced in a political learning environment. This book explores the important symbolic components of processing that citizens utilize when they are lacking significant information, and it demonstrates how our Millennial students also utilize such predispositions. Furthermore, it provides findings on how learning impacts that relationship. I explore countervailing forces of emotion and reason and look at how Millennials have exhibited both in light of emerging and seminal events, and how this relates to policy concerns. Indeed, these are the debates where students may need the most guidance as they sort through unfamiliar terrain, trying to utilize related information to formulate conclusions rather than rely on the host of emotional cues emanating from the mediated political environment.

In an early twenty-first century filled with profound change, crisis, symbolic, and, at times, threatening imagery, this book investigates how political knowledge and learning can provide Millennials with a reasoned counter to the often emotion-laden symbolic banter about politics and government swirling around them. Millennials' trust in government, confidence in the president, and conceptions of national identity can provide a symbolic connection to our nation, its leadership, and institutions, and can assist them in formulating related policy choices on issues of concern. Yet it is important to understand how political knowledge gains, as part of an introduction to US politics course, contribute to Millennials' policy reasoning and how such information is accessed.

Mediated Challenges and Possibilities

To more fully sort out the role of an introduction to US politics course in this learning equation, it is critical that we understand to what extent Millennials rely (or don't rely) on the diverse media sources now available in a 24/7 cable news environment and across extensive Internet resources when it comes to political information. Wattenberg (2008, 76) surmises, "Without reading a daily newspaper, watching the TV news, or otherwise following current events, even the best educated people will probably not pick up much knowledge about the political world. . . . Given their relative lack of exposure to political news and current events, young people should be falling more and more behind their elders in terms of political knowledge despite their relatively high levels of educational achievement." Bauerlein (2008) argues that young adults now have the choice to avoid current events and civic knowledge, which puts even more onus on educators to reach these developing minds when the opportunity is available and before bad habits are set.

While I explore how a variety of media sources relate to our students' political knowledge, I proceed with the assumption that media sources do not construct but, instead, work to integrate the salient political events that connect to the interests of our Millennial-age students. If Millennials simply choose to avoid certain political topics in the media because they have no inherent interest in them, we cannot impose interest simply by introducing media coverage. Media resources work most effectively for Millennials when they are combined with identified salient political events to build interest.

Surveillance knowledge, in particular, lags behind that of older age demographics because Millennials are less likely to pay as much attention to news media. However, once properly exposed to information, people learn about politics (Neuman, Just, and Crigler 1992; Iyengar and Kinder 1987). But with so many media choices and distractions, the classroom is arguably one of the few enduring places in which the younger generation and thus future citizens may collectively experience and consistently consider significant political events. And the introduction to US politics course is one of the logical places to consider related newsworthy events in a way that presumably aims to work with and stimulate political learning habits and related connections.

While this book explores how our Millennial-age students can still make use of more traditional media sources such as TV news, it also examines the emerging importance of Internet use and even soft news/entertainment media to focus Millennial attention on salient events, surveillance learning, and political interest. There is an ongoing debate over the positive and negative aspects of the Internet (Anderson 2004; Loader 2007; Tapscott 2008) and the distractions and possibilities of entertainment media (Baum 2002; Mindich 2005; Prior 2005). When it comes to Millennials' political knowledge and engagement, I argue that it is not the media technology but the accessible and relevant use of media sources that enhances related learning and engagement. This book explores how the integrated use of multimedia sources in introduction to US politics courses significantly relates to and connects with attentiveness to political events, surveillance knowledge, and interest. Relevance and accessibility are key factors for these students as they seek media resources for related knowledge and engagement connected to their own attentiveness and interest.

Little attention has been paid to understanding how to connect related political knowledge, interest, and media resources for this generation. Rather, many bemoan the fact that these young adults do not possess the requisite knowledge, and the idea that information acquisition has changed so dramatically that we must adapt to this new method of learning and reasoning is lacking. This book explores how knowledge and interest relate to political knowledge and how both long-standing and new technologies can also work in support of this dynamic rather than against it.

Connecting Political Interests and Engagement

There are important implications in understanding how our Millennial-age students learn to think about and access related political information about US politics and government. More knowledgeable and informed citizens are more likely to actively engage in politics and community (Nie, Junn, and Stehlik-Barry 1996; Skocpol and Fiorina 1999; Yates and Youniss 1998). Political participation also enhances political knowledge, so the two are mutually reinforcing (Verba, Schlozman, and Brady 1995). In this book, I also explore how attentiveness to salient political events, media sources, and political knowledge—namely surveillance knowledge—significantly relate to our students' political participation.

Importantly, I examine how our students' attentiveness to salient political events is also connected to interest in politics, which, in turn, leads to greater participation in political life, such as we've seen in recent presidential elections. However, despite heightened interest in national politics, Millennials continue to demonstrate much higher levels of community volunteerism than engagement in the very national-level issues that appear to captivate their attention, presenting a potential disconnect between community involvement and active political participation. I contend that it is thus important to account for multiple dimensions of our students' political interest in order to more effectively connect Millennials' relevant interests, related knowledge, and attentiveness with opportunities for participation at the local and national levels, and even in the expressive dimensions of politics, including political film, music, and protest. Throughout this book, we explore how engaging our Millennial-age students in US politics involves identifying and integrating the emerging political events that have their utmost attention. This attentiveness connects to a Millennial construction of interests, attitudes, and perspectives, which can facilitate political learning within and beyond the classroom. Many studies have contended that the younger generation cares less and less about US politics, learning about it, or being involved in it. I take the approach that it is not so much that they don't care as it is about facilitating connections with the events that capture their attention. It is about connecting with their interests, identifying the most accessible media sources, and utilizing the learning environment to help them effectively process policy issues and debates of perceived importance.

It is critical to recognize how to link an introduction to US politics with the political world Millennials inhabit. Zukin et al. (2006, 93) note that for the Millennial-age group, "lack of involvement seems to be more due to a lack of relevancy than rejection." This book demonstrates that Millennials are far from politically disengaged while adding that introduction to US politics courses can play a significant role in facilitating critical "new Millennial" political connections.

Political Higher Learning

How, what, and where Millennials learn about and apply their knowledge in US politics is a concern that is directly relevant to the educational environment. Millennials have been entering our nation's campuses in increasing numbers, with encouraging trends in political interest and participation during the first decade of the twenty-first century, and there is continuing concern regarding their pre-college level of civic knowledge (NAEP 1998, 2006, 2010). Serving as a de facto nation's report card across multiple subjects, including civics, National Assessment of Educational Progress (NAEP) findings continue to show well over one-third of high school seniors testing below what William Galston (2004, 264) has claimed is "the working knowledge that most citizens need," "indicating near total civic ignorance," and "without any discernible payoff in increased civic knowledge." NAEP civic reports have put about one-quarter of twelfth graders at or above the basic level of civic proficiency, with the ability to do things like "identify a leadership position in Congress" or "identify and explain a constitutional principle." Importantly, Niemi and Junn (1998, 29) conclude from the NAEP results, "It is when matters are outside a student's experience, they are less aware and unable to apply lessons learned in the classroom."

Scholars from John Dewey (1916) in *Democracy and Education* to Harry Boyte (2005) in *Everyday Politics: Reconnecting Citizens with Public Life* have discussed the vital relationship among public education, civic life, and American democracy. For some time, however, questions have been raised over just how effective civics education is in civic learning (Corbett 1991; Erickson and Tedin 1995; Jennings and Niemi 1974; Ravitch and Viteritti 2001), while others argue that civics education can be connected to a wide range of political learning (Levine 2007a; Milner 2002; Reeher and Cammarano 1997; Torney-Purta 2002). Whatever the pre-college civic learning impact, Macedo and others note in *Democracy in Risk* (2005, 1), "citizens need public information, but the number of civics courses taken in public schools has declined by two thirds since 1960."

With increasing concern over civic learning and engagement at the pre-college level, attention has also turned to higher education. For example, in 1999 the *President's Fourth of July Declaration on the Civic Responsibility of Higher Education* orchestrated by Campus Compact, a national coalition of more than one thousand colleges and universities, called on higher education to take seriously its commitment to civic learning and democratic renewal (Longo 2007, 9). In 2006, *The Coming Crisis in Citizenship: Higher Education's Failure to Teach America's History and Institutions* by the Intercollegiate Studies Institute (ISI) reported on a survey of fourteen thousand freshmen *and* seniors at fifty colleges and universities conducted by the University of Connecticut Department of Public Policy. The average college senior failed in all four subjects of America's history, government, international relations, and market economy, and did little better than the freshmen, in which certain types of civic knowledge would stick and slightly increase while others would not.

Despite the increasing demand for college education, there has not been a corresponding rise in overall civic knowledge, though it is not worse overall (Delli Carpini and Keeter 1996; Pew 2007). However, Macedo et al. (2005, 30) conclude, "the fact that political knowledge has held steady in the wake of a massive increase in education is really a net loss." It balances out since college graduates are about as knowledgeable as high school graduates were about fifty years ago, and high school graduates are at about the level of high school dropouts of that period (Galston 2007, 630). Our nation's universities are enrolling more students, but questions remain as to just how much our undergraduates are learning about US politics, what we can do to improve this learning curve, and how this relates to sustained political interest and engagement.

Higher civic education efforts cross discipline and department lines, with the recognition that there is no course that can claim to be the ultimate resource for civic learning. Students are found to learn about and engage in civic life in different ways, stimulated by different instructors, topics, methods, and avenues of awareness and participation (Colby et al. 2003; Jacoby et al. 2009; Youniss and Levine 2009). Yet as Anne Colby and others reason in *Educating for Democracy* (2007, 41), "more explicit attention to political learning is necessary if we are to take full advantage of higher education's opportunities to prepare thoughtful, skilled, and active citizens."

While it is useful to compare college freshman and college senior civic knowledge to determine *if* learning has occurred, it does not provide us with *how* and *why* our college students learn and retain certain types of political information. Furthermore, we are left wondering how increases in political learning are related to other political attitudes, interests, and engagement. And what about the influence of unforeseen and evolving political events during the learning experience as new and developing information is inevitably transmitted via diverse media channels to our students? How do our Millennial-age students learn political foundations while incorporating emerging political information into evolving understanding, policy decisionmaking, and engagement in US politics? How do we integrate the most salient millennial events, our students' attentiveness to and knowledge of them, their ability to reason through critical policy choices to facilitate related action, and engagement as part of an introduction to US politics?

Entering US Politics

Although there is no universal laboratory setting to explore the nature and impact of political learning on Millennial-age students, the introductory US politics course offered across all college campuses provides one of the more familiar environments in which students are exposed to enduring principles and evolving political information directly relevant to US politics and government. While there may be a stronger interest than average in politics, or at least a curiosity about it, that leads a student to enroll in such a course, a student's presence is more likely the product of a general education requirement that compels students across all majors, diverse levels of political interest, and knowledge to step into this class. Across nearly all US colleges and universities, introduction to US politics is one of the core course choices available as part of a general elective requirement. While it is somewhat self-selecting, it provides about as broad a cross section of the Millennial-age cohort possible in any given learning context.

It also represents for many adults the last time that they think and discuss US politics at such length. Thus in its own way, the introduction to US politics course is a civic clearinghouse for students and future citizens as they make their way through higher education and into the "real world." The rest will be material they learn (or do not learn) on their own as citizens, as news consumers, and as active or inactive participants in the body politic.

Studies have pointed out how introductory courses in politics, namely the introduction to US politics course, can impact student political learning and engagement (Bernstein 2008; Colby et al. 2007; Huerta and Jozwiak 2008). Such studies, however, have tended to focus on one point in time, even on multiple campuses in the same year, which provides for a more static political context. Thus we may be able to consider the recent impact of an election, a crisis, or an event, but we cannot really examine similar or differing information contexts and changing circumstances over time.

In this book, we are able to examine the US politics dynamic over multiple semesters and years, and thus different political contexts for an emerging generation. In this regard, the data collected and examined here allow us to explore how new millennial events and debates outside of the classroom intersect with developing perceptions and knowledge within it. This is not to suggest that students will only learn about US politics within such a course. As we have discussed, there is debate over whether any class or classes can directly enhance overall civic learning. However, a US politics course provides a unique opportunity to examine how and what students can learn and retain about politics and how intervening political events and information contribute to evolving understanding, interest, and engagement.

Collecting Data at an Introductory Level

On our own college campus at the State University of New York (SUNY) at Fredonia, we set about surveying the hundreds of students each semester enrolled in our introduction to US politics courses to gauge political attentiveness, knowledge, and engagement. We began at the end of the Clinton presidency amid not only the 2000 presidential election but also the historic campaign of First Lady Hillary Clinton for US senator from New York. We continued to survey students entering and completing our US politics courses but couldn't have anticipated many of the dramatic and historic events that would transpire over a relatively short period. Just as a new century was dawning, our students were introduced to US politics with the 2000 recount, 9/11, a war in Iraq, a contentious 2004 reelection, the Obama candidacy and victory, rapid technological change, and a host of other events, issues, and factors.

In fall 2000, we began collecting anonymous and voluntary surveys with paper-and-pencil administration for students completing our US politics courses. From fall 2001 to fall 2005 and in fall 2008, spring 2009, and spring 2010, we collected questionnaires from students both beginning and completing the course. Students were provided approximately 15 minutes to complete the surveys in class with their instructor present (see Appendix A for question wording and design). Students entering in the fall were surveyed at one point during the first week of the course, late August to early September. Students exiting in the late fall were surveyed at one point during the final two weeks in early to mid-December. Students entering the course in the spring were surveyed at one point during the first week, late January to early February, and students exiting in late spring were surveyed at one point during the final two weeks, early to mid-May.

In all, we collected 2,752 surveys for students entering over sixty different course sections with ten different instructors of the introduction to US politics courses at SUNY Fredonia across the period of the study. We collected a total of 2,664 surveys for students completing the US politics courses at SUNY Fredonia, fall 2000–fall 2005, fall 2008, spring 2009, and spring 2010. Where surveys were collected at the beginning and also the completion of the course, a unique identifying code was utilized to match pre- and post-course surveys of individual respondents. There were 2,019 US politics students at SUNY Fredonia who completed both entering and exiting surveys. Overall, 51 percent of our survey respondents are female students and 49 percent are male.

The university Human Subjects Committee approved the questionnaire for in-class use.

The class enrollment for our US politics sections averages about fifty students, with a few in the one hundred range, an enrollment figure that clearly varies across college campuses. SUNY Fredonia is one of thirteen university colleges in the State University of New York system. The campus enrolls just over five thousand undergraduate students. As the westernmost SUNY campus, Fredonia is close to the shores of Lake Erie and the borders of Pennsylvania and Ontario, Canada. It is about equal distance—about 50 miles—from Buffalo, New York, and Erie, Pennsylvania. The campus draws its enrollment predominantly from New York state, with the heaviest student representation from the surrounding Erie, Monroe, and Chautauqua counties. The student body has a healthy mix of urban, suburban, and rural populations. And state legislative representation from which these students are predominantly drawn closely reflects the national Republican and Democratic balance. Chautauqua County, home to SUNY Fredonia, has been one of the most reliable county barometers nationwide in presidential elections. Since 1980, the county has voted for the presidential winner in every election.

The general region has also served as a valuable resource for classic studies on the US electorate. For example, Bernard Berelson, Paul Lazarfeld, and William McPhee's 1954 book, *Voting: A Study of Opinion Formation in a Presidential Campaign*, depended on a study of the Elmira, New York, population during the 1948 election. In an influential book published in 1976, *The Unseeing Eye: The Myth of Television Power in National Elections*, Thomas Patterson and Robert McClure utilized panel surveys of six hundred respondents in Syracuse, New York, during the 1972 presidential election.

Our region, campus experience, student body, and courses have some unique characteristics. Thus this book relies as well on student surveys we conducted at several other universities and integrates national survey findings on the undergraduate population and on the broader Millennial Generation as a critical lens through which to consider our own survey results. We also extended our survey across the country to 398 students completing introduction to US politics courses at the University of California at Santa Barbara in spring 2003, fall 2004, and summer 2008. A total of 108 students were surveyed at the end of the course in the spring 2001 semester at the University of Wisconsin at River Falls. Across the Atlantic Ocean, we surveyed 369 students entering the introduction to politics course at Northumbria

University in the United Kingdom for the fall 2003, spring 2004, spring 2005, and fall 2005 terms. We also surveyed one hundred students from across the SUNY system participating in the SUNY Washington internship program, fall 2006–summer 2007.

All in all, we collected 6,429 college student questionnaires across the time period, fall 2000–spring 2010. Each questionnaire distributed to students consisted of approximately 75–80 items, including multiple measures of political attitudes, preferences, attentiveness, behavior, and knowledge (see Appendix A for wording). Most questions were based on the National Election Studies and General Social Survey, but others were constructed to measure more specific views of breaking events and critical moments in domestic affairs, foreign affairs, and political leadership.

What students bring to the US politics experience is a critical part of how they may in turn process information and engage related material. Students will have different interests and majors that may facilitate certain predispositions to retaining information. But most students are in the same boat as they enter the US politics course. Overwhelmingly they are taking the course as part of a general requirement. For instance, in any given semester, approximately 5 percent of our SUNY Fredonia students in the introduction to US politics course are majoring in political science, about 1 percent have a political science minor, and only about 3 percent are considering a major in political science. Even for those very few students already established as political science majors or considering it as a minor, this is an initial introduction to the subject, and our survey results show they have no inherent differences from, say, music majors when it comes to preexisting levels of political knowledge, interest, attentiveness, and so on.

On average, introduction to US politics course sections at SUNY Fredonia enroll forty to fifty students, but the fall 2000, fall 2004, and fall 2008 terms each had one section with 100–120 students enrolled. With the exception of fall 2003 and spring 2004, three different instructors in each semester would distribute the questionnaires to their US sections. Overall, ten different political science instructors distributed surveys to their respective classes at SUNY Fredonia, fall 2000–spring 2010.

With over sixty course sections and nearly three thousand different students surveyed at SUNY Fredonia alone, the objective was to identify the relationship between and impact of variables independent of individual course differences. Despite some instructional differences, course readings, assignments, and debate and discussion opportunities, expectations were remarkably similar across faculty and courses (see

Appendix B). We were able to measure variables of interest through an extensive student survey in order to assess relative learning impacts and connections for our Millennial-age students across the courses.

Admittedly, our surveys of US politics students do not fully represent Millennials or even the national college population. An introduction to US politics course on select campuses provides only a limited window on fully understanding an emerging generation's voice. It does, however, provide a firsthand look at how salient events *and* related learning impact developing political interests, preferences, and action for cohorts of this age group. It allows us to simultaneously examine the interplay of the instructional and broader information environment over multiple time periods in a relatively familiar setting. We can consider how higher education and the widespread introduction to US politics course, in particular, might play a critical role with regard to political understanding and engagement beyond college and the classroom experience.

To examine our US politics students with a proper recognition of the broader national population, this book considers both our student surveys and national representative surveys (e.g., Graber 2001; Lewis 2001). Our own surveys provide for a detailed and pointed texture drawn from the unique opportunity to survey our students through numerous and even unexpected critical events in a familiar yet evolving environment. At the same time, we include a national survey backdrop to illuminate and confirm observed dynamics and particular trends essential to understanding how the early new millennium has shaped the political mindset of an increasingly impactful generation. National surveys include findings and trends from Harvard University's IOP, UCLA's HERI, the Center for Information and Research on Civic Learning and Engagement (CIRCLE), the NAEP, the Pew Research Center for People and the Press (Pew), the American National Election Studies, and the General Social Survey (GSS).

The Organization of the Book

This collection of survey findings provides insight into how Millennials and their respective college populations have learned, responded, reasoned, and participated at a national and at a more local level in an eventful first decade of the twenty-first century. In Chapters 2 through 4 of this book, much of the contextual backdrop is the two terms of the George W. Bush presidency, an eventful period without a doubt in US politics, regardless of how one assesses it. But what followed is perhaps an even more memorable time for Millennials as they embarked on an understanding of US politics and government as Barack Obama won the 2008 election and was sworn in as the nation's first African American president. In Chapters 5 and 6, I examine how the earlier millennial experience of our students and of this generation ultimately evolved into the levels of youth interest, attentiveness, participation, and impact that stunned many observers during the 2008 presidential campaign. Beyond this historic mobilization around a highly salient political event and process, I consider how Millennials can also connect their attentiveness to other emerging events, related political learning, interests, and unique preferences with other opportunities for sustained political engagement.

In Chapter 2, I examine how significant moments in the new millennium relate to what interests our college students and what they know about US politics. The chapter considers how attentiveness to high-profile events, including recent elections, the 9/11 attacks, and war in Iraq, relate to how and what students learn about US politics and government. Political events and processes outside of the college classroom are important to what is accessible and recognized within it. Surveillance knowledge of foreign and domestic political figures and facts, more than standard textbook knowledge, is connected to interest and attentiveness, which raises questions about the most appropriate ways to best facilitate political learning and engagement.

The sudden and dramatic events from 9/11 to the war in Iraq visited upon the younger generation in this new century provoked compelling challenges but also learning opportunities. In Chapter 3, I consider how our students have made sense of a dizzying array of historic events, policy questions, and debates in which we pay particular attention to attitudes, learning, and preferences on the evolving issue of war in Iraq. Studies find that for many of us, confusing decisions about domestic and foreign policy are often simplified through information shortcuts, which include emotive attitudes, symbolic predispositions, and political cues. Attentiveness to critical, if not crisis, events can reinforce information that can stimulate learning and retention. However, dramatic events can also provoke emotional reactions that can bypass citizen scrutiny in favor of more convenient symbolic attachments and accessible cues. Like the general population, many of our students were swept up in the imagery and emotion leading from 9/11 into war in Iraq. But as our surveys of US politics courses uncovered over the dramatic first years of the war, political learning also shaped how these emerging citizens understood and reasoned about the most important of policy decisions a government can make.

How students receive political information both inside and outside of the classroom is a critical factor in how they will process it. And once we leave the educational setting, the wide-ranging media is the likeliest source of information consumption updating an understanding of politics and policy. Chapter 4 explores how evolving media use among younger adults provides challenges and opportunities for political learning, interest, and engagement. With noticeable changes in media sources just since the start of the new millennium, this chapter examines the debate over consumption patterns and what it means for information dissemination across the younger population as well as more specifically within the US politics instructional environment. Our findings show that higher levels of attention to TV news or Internet news are both related to higher political knowledge, with an emphasis on surveillance knowledge gains. Yet despite the fears that youth are wasting most of their time online with social networking sites, students with higher levels of net use also demonstrate greater political knowledge entering and exiting our US politics courses. As young adults develop new media habits, I also find that students may learn while laughing, as *Daily Show* attentiveness is strongly linked to political knowledge and learning. Moreover, it is the instructional environment providing for the incorporation of the multimedia experience that most successfully appears to generate political interest, attentiveness, and knowledge, three key factors that rely on each other to forge the active citizen.

In Chapter 5, I investigate how political learning and interest translate into participation and engagement for our students and this Millennial cohort as we transition from the Bush to the Obama era. There have been consistently higher levels of volunteerism for young adults at the community level, but whether such involvement will translate into broader and enduring political participation is of concern. How to encourage voting participation is explored, but the chapter examines why it is critical to extend understanding of US politics beyond presidential elections for democratic citizenship to really take hold in developing minds. There is higher interest in national than in local politics but a potential disconnect about how to translate such interest into action. The instructional environment is important in cognitively linking interest, knowledge, and participation, yet colleges can facilitate further opportunities outside of the classroom in public service. The foundation was laid for the Obama presidency by events and attitudes transpiring in the early new century, but the translation of those views into civic action for the emerging generation is a work in progress.

"Democratic Directions for a New Millennial Generation," Chapter 6, sums up competing attributes of the generation coming of age in the twenty-first century and discusses challenges and opportunities in stimulating higher levels of related Millennial political knowledge, interest, and participation. A recognition and understanding of how this generation demonstrates consumer and civic components, private and public predispositions, distraction, and deeper considerations is just one of the seeming contradictions that actually work together in translating thought into action for many of these developing citizens. Millennial attachment to their cohort, confidence in democracy, and reasoned debate for policy solutions appear to provide important democratic connections that stretch beyond partisan politics and an emphasis on the presidency as channels for political interest and engagement. There is a critical role here for the educational environment, particularly during times of eventful and dramatic transformation, to engage young minds in new democratic debates and possibilities. While educators can assist in identifying how best to interpret and engage the political world, in the end the responsibility rests with each new generation to utilize evolving resources essential to the future of US politics and democracy. As this book unfolds, it demonstrates how the first decade of a new century has already impacted the relationship between a Millennial generation, its student body, and the US body politic.

2

Learning About US Politics

What's a primary? Wow. I learned that once in school.
—*A New Hampshire college student
interviewed on MTV's* Choose or Lose, *2000*

To understand how Millennials learn about US politics, it is critical to understand when and how politics captures their attention. I have mentioned numerous studies that discuss what Millennial-age students do not know and why they lack interest and attentiveness. The objective here is to explore what our students are attentive to when it comes to US politics, what they are most likely to know, and why.

As significant events emerged over a new century's first decade, it became increasingly clear that these years would be different from the 1990s or the 1980s—twenty-some years of trending political disinterest for the younger generation. With the accumulating impact of 9/11, ongoing wars in Iraq and Afghanistan, an increasingly divisive presidency, and an incredibly polarized reelection, the twenty-first century's first decade echoed more closely the 1960s, a period of relatively higher interest, activity, and attentiveness for the youth of the United States.

In this chapter, I examine when and how Millennial college-age students have been paying attention to US politics and policy inside and outside of the classroom. It is important to understand that our students are more attentive to certain critical events and political processes and how that is related to knowledge and learning. Indeed, the "follows" (certain topics) measure has been interpreted by a number of scholars to convey exposure to the information environment around us (Dalton, Beck, and Huckfeldt 1998; Hetherington 1996). In particular, I consider how a surveillance of contemporary political events relates to political interest, awareness, and knowledge.

What our students are paying attention to can be particularly important, as they are also learning political foundations and processes. We would assume that a US politics course and textbook cover core foundations and processes, known as textbook knowledge. However, students are also introduced to contemporary facts and figures—surveillance knowledge—that can also be reinforced through the mediated political context outside of the classroom.

While textbook knowledge provides an important foundation for any educated citizen, this chapter also examines how surveillance knowledge appears most responsive to the changing political context and salience of political events and processes. We learn more when paying attention for some length of time (Page and Shapiro 1992, 12), whether watching TV at home or sitting in a lecture hall on campus. It is important to understand these distinctions to more fully comprehend what our students are retaining about politics and how it relates to political interest and attentiveness.

Furthermore, surveillance knowledge is a more significant aspect of the knowledge gap for Millennials relative to their elders. For example, Zukin et al.'s *A New Engagement? Political Participation, Civic Life, and the Changing American Citizen* (2006) reports that the April 2002 National Center for Education Statistics (NCES) survey found 30 percent of DotNets to be similarly informed (or perhaps similarly uninformed) as other age groups (Gen X, 29 percent; Boomers, 35 percent; Dutifuls, 32 percent) on textbook knowledge such as the margin to override a veto, but note (83) that where "DotNets fall behind their elders, including Gen X, is on factual knowledge that requires regular surveillance of the political landscape, such as naming public officials or knowing that Republicans have a majority in the Senate." However, studies have paid little attention specifically to surveillance knowledge, particularly when it comes to its important connection with attentiveness to salient political events and interest.

Relevance is a key factor in awareness and learning for any young cohort's introduction to US politics. Students, and citizens for that matter, learn and retain more information about what they find interesting and important to their lives (Delli Carpini and Keeter 1996; Iyengar 1990; Lupia and McCubbins 1998). Thus it is important to understand the events that pique interest for this generation beyond the historical events that stimulated related attentiveness for previous generations. Understanding the contemporary political context, related political figures, processes, and facts is a key element of recognizing what our students are absorbing outside of the classroom and most likely to retain within the learning environment.

Related Attentiveness and Awareness

It is critical to understand the events important to any generation in order to recognize how relevance is related to attentiveness and awareness. There are critical and salient moments for each generation, such as Pearl Harbor, the JFK assassination, the Cold War, and Vietnam, just as there are new defining events for a Millennial Generation. For example, Martin Wattenberg (2008, 63) found through his examination of American National Elections Studies findings in the 1960s that more of those under 30 years of age (77 percent) had heard of the 1964 civil rights bill than those 65 years of age or older (66 percent) or those 45–64 years old (72 percent). As for the antiwar demonstrations at the 1968 Democratic nominating convention in Chicago, which was essentially a youth-driven confrontation with the "powers that be," 90 percent of those under 30 had heard about it, higher than any other age group. As the "whole world is watching" chant was born when Mayor Daley's anti-riot police descended on the youthful protesters gathered in Chicago's Grant Park, it turns out the younger generation was particularly tuning in to this conflict.

By the end of the Cold War in the late 1980s and early 1990s, there was an increasing age gap in awareness of domestic and foreign affairs. The Millennials came of age in a time when Ronald Reagan had famously stood in front of the Berlin Wall and implored, "Mr. Gorbachev, tear down this wall" (Wattenberg 2008, 62). Meanwhile, a 1990 National Election Study (NES) survey found that only 27 percent of Americans younger than 30 had "heard a lot" about the changes taking place in the Soviet Union and Eastern Europe, compared with 53 percent for those 65 years or older, and dropping by seven points in awareness for each younger age group (Wattenberg 2008, 62). Apparently this was a more meaningful moment for those who had come of age in the World War II era, during the construction of the Berlin Wall and dramatic events like the Cuban Missile Crisis.

In the first year of the new millennium, the 9/11 attacks had the intense attention of the emerging Millennial generation, including our students. A Pew survey report in December 2001 found that 61 percent of adult Americans nationwide under age 30 said they were following the story very closely. In our US politics courses at SUNY Fredonia, fall 2001–fall 2005, the amount of entering students who paid a lot of attention to the 9/11 attacks dwarfed other categories, with a high of 94 percent in the early aftermath of the attack in fall 2001 and remaining above 80 percent for entering students in the courses until 2004. Granted, these were New York state residents, with some residing in the New York City area, but the attacks had long-lasting resonance for Americans and youth across the nation (Harvard IOP 2002). And for our students, the early relevance and lasting impact were higher and consistent across subsequent years when compared with those paying "a lot of attention" to even the 2004 presidential election (see Figure 2.1).

In the first years of the new millennium, 9/11 was a cataclysmic event preceded and followed by a series of very visible crises and historic moments, from the 2000 election to Katrina. Across the nation, younger Americans were paying a great deal of attention to politics in a way we had grown unaccustomed to in recent years (e.g., Harvard IOP 2005; HERI 2006). Along with 9/11, the war in Iraq, and the 2000 and 2004 elections, these were highly salient times when it came to particular aspects of US politics and policy. Students paid particular attention to key political moments, the most visible, dramatic, and grand events in the news cycle. However, they weren't as likely to pay a lot of attention to the 2002 congressional elections or even the 2004 presidential primaries (see Table 2.1).

It is important to distinguish perceived relevance—not simply the dramatic event—as it is related to attentiveness. For 334 students entering our

Figure 2.1   Attentiveness upon Entering a US Politics Course

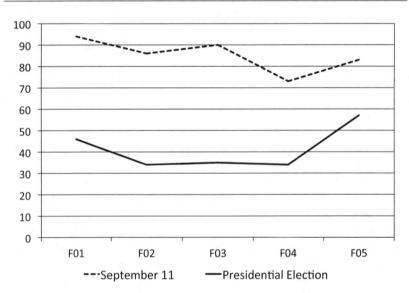

Notes: Trend lines indicate the percentage of SUNY Fredonia students beginning US politics courses who are paying or have paid "a lot of attention" to the September 11 attacks and to the 2000 presidential election (F01–F03) and the 2004 presidential election (F04 and F05). The question wording is given in Appendix A.

US politics courses at SUNY Fredonia in fall 2005, 57 percent claimed to have paid a lot of attention to the 2004 presidential election, with fully 90 percent claiming to have paid at least some attention. While 83 percent in fall 2005 claimed to have paid a lot of attention to 9/11, only 27 percent claimed to pay a lot of attention to terrorist attacks that took place in London on July 7, 2005, or 7/7 as it is referred to in England. In our survey of 133 Northumbria University students in Newcastle, England, entering an introductory politics course in fall 2005, 74 percent had paid a lot of attention to the London bombings.

Attentiveness and Political Knowledge

What grabs students' attention (and what does not) helps to explain important differences in related political knowledge. Describing the intervening impact of 9/11, Marcus Prior (2002, 524) argues, "The immediate threat and the uncommonly high levels of interest, combined with a ready supply of information, created a situation in which learning was bound to occur . . . knowledge of foreign affairs contrasted markedly with knowledge before 9/11."

Attentiveness is a key element of information exposure to and learning about politics, in the general population or in the classroom. John Zaller (1992, 21), for example, notes political awareness is "best measured by simple tests of neutral factual information about politics . . . to capture what has actually gotten into people's minds." In the assessment of our students' political awareness and learning we utilized many commonly accepted measures of political knowledge (e.g., Delli Carpini and

Table 2.1 Attentiveness upon Exiting a US Politics Course

	Some/A Lot (%)	A Lot (%)	Term	N
9/11 attacks	98	86	F01	235
2004 presidential election	97	70	F04	297
Launch of war in Iraq	93	60	S03	185
2000 presidential election	92	60	F00	243
Launch of war in Afghanistan	91	47	F01	235
Hurricane Katrina	85	54	F05	215
2004 presidential primaries	50	18	S04	88
Statewide/congressional elections	35	8	F02	325

Notes: Figures indicate the percentage of SUNY Fredonia students completing US politics courses who paid "some/a lot of attention" to the events listed above. Questionnaires were distributed during the final week of fall (e.g., F01) and spring (e.g., S04) courses, in December and May of respective years. The question wording is given in Appendix A.

Keeter 1996; Robinson, Shaver, and Wrightsman 1999), but also developed several measures specific to knowledge on issues and figures related to particular topics such as the war on terrorism and war in Iraq. We also utilized a combination of open-ended and closed-ended questions, along with "Don't Know" response options for a mix of the questions (see Appendix A for question wording).

In general, open-ended questions are considered more difficult for respondents to answer correctly when information must be recalled rather than simply recognized (Mondak 2001; Tedin and Murray 1979). For example, only 36 percent of adult respondents were able to volunteer Putin's name according to an April 2007 Pew report that asked, "Who is the president of Russia?" But 60 percent correctly selected Putin when the question was worded: "Can you tell me who is the president of Russia: Is it Boris Yeltsin, Vladimir Putin, Mikhail Gorbachev, or is it someone else?" Similarly, only 21 percent correctly answered that Robert Gates was the secretary of defense to an open-ended question in our survey, compared with 37 percent who did so when asked to choose whether Gates was the defense secretary, a senator from Michigan, the chairman of General Motors, or held another job.

On other questions, the differences attributable to alternative formats are less dramatic. In an April 2007 Pew survey report, about three in four (76 percent) were able to volunteer unaided that the Democrats controlled the House of Representatives. Eighty-two percent of Pew respondents answered correctly when asked which political party controlled the House followed by the prompt, "Is it the Democratic Party or the Republican Party?"

Some studies have found question types, namely the use of "Don't Know" options, to have little to no measurable effect on knowledge differences (Sturgis, Allum, and Smith 2008). Others contend such question options do impact respondents' answers (Mondak and Davis 2001). At times, "Don't Know" options have been encouraged, so as not to force choices by respondents (Delli Carpini and Keeter 1996). It is not the objective here to determine question-wording effect on political awareness and knowledge, but rather to use a variety of question-wording options to demonstrate the importance of context and perceived relevance connecting our students' political awareness with learning.

The salience of figures, processes, and events, coupled with perceived relevance, is a critical element in political knowledge. How one asks a question may have less to do with political recall than the respondent's own interest or the information's personal relevance. In a television clip of the game show *Who Wants to Be a Millionaire* hosted by Regis Philbin, a confused contestant stares down at the question, "Which of the following is described in Article I of the Constitution?" The contestant has already used the option to eliminate two of the four multiple-choice answers, which were the CIA and the courts. Left with two choices, the legislature and the executive, the perplexed man then uses another lifeline to phone a former law school friend. Shakily the friend replies she thinks the answer is the legislature but she is far from certain, which he accepts as the best choice since he clearly has no idea.

When viewing this clip in a US politics course, students are astounded when it is revealed that this lawyer just won $64,000 for answering the most basic US politics course question correctly, albeit after using two of his lifelines. But even more revealing is how the contestant, who Regis also notes was voted *most likely to succeed* in high school, handles the very next question. Asked to choose which musical artist had won the most Grammy awards, the man barely pauses as he confidently announces Aretha Franklin, good for $128,000!

The contestant had essentially flunked the most basic example of textbook knowledge of US politics but aced what could be referred to as surveillance knowledge when it came to an understanding of changing pop cultural figures and recognition. Textbook knowledge is the type one would expect in a traditional US politics course, consisting of understanding enduring processes and institutions, such as US Senate term length. Surveillance *political* knowledge is more about an understanding of the contemporary issue environment and current affairs. Such contextual information can change, such as party control of the US House. Surveillance knowledge is also more likely to change in connection to related salient events, attentiveness, and interest, as we discover with regard to our Millennial-age students.

Learning Relevance

Whether or not the *Who Wants to Be a Millionaire* contestant knew such textbook political knowledge at one point during high school or college or even law school, its relevance in his life had clearly escaped him. Although many people would find such a lack of knowledge concerning (not only for an average citizen, but particularly for a practicing attorney), the fact is that most attorneys probably learn more about the articles of the Constitution in an introduction to US politics course than in the study of contracts and torts in law school. Law students are training to be lawyers but not necessarily politically informed citizens.

We would hope that political textbook knowledge is more accessible for our students entering an introduction to US politics course. However,

NAEP findings also show that high school seniors do better retaining general facts (how a bill becomes law in Congress) but have a more difficult time with concepts, such as executive vs. legislative functions, or particular details. For example, about 74 percent know that Congress belongs to the legislative branch and the president belongs to the executive. Just about half of high school seniors know that the president nominates federal judges, and about one-third know a US senator's term is six years.

While most of our students entering US politics courses during fall 2001–fall 2005 understood that the Supreme Court of the United States determines whether laws are unconstitutional, there was much less knowledge when it came to who appoints federal judges, and only a minority could identify the length of a US Senate term (see Figure 2.2). The results also demonstrate how multiple-choice options do not guarantee more accurate responses. For example, more students were able to recall that the president appoints federal judges than were able to choose among different options with regard to US Senate term length.

When it came to elements of surveillance knowledge, open-ended written identification of Osama bin Laden as the principal suspect in the

Figure 2.2   Textbook Knowledge upon Entering a US Politics Course

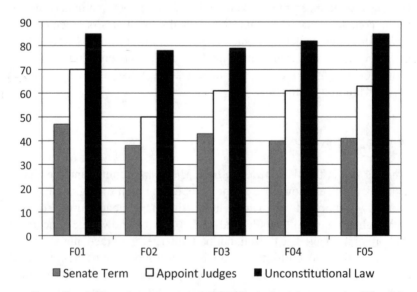

Notes: Bars indicate the percentage of SUNY Fredonia students entering US politics courses in each semester who are able to identify in closed-ended questions "the length of a US Senate term" and "whose responsibility it is to determine if a law is unconstitutional," and the percentage of students who are able to recall in an open-ended question "whose responsibility it is to appoint federal judges." The question wording is given in Appendix A.

9/11 attacks was at levels of almost universal recognition for our students *entering* the US politics courses at SUNY Fredonia. While this was at its highest levels in the near aftermath of 9/11, recall of bin Laden never dipped below the high seventies in the four years following the attacks. While this seems logical based on the overwhelming attention to bin Laden as enemy number one of the United States in the media and on political leadership in the early war on terrorism (Prior 2002), this level of consistent recognition is unheard of for most high-level foreign policy figures in the United States.

Secretaries of State Colin Powell and Condoleezza Rice and Defense Secretary Donald Rumsfeld were arguably three of the more visible figures in the Bush administration, but an understanding of their relative positions was dwarfed by the recognition of bin Laden for incoming students in an introductory course in US politics (see Figure 2.3). Although much more limited recall was consistent for these figures, high media points and crises ranging from the initial 9/11 attacks to critical moments in the war in Iraq did appear to boost knowledge, particularly as media attention and general public opinion became more negative and divided

Figure 2.3   Recalling Foreign Policy Figures

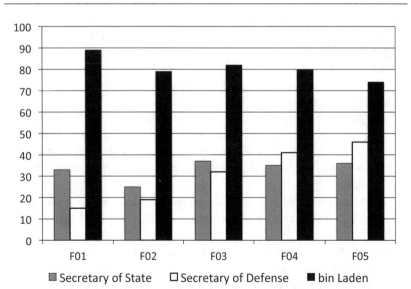

Notes: Bars indicate the percentage of SUNY Fredonia students entering US politics courses in each semester who are able to recall, in an open-ended question, the job or political office held by Colin Powell/Condoleezza Rice and Donald Rumsfeld and the last name of the primary suspect in the 9/11 terrorist attacks. The question wording is given in Appendix A.

about the roles and strategies of these key political figures. This appeared particularly true for increasingly combative Defense Secretary Rumsfeld. In his case, our students' awareness of who he was increased as his negative visibility increased.

Table 2.2 shows the US politics learning curve for surveillance knowledge items as well as that for textbook knowledge. Recall of political figures by students entering our US politics courses appears quite reflective of the perceived relevance and likely mainstream media attention afforded (or not) to public officials. Our students were far more comfortable recalling the high-profile US senator Hillary Clinton from New York than they were identifying the length of her US Senate term, even when provided with options. The students had much greater difficulty coming up with the names of both US senators from New York.

A surveillance knowledge learning curve was particularly large with regard to partisan control of the US House (the Republican Party throughout these surveys) as well as the ability to recall the chief justice of the US Supreme Court. As we discussed earlier, knowledge of the chief justice is extremely low for most Americans, and 43 percent is actually a pretty impressive level of recall for what seems to be a very obscure individual (despite his importance and stature) to most adult respondents. A 2004 NES survey found that 28 percent of 18- to 24-year-olds could identify Rehnquist as chief justice. Clearly, there are certain types of surveillance knowledge that students bring to a course based on media context and perceived relevance that can be reinforced within an introduction to US politics course.

In fact, knowledge recall of domestic political figures paled in comparison with our students' recall of figures from the war on terrorism, including bin Laden and the Taliban/al-Qaeda in Afghanistan. Such "foreign" figures were among the most recognizable for students both entering and exiting the introductory course on US politics. This is not surprising considering the heightened and sustained attentiveness outside of the classroom our students had with regard to the 9/11 attacks and war on terrorism.

Surveillance knowledge, by its very nature, is connected to the understanding and awareness of contextual political events and figures. And with higher alpha reliability scores (see Table 2.2), our students were more likely to coherently link in their minds their knowledge of domestic and foreign policy figures rather than enduring textbook facts. Therefore, it is particularly important to recognize how an awareness of salient events and processes relates to our students' surveillance knowledge. It is also important to understand how salient events are also connected to textbook gains when current events at least temporarily raise the visibility and perceived direct relevance of foundational processes and institutions.

As critical events arise, important learning opportunities present themselves for building increased surveillance knowledge as well as textbook knowledge and learning. Despite what educators may consider ideal, students are more likely to retain knowledge related to salient

Table 2.2 Political Knowledge and Learning in US Politics Courses

Fall 2001 to Fall 2005 Knowledge of:	Pre	Post	Change
War on terrorism political figures/facts			
Secretary of state	32%	43%	+11
Secretary of defense	29%	38%	+9
bin Laden as 9/11 suspect	81%	87%	+6
Taliban/al-Qaeda in Afghanistan	80%	84%	+4
Mean knowledge (0–4)	2.1	2.4	+.3*
Alpha reliability scale	.53	.57	
Domestic political figures/facts			
Chief justice of US Supreme Court	21%	43%	+22
One New York senator	67%	76%	+9
Both New York senators	20%	29%	+9
One vice presidential candidate	63%	75%	+12
Two vice presidential candidates	39%	52%	+13
Party with control of US House[a]	48%	70%	+22
Mean knowledge (0–6)	2.5	3.4	+.9*
Alpha reliability scale	.61	.62	
Mean surveillance knowledge (0–10)	4.6	5.8	+1.2*
Alpha reliability scale	.72	.72	
Textbook knowledge			
Length of Senate term[a]	41%	53%	+12
Court determines if law unconstitutional[a]	81%	86%	+5
President appoints federal judges	60%	77%	+17
Mean knowledge (0–3)	1.8	2.2	+.4*
Alpha reliability scale	.39	.41	
Mean total knowledge (0–13)	6.4	8.0	+1.6*
Alpha reliability scale	.75	.76	

Notes: The column figures are based on the pooled data of 1,558 student respondents both entering (pre) and completing (post) US politics courses at SUNY Fredonia, fall 2001–fall 2005. The Taliban/al-Qaeda Afghanistan question was not included in fall 2001 results, otherwise all items were included in pre and post questionnaires. The question wording is given in Appendix A. * $p \leq .001$ for paired sample t-tests.

a. A closed-ended question (e.g., multiple choice); all others are open-ended questions (e.g., write-in answer).

events with perceived relevance to their lives outside of the course. Thus it is important to understand in what circumstances political knowledge and learning appear most responsive to contextual factors.

In this chapter, I examine three particularly prominent examples connected to very high surges in student attentiveness and learning, including the dramatic conclusion of highly visible elections in 2000 and 2004, a highly salient war on terrorism and in Iraq, and the recognition of the most visible figures associated with these high-profile events and processes. Similarly, I demonstrate what types of political processes and related political figures are less likely to stimulate related knowledge acquisition and learning. And finally, there are the celebrity figures our students (and citizens in general) recognize for no other reason than that they are in the media spotlight, a category that provides little basis for extended learning when these figures are not associated with political foundations, institutions, processes, and larger political events. The key here is to link the perceived relevance of political processes and events with political attentiveness, knowledge, and interest.

Electoral Understanding

Every four years a great deal of attention focuses on the presidential campaign. The election cycle is considered one of the more information-rich environments for citizens when it comes to US politics, particularly as we near Election Day in the presidential general election (Alvarez 1997). For many young Americans, this is the first and perhaps only time they are asked to think about and consider US politics and their role in it as a voter.

For our US politics students, attention, interest, and knowledge increased and coalesced as we headed into the fall presidential campaigns. Like Americans in general, our students tended to start paying attention to politics when it seemed to matter most in their eyes, or perhaps when it was most difficult to avoid. As for the presidential primary process, Macedo et al. (2005, 3) argue, "its lengthy and episodic nature discourages sustained attention and continued political learning." For example, it was difficult to even communicate to 18- to 24-year-olds that George W. Bush was a candidate as the 2000 primary season began (Pew, February 2000). By the time the 2000 Florida electoral recount battle reached the Supreme Court, identification would be far less of a problem (Pew, November 2000).

At the end of the fall 2000 term, 60 percent of our US politics students claimed to have paid a lot of attention to the 2000 election, and 92 percent at least some attention. And as the *Bush v. Gore* Supreme Court decision wound a historic election to its dramatic conclusion, 60 percent could recall both vice presidential candidates (76 percent at least one), the highest number for this category until our courses during the fall 2004 election.

Moreover, heightened attentiveness provided opportunities to increase and sustain related surveillance learning across other political and/or governmental figures. Our US politics students' ability to recall Chief Justice William Rehnquist was at its highest numbers following the fall 2000 election (62 percent). At the end of the spring 2001 courses our students at SUNY Fredonia had 57 percent recall of the chief justice, a figure quite similar to the 59 percent recall of the chief justice in our spring 2001 survey of students at the completion of an introduction to US politics course at the University of Wisconsin, River Falls. Our student recall of the Supreme Court justice would not crack 50 percent again until Rehnquist's death opened up a seat on the bench for John Roberts. By the end of the fall 2005 course, 61 percent of our SUNY Fredonia US politics students could recall Rehnquist's role.

This is an impressive number considering the knowledge most Americans possess when it comes to the Supreme Court and governmental figures in general. For example, in an August 2006 national survey conducted by Zogby International, only one-quarter of adult respondents could name two of the Supreme Court justices while three-quarters of adult respondents could name two of Snow White's seven dwarfs. Related surveillance knowledge and learning was at its highest levels when our students' own attentiveness was at its highest with regard to particularly salient events and processes.

Exposure to the US politics learning experience helps to reinforce awareness and increase knowledge by building on an already salient event in our students' minds and drawing even more attention to it as part of the course. In spring 2004, those students claiming to pay a lot of attention to the presidential election rose from 34 to 70 percent by the end of the term and 82 to 97 percent (9/11-type numbers) for those paying at least some attention. By the end of fall 2004, 78 percent of our students claimed to have paid a lot of attention to the 2004 presidential election, with another 18 percent paying at least some attention.

And this wasn't an isolated case in our courses in western New York. In surveys distributed to 237 students at the close of an introductory US politics course at the University of California at Santa Barbara (UCSB) in December 2004, 71 percent of students claimed to pay a lot of attention to the presidential election (with another 27 percent at least some). Even though both campuses were hardly in what one could consider swing states during the 2004 presidential election, there was still tremendous attention to the election on both coasts.

With increasing attention to the 2004 election, knowledge of not only the sitting vice president but also the Democratic vice presidential candidate soared. At the end of fall 2004, 78 percent of SUNY Fredonia students in the US politics courses could name both VP candidates, and 86 percent at least one. This was a significant bump from the 48 percent who could name both VP candidates at the beginning of fall 2004, with 68 percent able to name at least one. In our survey of UCSB students at the end of fall 2004, 85 percent were able to name both vice presidential candidates, and 92 percent at least one (overwhelmingly Cheney).

For highly salient political events with perceived direct relevance, our students' attentiveness to the 2000 and 2004 elections also impacted related items of textbook knowledge, with students able to connect heightened attentiveness to course learning. When posed a multiple-choice question at the end of class in fall 2000 and spring 2001, 97 percent of SUNY Fredonia US politics students answered correctly that the Electoral College selects the president, by far the highest number in the time periods covered. In fall 2000, 78 percent of our SUNY Fredonia students had also correctly chosen 270 as the minimum amount needed to secure an Electoral College majority.

Universal understanding that the Electoral College determines the president-elect was available for our SUNY Fredonia students entering the fall 2004 course (94 percent) and the fall 2005 course (89 percent). At the end of the spring 2003 quarter in early June at UCSB, 44 percent of 101 US politics students correctly identified the Electoral College majority number at 270, whereas at the end of the fall 2004 quarter at UCSB, 87 percent could identify the number. Similarly, at the end of the spring 2003 semester, 55 percent of SUNY Fredonia students in the US politics courses could identify the Electoral College majority, and 80 percent in fall 2004. In those cases where entering knowledge of the Electoral College majority was measured, the learning curve at the end of the course averaged 24 points, one of the higher knowledge gains on items measured. However, it was clear that our students' knowledge of the Electoral College majority was at significantly higher levels when their own attentiveness to the presidential election was at its highest.

Attention to the elections appeared to also boost understanding and learning for other components of surveillance knowledge. The fall 2004 semester was a high point in knowledge of US House partisan control at nearly 90 percent, a gain of 35 points from entering knowledge for our SUNY Fredonia students (see Figure 2.4). Knowledge of House control for UCSB students in US politics at the end of fall 2004 was at 92 percent. The largest increases in House control knowledge for our students occurred during the fall 2004 and fall 2002 elections, when learning these facts was likely reinforced by our students' attentiveness to actual and directly relevant results reported as part of the election cycle.

Our students' attentiveness was simply much higher when it came to the height of the presidential elections than it was for the midterm election. During the fall 2002 election cycle, 33 percent of our SUNY Fredonia students entering US politics claimed to pay at least some attention to the statewide elections, a figure moving to 45 percent by the end of the

Figure 2.4   Exiting Knowledge of the Electoral College and House Control

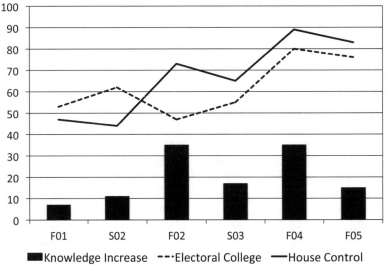

Notes: Trend lines indicate the percentage of SUNY Fredonia students with knowledge of the Electoral College majority rule of 270 electoral votes and knowledge that Republicans controlled the House at the end of the term in US politics courses. Bars indicate the percentage point increase in students' knowledge from when they first entered the course. We did not ask the Electoral College majority question in fall 2003 and spring 2004. The question wording is given in Appendix A.

fall 2002 term but still far below those of the 2000 and 2004 fall terms. And relatively lower levels of attentiveness to related processes equaled lower levels of related knowledge. Despite the fact that Republican incumbent George Pataki was up for a third term and his challenger H. Carl McCall was the first African American comptroller of New York state, only 36 percent of our students could recall both candidates' names at the start of fall 2002, and 49 percent at the end of the term.

By the beginning of the spring 2003 term, 25 percent of our US politics students claimed to have paid some attention (and only 6 percent a lot) to the New York gubernatorial election, whereas 69 percent claimed to have paid at least some attention (and 24 percent a lot) to the more distant 2000 presidential election. Not surprisingly, then, only 31 percent of our students entering the spring 2003 course could name both gubernatorial candidates, compared with 50 percent who could name both VP candidates from the 2000 presidential election. With a lower starting knowledge of these state officials, only 37 percent could recall both gubernatorial candidates by the end of the spring 2003 course, a number that increased to 63 percent for the 2000 VP candidates.

At the end of spring 2003 in June, we also asked UCSB students in the introduction to US politics course if they paid much attention to the 2002 California gubernatorial election. At over $100 million spent, the California gubernatorial election was the most expensive in state history. Yet only 8 percent of these students claimed to have paid a lot of attention and 23 percent some attention to the gubernatorial election, whereas 83 percent had paid at least some attention to the 2000 election.

Fifty-five percent of these UCSB students could name both of the vice presidential candidates in the 2000 election, but only 26 percent could name more than one of the California gubernatorial candidates in the 2002 election. Overall, 59 percent could recall at least one of the 2002 gubernatorial candidates and 76 percent at least one of the 2000 VP candidates. Only 24 percent of these UCSB students could name both US senators from California, with another 59 percent able to name at least one of them.

Furthermore, our students' relatively higher level of attentiveness to the presidential election than to the midterm election also translated into higher textbook knowledge levels of items such as the Electoral College and surveillance knowledge such as US House control in fall 2004 when compared with fall 2002. It is clear that certain political events and processes, namely the height of a highly visible presidential election, will hold the attention of our college-age Millennials, while other political events such as the midterm election are far less likely to do so. Far more than these obvious differences, it is important to recognize how differing levels of attentiveness to such processes also directly relate to political knowledge and learning. Despite our best efforts to educate our students at times apart from external context and changing political events, we must contend with students' own attentiveness to the events and related figures that they deem most recognizable and familiar in their perception of the political world.

Domestic Recognition

It is important to understand whom our students are likely to know compared with whom they do not in order to recognize and sort out the awareness impact of external factors such as the media and what role an introduction to US politics can play in filling such knowledge gaps. This helps to inform educators about where we may need to strengthen identification of lesser-known political figures and develop connections to build awareness and recognition in our students' understanding of the broader political process.

For example, one of the most well-known political figures among our SUNY Fredonia US politics students was California's governor, Arnold Schwarzenegger. The self-described "governator" had been elevated to the position in California's recall election of 2003, a far greater media spectacle than the 2002 election in which incumbent Gray Davis had been reelected. Entering the US politics course in western New York, the ability to recall the name of the California governor was at 87 percent in spring 2004, 93 percent in fall 2004, and 92 percent in spring 2005. Perhaps former New York governor Pataki would have been better known if he had been an action hero rather than a former New York state legislator.

Our students were simply serving as an example of political awareness and knowledge prevalent in the general US population in direct proportion to mainstream media attention and perceived celebrity. In an April 2007 Pew report, more than nine in ten Americans (93 percent) could identify Arnold Schwarzenegger as the California governor or a former action-movie star—both responses were counted as correct in the scoring. Not to be outdone, 93 percent named Hillary Clinton as a US senator, a former first lady, a Democratic leader, or a candidate for president. Sixty-four percent could identify singer and actress Beyoncé Knowles, 62 percent NFL quarterback Peyton Manning, 21 percent Defense Secretary Robert Gates, and 15 percent US Senate Majority Leader Harry Reid.

Like LeBron or Madonna, the former first lady and US senator from New York had become well enough known to go by just her first name. Whereas 45 percent of our SUNY Fredonia US politics students had claimed to pay some attention to the 2002 statewide New York elections by the end of the fall 2002 term, 72 percent had claimed to pay at least some attention to the 2000 race for the US Senate seat from New York by the end of the fall 2000 course. Eighty-four percent of students could recall at least one of the US Senate candidates from New York at the end of the fall 2000 term, and it was overwhelmingly Hillary.

Hillary Clinton was the major reason for the high level of familiarity and attention given the fact the race had gained national attention coverage at times rivaling the presidential race in its early stages. This sort of attention also seemed to boost knowledge of US Senate term length. At 68 percent at the end of the fall 2000 course, it was the highest exiting score on the question for students, fall 2000–fall 2005. A highly visible Senate race with a well-known figure for this age group provided an important opportunity to engage students in related areas of learning, and the facts stuck.

There are unique opportunities to build learning around recognizable events such as the height of a presidential election and identifiable figures such as Hillary Clinton that can connect recognition with related knowledge and learning. However, widespread awareness of political figures, beyond the president, is rare, and in most instances salient events must be used in conjunction with heightened student political attentiveness to build recognition of lesser-known elected officials.

For instance, UCSB students completing an introductory course in US politics were much more likely to recall the names of both vice presidential candidates from the 2000 and 2004 elections than to recall their US senators. In spring 2003, 55 percent of these UCSB students could name both of the 2000 vice presidential candidates and 24 percent could recall both Feinstein and Boxer. By the end of fall 2004, 85 percent of UCSB students in the course could name the VP candidates and 43 percent both of the US senators, a knowledge gap of 42 points.

With the rare exception of high-profile national figures such as Hillary Clinton, Millennial awareness of political figures is driven far more by attentiveness to highly visible processes such as the presidential election than is awareness of any midterm election or nonpresidential political leadership.

Moreover, while the senator vs. vice presidential candidate recognition gap favored First Lady Hillary Clinton with SUNY Fredonia students in fall 2000, the SUNY Fredonia gap was almost identical to that of UCSB in fall 2004, with a 41-point recognition advantage to the vice presidential candidates. Dick Cheney had reached a particularly visible level for the younger generation and Americans in general by the 2004 election, well beyond recognition of this Washington insider in 2000. Cheney had emerged from relative obscurity, when he was charged with selecting a vice presidential running mate for George W. Bush, to one of the most polarizing figures within the Bush White House, and he became a figure of much late night comedy banter, including references to Cheney in villainous imagery such as *Star Wars'* Darth Vader.

With such visibility and awareness more associated with the central figures within the White House than on Capitol Hill, it is little wonder that our *Who Wants to Be a Millionaire* contestant could not distinguish whether the executive or legislature was the first article listed by the founders in the US Constitution. After all, with the rare exception of first-name celebrity political figures like Hillary and Arnold, the White House receives the overwhelming focus of the media and thus our students' awareness of US politics.

According to a 2004 NES survey, only 25 percent of 18- to 25-year-olds could name their own candidate for the US House, and that figure was only 16 percent in what would be a contentious 2000 election. In a multiple-choice example, our SUNY Fredonia students entering US politics courses in fall 2001–spring 2004 were asked to select whether Dennis Hastert was US attorney general, Speaker of the House, Senate majority leader, or a US senator from New York. The correct answer was at 31 percent in fall 2001, 26 percent in spring 2002, 27 percent in fall 2002 and spring 2003, 32 percent in fall 2003, and 27 percent in spring 2004.

With relatively lower entering knowledge of such figures, this does present an opportunity to increase our students' knowledge of such less familiar political figures as they learn about their respective congressional role as part of a typical introduction to US politics course (see Appendix B). There was a strong learning curve on the question for our students by the end of the US politics course, moving to 46 percent in fall 2001, 47 percent in spring 2002, 36 percent in fall 2002, 46 percent in spring 2003, 47 percent in fall 2003, and 39 percent in spring 2004. On average, students came into the course with 28 percent name recognition of the Speaker of the House and ended the course at 44 percent recognition, a 16-point increase. At the end of the spring 2003 UCSB US politics course, name recognition of the Speaker of the House was at 50 percent compared with 46 percent of SUNY Fredonia students.

Overall, our 435 House members toil in relative obscurity with rare exceptions, including a scandal-crossed member in the vein of Democrat

Gary Condit of California in 2001 (the missing intern scandal) or Republican Mark Foley of Florida in 2006 (the male page scandal), or a vociferous or media-friendly House Speaker (e.g., Tip O'Neill, Newt Gingrich). House member Nancy Pelosi was plucked from relative obscurity when she was elevated to the position of the first female Speaker of the House and became the most visible point of opposition to the Bush administration after Democrats regained Congress in 2006. According to a March 2008 Pew survey report, 74 percent of adult respondents nationwide could identify Pelosi as the House Speaker, which was a big leap from the 49 percent who could do so a year earlier in an April 2007 Pew report. On the other hand, only 24 percent could identify Harry Reid, who was elevated to US Senate majority leader after the 2006 takeover of Congress, albeit a slight bump up from the 15 percent who could identify him according to an April 2007 Pew report.

Our students likewise are familiar with certain political figures but could not name others, simply because we don't see them as often across the media spectrum. Conflict and controversy generate coverage in the modern media, which facilitates awareness of certain political figures but not others. We get to know presidential candidates at the height of presidential elections when the quadrennial spectacle heats up. Drama and action seared Arnold into our public consciousness and particularly young minds living in a media-saturated world. It was the same when the names bin Laden and Saddam brought a distant world home suddenly to young learners blitzed by breaking events and dramatic narratives.

Foreign Familiarity

The 9/11 attacks and ensuing war on terrorism exhibited levels of attentiveness to connect these salient events to related items of knowledge and learning. For our students, attentiveness to the 9/11 attacks and the war on terrorism was related to high levels of surveillance knowledge of particular figures and related facts. However, the findings also demonstrate once again how recognition of the most visible media figures can also be in the forefront of our students' minds, making it all the more important to draw learning connections to the broader array of political leaders involved in policymaking. High attentiveness to a particular event, such as the height of the presidential elections or even war, provides a critical opportunity to build on our students' established attentiveness to facilitate a broader array of related learning and knowledge.

By the end of fall 2001, 47 percent of our SUNY Fredonia students of US politics were paying a lot of attention to the war in Afghanistan and 91 percent were paying at least some attention. And for our students both beginning and completing US politics courses, there was nearly universal recognition of Osama bin Laden as the principal suspect or mastermind in the terrorist attacks on the World Trade Center and Pentagon. There was also a consistent and stable understanding that the principal adversary in Afghanistan, as part of the war on terrorism, was the Taliban and/or the al-Qaeda terrorist network. As the war on terrorism extended into a war in Iraq, our students also exhibited almost universal recognition of Saddam Hussein as that nation's leader or former leader.

On the other hand, there were key US foreign policy figures about whom the students were less informed, important players in the Bush administration. For example, average recall of the secretary of state was at 32 percent for our US politics students entering the courses from fall 2001 to fall 2005 and at 29 percent for naming the secretary of defense. This isn't that far removed from the general public. According to Erikson and Tedin (2007, 62), in 1990 the General Social Survey reported that 34 percent of adults could name Jim Baker as secretary of state. They also reported that in 2000 the Gallup Poll found only 33 percent could name Madeleine Albright as secretary of state, even though Albright was the first female to hold that position and was involved in a number of high-profile situations, including the conflict in Yugoslavia.

Based on data from Pew Research, Zukin et al. (2006, 82) found that 28 percent of DotNets could name the secretary of state in May 2002, compared with 42 percent of Gen X, 57 percent of Boomers, and 54 percent of Dutifuls. For those too young to remember the Persian Gulf War, the former chairman of the Joint Chiefs of Staff Colin Powell, a CNN regular during the conflict, was relatively unknown. And with no discernible connection in our students' minds when it came to thinking about these figures beyond a course in US politics, knowledge levels were lower when there was less perceived relevance. However, as war with Iraq became more of this generation's war—with friends and family in line to do the fighting rather than as an abstract history lesson—knowledge of key figures in the war spiked.

Thus it is critical to take advantage of our students' attentiveness to salient events to build related knowledge when these opportunities arise as part of the US politics course experience. During the spring 2003 semester when the war actually commenced, our SUNY Fredonia US politics students' recall of Colin Powell as the secretary of state doubled from 24 to 48 percent. Students' recognition of Donald Rumsfeld as secretary of defense rose by 21 points, from 19 to 40 percent. Recall of Rumsfeld and Powell was at 37 percent and 44 percent for the UCSB students surveyed in a US politics course at the end of the spring 2003 quarter. The learning curve on these US foreign policy figures was at the highest for our SUNY Fredonia students during this spring 2003 semester, when the war actually began, compared with surveys distributed across fall 2001–fall 2005.

Our students had much more ground to make up with regard to not only US foreign policy officials but also domestic political figures when compared with the most visible adversaries like Osama and Saddam. Whereas recall of these visible foreign "villains" was already high and thus relatively unchanged for students over the term, the learning curve was substantial with respect to key US political leaders. While recognition of domestic and foreign figures surged dramatically after a term of US politics, recall of Saddam and bin Laden still generally topped the list for students, not only at SUNY Fredonia but also at UCSB.

This was true not only for students surveyed at the end of spring 2003, just two months after the launch of the war in Iraq, but also for those students surveyed a month after the 2004 presidential election. As Table 2.3 demonstrates, recall of a vice presidential candidate was particularly high for both campuses at the end of the fall 2004 term when compared with the conclusion of spring 2003. And SUNY Fredonia students had a much higher recall of one US senator than did UCSB students of their own, likely because the course reinforced an awareness of the

Table 2.3   Recall of Figures at the End of a US Politics Course

	S03 (NY)	S03 (UC)	F04 (NY)	F04 (UC)
Saddam	86	85	82	83
bin Laden	86	78	81	83
One US senator	71	49	74	64
One VP candidate	63	77	85	92
British prime minister			56	63
Speaker of the US House	46	50		
Secretary of state	48	44	41	58
Secretary of defense	39	37	41	49
Chief justice	43	45	41	41
N	185	101	297	237

Notes: Column figures indicate the percentage correctly recalling the political figures listed above for students completing spring 2003 and fall 2004 US politics courses at SUNY Fredonia (NY) and UCSB (UC). The question wording is given in Appendix A.

already incredibly visible Senator Hillary Clinton. There were slight differences in recall of other political figures for the two campuses, but it was clear which political figures both sets of students were more likely to recognize during the dramatic beginning of the war or aftermath of a very divisive election. These findings show what surveillance knowledge our students are likely to consistently hold as a result of the most identifiable media figures. The US politics course can work within an evolving context to increase related knowledge and learning in terrain less familiar and accessible to Millennials who are attempting to find their way into the political world, domestically and abroad.

Learning Reinforcement

Our students most consistently identified figures and facts likely most accessible in the contextual environment outside of the course based on their attentiveness and interest in current and ongoing salient events. However, the findings also suggest that the US politics course plays an important role in political learning, particularly related to otherwise less familiar but critical political figures. As instructors, we need to recognize that our students' familiarity with US politics does operate within an environment in which information is influenced by external sources, namely the media. At times, these forces can be in contention, but more often than not they can be used to facilitate learning overall. With a more solid understanding of US politics and more consistent exposure in the course, students can seize on images in the media and vice versa to build recognition. When they do, we see the impact on surveillance knowledge, which increases during these key periods of media saturation on related topics.

Figure 2.5 demonstrates how learning about foreign policy figures increased dramatically for our SUNY Fredonia US politics students in spring 2003 when compared with spring 2002 and fall 2002. Furthermore, foreign surveillance knowledge levels surged higher overall and trended consistently higher for the ensuing year in fall 2003 and spring 2004. Students were recalling the related figures at a consistently higher level, not surprisingly at the high point of the early war in Iraq effort. A more direct relevance appeared to enhance recall of such political information, not unlike the rise in knowledge attached to the height of presidential elections. Moreover, this foreign policy learning surge also spilled over into domestic surveillance knowledge. There were particularly noticeable learning increases during the fall 2003 term with the war well under way and debate increasing, and in fall 2004 at the height of one of the most

contentious presidential elections in decades. Furthermore, domestic surveillance knowledge levels trended upward and did not return to pre–Iraq
War or pre-2004 election levels as students encountered the Katrina crisis
when they entered the fall 2005 term.

Textbook knowledge and learning, on the other hand, remained relatively unaffected by the war in Iraq and the contentious 2004 election.
Foundational knowledge, while critical to understanding politics and government, does not necessarily connect students to the evolving world
around them. Furthermore, this disconnect can occur at the most critical
moments when the outside world could be an incredible teaching resource.

Our findings show how surveillance knowledge is particularly connected to interest and attentiveness. The variables work hand in hand, far
more than does the relationship among textbook knowledge, interest, and
attentiveness. As Table 2.4 demonstrates, surveillance knowledge is
related more to political interest and attentiveness than is textbook knowl-

Figure 2.5   Sorting Out Surveillance and Textbook Knowledge

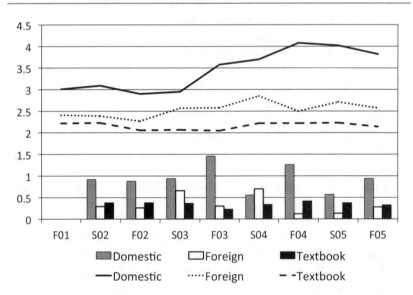

Notes: Where the scale of domestic politics knowledge is 0–6, foreign affairs knowledge is 0–4, and textbook knowledge is 0–3, trend lines show exiting mean scores and bars
show mean increases from entering mean scores for SUNY Fredonia students in US politics
courses. The mean scores are derived from the knowledge items and scales listed in Table
2.2. Mean increases are not displayed for fall 2001 because students were not asked about
the Taliban's role in the war in Afghanistan as they entered the fall 2001 course. The question is included in the exiting score trend lines since the end of fall 2001.

edge for our students entering US politics from fall 2001 to fall 2005. Students connected their broader political interest and more specific attentiveness to the election to their recognition of key political figures and realities more than to their grasp of enduring constitutional foundations and institutions. For example, the connection was much more significant among political interest, attention to the election, and surveillance knowledge of the US senators from New York than any relationship with textbook knowledge of US Senate term length.

Our students were more likely to link political interest and attentiveness to the presidential election with the recall of relevant candidates than the understanding that it takes 270 electoral votes to win a bare majority in the Electoral College system. Interest and attentiveness were far more important for our students in identifying which party controls the House than in understanding how many overall members serve in this representative chamber. Interest and attentiveness were more significantly connected with surveillance knowledge of the chief justice of the Supreme Court than with the textbook understanding that the US Supreme Court is

Table 2.4 Interest, Attentiveness, and Knowledge upon Entering US Politics Courses

	Political Interest	Election Attention
Presidential appointment power	.220	.175
Recall secretary of state	*.256*	*.224*
US Senate term length	.084	.112
Recall US senators from New York	*.298*	*.298*
Determines constitutionality	.149	.079
Recall chief justice	*.194*	*.137*
Electoral College majority rule	.158	.124
Recall vice presidential candidates	*.338*	*.296*
Number of members in the US House of Representatives	.088	.061
Identify House party control	*.139*	*.230*

Notes: Column figures are Spearman's Rho correlation coefficients (all p ≤ .001) indicating statistically significant relationships between item knowledge and national political interest/attentiveness to the presidential election. Measures of surveillance knowledge are in italics. Political interest measured a four-point scale of levels of interest in national politics, and election attention measured a four-point scale of levels of attention to the presidential election. Results are based on pooled data of 1,558 SUNY Fredonia student respondents for fall 2001–fall 2005, except for "Number of members in the US House" (fall 2001 only) and "Electoral College majority rule" (the question was not asked in fall 2003 or spring 2004).

the branch that determines whether a law is unconstitutional. Again and again, it was clear that our students' own political attentiveness and identified political interest, while significantly related to textbook knowledge, were connected most significantly to surveillance knowledge and learning.

Conclusion

It is critical to understand what our Millennial-age students are paying attention to as they enter US politics, and how their related awareness and interest can most effectively connect with political learning. What do we accomplish if students learn the basic foundational knowledge of government but do not connect it to specific electoral attentiveness or broader political interest? What if students cannot identify contemporary political figures and realities that impact enduring rules and processes? Such connections are critical for students to more fully understand US politics and to take these lessons beyond the course into their emerging roles as citizens.

It is important to recognize how our students' political interest and attentiveness to salient events can facilitate political knowledge and learning. The results here show how surveillance knowledge increases in line with students' attentiveness and interest far more than with regard to textbook knowledge. This provides important insight into how to connect critical aspects of political interest and learning as part of the educational environment. Instruction can facilitate connections among students' perceived interest in contemporary political events, surveillance knowledge, and a foundational understanding of US government and process. There are certain types of surveillance knowledge that are most accessible in our students' minds. As student learning is related to attentiveness and interest, an effective learning environment will integrate relevant salient events and processes to enhance the learning curve across related items of knowledge. Attentiveness to salient events also boosts knowledge across other areas of US politics and government as our students connect heightened political interest with broader political learning when these connections are strengthened.

Knowledge begets knowledge. Foundational knowledge helps to put surveillance knowledge into a proper context within a classroom environment and in our roles as citizens. While foundational knowledge is important, surveillance knowledge helps us to make sense of politics as it transpires around us, to understand context and how to apply it to given debates facing the country or our community. It is not enough to simply understand how a veto works and not the politics behind it and the figures involved. There will be political events that grab our students' attention and open up learning opportunities. Rather than a distant mechanism accessed only through textbooks, understanding direct relevance and workings of politics and processes provides for related learning.

At the same time, these findings demonstrate that our students find particular political figures and processes to be far more accessible than other figures when it comes to political attentiveness and knowledge. What our students know and their acquisition of related knowledge are a critical part of understanding how these Millennials process often-limited political information in order to reason through political and policy debates as learning exercises and as real-life issue concerns. Thus, political knowledge gained as part of an introduction to US politics provides valuable information beyond what our students receive in the mediated political environment and can contribute significantly to their being able to sort through the most salient policy choices facing this generation.

3

Reasoning in
a World of Politics and Policy

I think we should just trust our president in every decision
he makes and should just support that, you know.
—*Britney Spears speaking with*
CNN Crossfire *host Tucker Carlson, 2003*

The sudden and dramatic events from 9/11 to the war in Iraq visited upon the Millennial Generation provided for compelling challenges as well as learning opportunities. Attentiveness to salient, if not crisis, events can reinforce political information that can stimulate learning and retention, as I discussed in Chapter 2. Crises also provoke emotional reactions that can cause citizens to bypass scrutiny and, instead, rely more on familiar symbolic attachments and inflated trust in political leaders and government mechanisms. This, too, can be a tenuous relationship, one shaped by crisis and not by mutual commitment to civic discourse and communication. When such crises dissipate, citizens can remain disconnected from the critical policy choices in which they never truly engaged. Thus, knowing or learning how to sift through information and to counter emotional overload when formulating judgments can be a critical part of how one thinks about US politics as a student. These learned skills can then be carried forward into students' lifelong roles as informed citizens.

Political knowledge has long been understood to be critical to broader notions of political sophistication, intellectual engagement with politics, and political awareness (Converse 1964; Zaller 1992). Higher levels of knowledge help people to more effectively process, assimilate, and retrieve new information (Berent and Krosnick 1995). Galston (2007) argues, "Unless citizens possess a basic level of civic knowledge . . . it is difficult for them to understand political events or to integrate new information into an existing framework."

This is particularly important, as numerous studies show that most Americans rely extensively on information shortcuts, including political cues and feelings, to make sense of the political world when faced with unfamiliar situations (Kuklinski 2001; Neuman et al. 2007; Popkin 1991). Furthermore, when people are better informed, research shows they tend to reach different political or policy decisions than when they are poorly informed (Althaus 1998; Bartels 1996).

When it comes to foreign policy concerns in particular, emotion has often guided the average citizen's reasoning (Almond 1960; Hurwitz and Peffley 1990). Emotions (or affective attitudes) also influence domestic policy preferences when there is limited information (Dolan and Holbrook 2001; Sniderman, Brody, and Tetlock 1991). In Chapter 2, drama drew our students into awareness of certain events, related political facts, and figures. Some degree of emotional arousal is found to encourage people to pay attention to other kinds of information in a situation (Marcus, Neuman, and MacKuen 2000). The question is, how do we build understanding and facilitate reasoned judgment beyond an emotional hook and response? This is where a US politics course can build on Millennial interest and attentiveness in particular events and processes. It can provide for reinforcement and development of a more comprehensive understanding of related political information and policy connections.

There is certainly no shortage of emotion in the modern mediated political environment, from the variety of cable news sources and the blogosphere to the emotion-laden banter across Twitter and the like. For Millennials, there are the ongoing heated debates over issues ranging from war in Afghanistan to health care. Hype-laced banter saturates cable news shows and the US political exchanges beamed out of the halls of Congress and at the White House gates. It is not surprising then that misperceptions abound in such an information-bombarded environment. And as younger Americans are exposed to the political drama, relevant political learning becomes all the more important in sorting out the debate and related policies. This chapter explores how an introduction to US politics can provide a cognitive understanding of how to reason through current and future debates, even as the emotional volume threatens to drown out the application of political knowledge.

How and what our students learn are critical as they encounter policy debates and develop means of processing related information in a saturated news environment rife with symbolism and emotional cues (Lakoff 2008; Westen 2007). This chapter examines the shape and influence of our students' symbolic predispositions, that is, not only their existing knowledge, but also their feelings and attitudes regarding related political figures, institutions, and country, and how learning impacts their policy reasoning. Beyond the classroom—and even within it—our students navigate the political world through a prism of predispositions established at a young age and crystallized over time. There are attitudes that are responsive to the changing political environment, and some draw on a more familiar and stable reservoir of affective attitudes. It is important to understand the shape of these Millennial attitudes over time and how each of them influences student learning.

This chapter examines how acquiring fact-based knowledge can lessen the impact that emotions and predispositions play in shaping views on policy. In this analysis, I pay particular attention to the war in Iraq, a seminal event in Millennial lives and one that allows us to examine the interplay among learning, attitudes, and preferences. War and crisis are among the few types of events and processes with widespread public awareness and salience, particularly for young adults (Bennett and Manheim 1993; Delli Carpini and Keeter 1996). With many families directly affected by the conflict and probably an age cohort serving in combat, college-age students have had a direct stake in this conflict, and that is reflected in their consistent attentiveness to the topic (Boettcher and Cobb 2006). This chapter's findings provide insight into how the perceived relevance of this current event relates to knowledge and how it is connected to other important Millennial attitudes and predispositions.

Importantly, our students (and Millennials overall) demonstrated relatively stable attitudes, dispositions, and preferences across a range of pressing policy concerns. Millennial support for particular policies remains remarkably stable through time and across the learning environment. There is clearly a Millennial view on critical policies, including health care, education, the environment, and defense spending. That said, I also explore how Millennial views respond to a shifting political environment and how the introduction of current events, such as the war in Iraq, relates to predispositions, perceptions, and attitudes such as confidence in the president and trust in institutions. With higher degrees of attentiveness, we can expect our students to be more aware of and receptive to the mediated political context (Zaller 1992), which I argue tends to reinforce the most accessible cues and predispositions.

It is important to understand how affective attitudes have related to new Millennial events, particularly those deemed of most concern and most threatening. These are most likely to trigger emotional responses and spark symbolic predispositions in the evaluation of related domestic and foreign political figures, nations, and policy decisions. It is here that I contend the learning environment can be critical in linking political information with Millennial interest in salient events. It reduces the reliance on affective attitudes in related policy reasoning in even the most emotion-laden issue debates. In the evolving political environment, I also consider other emerging policy concerns, potential threats, and challenges for Millennials as we make our way through the decade and into a more global outlook, which is also a defining characteristic of this generation.

An Age-Old Affective Connection

From an early age, Americans come to rely on affective attachments when formulating views on policies concerning the nation (Sears 2001). There is the emotion attached to witnessing a flying flag, the pride or anger listening to a president addressing the nation, the enthusiasm and fear attached to a nation's military entering into war, and the belief and trust that one's nation and leaders represent and serve the public good and the country (Westen 2007). Emotion, related symbols, and cues played a profound role for many Americans, including Millennials, as they sought to make sense of the 9/11 attacks and the war on terrorism (Small, Lerner, and Fischhoff 2006).

On the one hand, political trust and symbolic attachments to the nation can be key attributes of healthy citizen development and participation (Huddy and Khatib 2007; Putnam 2000). Without such connections, it is hard to form a lifetime commitment to public interest, whether at the community or national level. We must see the capacity of government to effectively and legitimately respond to our concerns in order to cognitively engage the political and civic process. On the other hand, political trust often functions for many as an information shortcut when it comes to policy judgment across a range of topics (Brewer et al. 2004; Hetherington and Globetti 2002). We may be more likely to support government programs and policies when there is relatively higher political trust and to rely on this reservoir of confidence when we feel less than informed on the details of the topic.

American trust in government was nearly severed after the political fallout from Vietnam and Watergate. In the early 1960s, about three-quarters of citizens trusted the government to do what is right, but by the turn of the millennium it was far below half, as low as 25 percent in the mid-1990s (Pharr, Putnam, and Dalton 2000). National Election Studies figures show that trust in the government in Washington to "do the right thing most of the time" was at 42 percent for 18- to 25-year-olds in 1976 and 45 percent for this age group in 2000. For all of their youthful rebelliousness, there is no systematic evidence that younger Americans are more or less likely to trust their government than are their elders (Galston 2007).

For our US politics students at SUNY Fredonia, those who felt that they could trust Washington at least "most of the time" had hovered in the low 30s from the tail end of the Clinton administration (32 percent in fall 2000) to 36 percent in late spring 2001 after the first few months of the Bush White House. Like most Americans, our students' trust in government spiked after the 9/11 attacks. Fifty-one percent of our US politics students surveyed in late September 2001 felt that they could trust Washington to do the right thing "most of the time or almost always," the highest level for our students surveyed from fall 2000 to fall 2005.

As Osama bin Laden remained on the run and weapons of mass destruction (WMDs) were not found in Iraq, fallout from the war on terrorism and war in Iraq affected trust in government and also confidence in major institutions, namely for the president and Congress. By 2002 the Harvard IOP found that trust in government, Congress, the president, and military had declined among the nation's undergraduates. As the 9/11 emotional surge began to dissipate, the military remained the most trusted institution (70 percent in 2002), and the president a distant second at 58 percent. Trust in the federal government was down 9 points from 2001, but remained 15 percentage points higher than 2000 levels among our nation's undergraduates (Harvard IOP 2002).

By fall 2004–fall 2005, entering students in our US politics courses at SUNY Fredonia once again had fallen to pre-9/11 levels of trust in Washington to do the right thing at least "most of the time," hovering in the low 30s. For 237 students finishing the fall 2004 term in US politics at UCSB, trust in government was at 36 percent. Despite a surge after 9/11, trust had dropped back to initial millennial numbers for both adults and college-age students in the wake of a polarized administration and increasingly divisive war.

Understanding these trends in trust helps us to recognize the relative impact of affective attitudes when it comes to our Millennial students' developing attitudinal framework and how it works or does not work in concert with cognitive reasoning. We explore how trust and the shape of other predispositions contribute to Millennials' attitudinal framework and policy reasoning as they are exposed to the symbolism-laden contextual environment while adding political information through course learning.

Grappling with Identity and Imagery

For many citizens, symbolic predispositions such as national identity help them to interpret policy decisions and governance in the face of limited information, particularly in foreign affairs or threats to the nation's security or sovereignty (Rankin 2001; Schatz, Staub, and Lavine 1999). And not surprisingly, Americans' sense of national identity surged following the 9/11 attacks (Li and Brewer 2004; Renshon 2005), reaching across the nation and onto college campuses (Harvard IOP 2002; Moskalenko, McCauley, and Rozin 2006).

In the weeks following the 9/11 attacks we first introduced commonly employed measures of national identity (e.g., Kosterman and Feshbach 1989; Sidanius et al. 1997) in our surveys of students in US politics courses. With self-placement on a 1–5 scale where 1 = strongly agree and 5 = strongly disagree, there was a strong and enduring patriotic dimension among student responses to the following three statements: (1) The US flag fills me with pride, (2) I would rather be a citizen of America than any other country, and (3) There is nothing particularly wonderful about US culture. A patriotism scale was constructed in which alpha reliability among the three items was at .75 for all students combined at the beginning of the course and at .80 when surveyed at the close of the term, demonstrating a very coherent, stable, and constrained attitudinal dimension of national identity.

Figure 3.1 demonstrates how pride in the US flag, in US citizenry, and in US culture was particularly high and connected in the direct aftermath of September 11 when the fall 2001 survey was first introduced to our US politics students at SUNY Fredonia. Pride in the US flag appeared more susceptible to the changing political environment for each new term of US politics students. It surged back up as we entered war in Iraq and dropped as the war dragged on and became more divisive as part of the 2004 election and early second term of the Bush presidency. The emotional connection to US citizenship and culture did show similar trends but far more consistency across the terms. These conceptions of national identity retained the general level of stability we have come to expect from symbolic predispositions even during eventful times.

For UCSB students surveyed at the end of a spring 2003 US politics course just after the war in Iraq had commenced, 71 percent agreed that they would rather be a citizen of the US, 66 percent disagreed that there is nothing inherently wonderful about US culture, and 54 percent agreed that the US flag fills them with pride. In fall 2004, following a divisive presidential election centered in many ways on the war in Iraq, the numbers of UCSB students completing a US politics course were at 66 percent,

65 percent, and 41 percent on the same three items, respectively. For SUNY Fredonia and UCSB students, symbolism attached to pride in the flag appeared most affected by the contextual environment.

Just as emotion can shape how we feel about our own country, it also can affect our perceptions of other countries, particularly nations considered some sort of potential threat. Although Iraq was a focal point of the Bush administration, the president also spoke of an "axis of evil" in a State of the Union address delivered in January 2002, lumping Iran and North Korea together with Saddam Hussein's regime. And in a 2005 Gallup Poll, North Korea and Iran received the least favorable opinion among Americans, at 13 and 12 percent favorability, respectively (Erikson and Tedin 2007, 108). Next up the list were Syria at 25 percent and Iraq at 29 percent. Great Britain topped the list for Americans at 91 percent favorability in the 2005 Gallup Poll.

When asked how they viewed countries on a scale where 1 = very negative and 5 = very positive, 49 percent of the UCSB US politics stu-

Figure 3.1 Patriotic Feelings upon Entering US Politics Courses

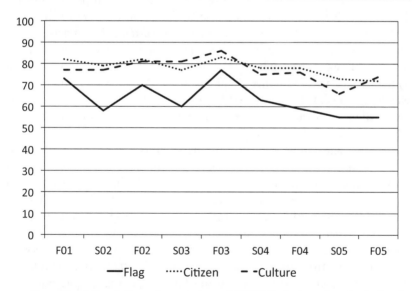

Notes: Trend lines indicate the percentage of SUNY Fredonia students beginning the US politics course with agreement or strong agreement that "the American flag fills me with pride" and "I would rather be a citizen of America than any other country," and disagreement or strong disagreement that "there is nothing particularly wonderful about American culture." The question wording is given in Appendix A.

dents surveyed at the end of fall 2004 had a negative view of Iran. Only 4 percent had positive views of Iran. Negative views of Iran were held by at least 50 percent, and as much as 62 percent of students completing the US politics course at SUNY Fredonia, fall 2003–fall 2005, held positive views in single digits.

Like most Americans, our students clearly had enemy images and friendly images of particular nations. For example, 64 percent of the UCSB students surveyed in fall 2004 had a positive view of Great Britain. As for our SUNY Fredonia students surveyed from fall 2003 to fall 2005, positive views of Great Britain were never lower than 61 percent (spring 2005) and were as high as 73 percent in spring 2004. Sixty-four percent of our SUNY Fredonia students surveyed had a positive view of Great Britain on average, while 3 percent had a positive view of Iran and 55 percent held negative views of Iran on average across these years.

There are distinctly negative and positive impressions that can be formed of nations, and such images can also influence awareness and knowledge acquisition, which in turn can impact learning and the formation of policy preferences. For example, students' apparent view of a long-standing "special relationship" between the United States and Great Britain carried over into their knowledge of the British prime minister Tony Blair. Recall of Tony Blair as the British prime minister for an open-ended question was no lower than 48 percent (spring 2004) and as high as 60 percent in fall 2005 for our SUNY Fredonia students surveyed entering US politics courses, fall 2003–fall 2005. For UCSB students surveyed as they completed US politics courses in fall 2004, recognition of Blair was at 63 percent. For both UCSB and SUNY Fredonia US politics students, Blair was a more consistently recognizable political figure than the US secretaries of state and defense.

At the same time, foreign villains such as Osama bin Laden and Saddam Hussein were among the most recognizable figures for our students, while Iran clearly had emerged as an identifiable enemy state in our surveys conducted from spring 2003 to fall 2005. Whether the parody of North Korean dictator Kim Jung Il in the all-puppet movie *Team America: World Police* by South Park creators Trey Stone and Matt Parker, or an earlier vilification of Saddam Hussein literally in bed with Satan in their first South Park movie, actually intensified or relaxed threat perceptions by young Americans laughing at such depictions is an open debate. However, key US political leaders and commentators did make a point of connecting Kim Jung Il and Saddam in an "axis of evil" with Iran, and publicly worried about Saddam's connections with al-Qaeda and terrorist attacks such as 9/11.

It is important to recognize the prevalence of symbolic predispositions, stereotypes, and images in how our Millennial students are actively constructing understanding of politics and policy, particularly in the less familiar realm of foreign affairs. In order to more fully understand the impact of course learning, it is critical to comprehend how the external political environment can encourage reliance on the most accessible cues and images when there is less direct access to related political information.

In one of his first public appearances following the 9/11 attacks, President George W. Bush climbed atop the rubble of the World Trade Center and through a bullhorn shouted out to the rescue workers below, "I can hear you, the rest of the world can hear you, and the people that did this will hear all of us soon!" A resounding chant of "USA! USA! USA!" followed, broadcast again and again to a nation reeling in shock and a Millennial generation suddenly coming of age with a defining event. In the year following the 9/11 attacks, the Bush administration was increasingly speaking about the threat posed by Saddam Hussein's Iraq. Administration officials and the president (in his 2002 State of the Union speech) evoked images of "our first warning in the form of a mushroom cloud," suggesting evidence of a nuclear weapons program, weapons of mass destruction, terror alerts, and terror plots. For a younger generation familiarizing itself with new and unfamiliar political terrain, such salient political rhetoric evoked threatening imagery linked to the most accessible symbolic predispositions. It also placed the president front and center as one of the most visible political leaders for Millennials seeking cues for how to evaluate the related policies before them.

For younger adults just beginning to learn about US politics and government, the president is a most accessible and identifiable symbol, and attitudes toward this political figure can be quite responsive to perceived changes in the political environment and debate. Our US politics students at SUNY Fredonia followed a similar trajectory to that of the general adult population. President Bush's highest approval ratings were at the end of the fall 2001 semester, just a few months after the September 11 attacks and two months following the launch of the war in Afghanistan (see Figure 3.2). Presidential approval drifted down before spiking back up to its second highest point during this period with the commencement of the war in Iraq.

During the fall 2001 and spring 2003 courses, presidential approval surged from entering levels for our US politics students with the intervening events of the start of the war in Afghanistan and the invasion of Iraq. By spring 2004, presidential approval for our SUNY Fredonia US

**Figure 3.2   Presidential Approval upon Entering
and Exiting US Politics Courses**

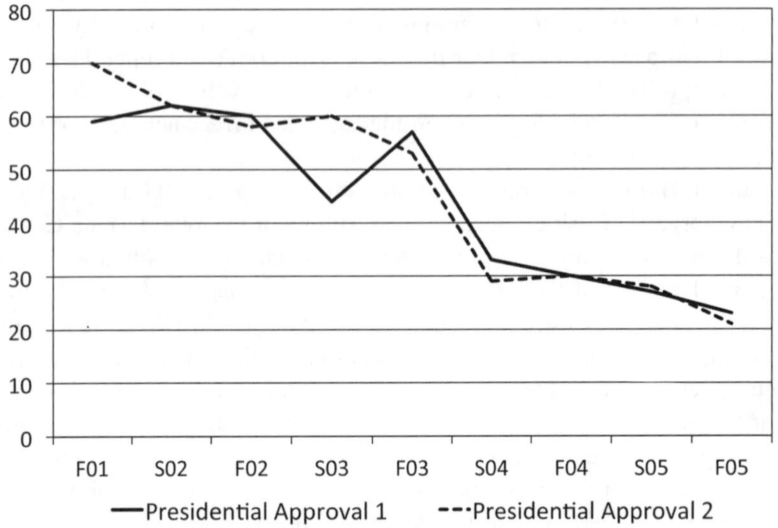

Notes: The solid line indicates the percentage of students entering and the dotted line the percentage of students completing the US politics courses at SUNY Fredonia who responded that they "approve/strongly approve" of President Bush's handling of his job as president. The question wording is given in Appendix A.

politics students had plummeted to about 30 percent before hitting the low 20s following Hurricane Katrina at the end of the fall 2005 semester.

Understanding how our students learn about and process politics and policy requires recognizing the intervening impact of political cues and affective attitudes. For the most part we find that Millennials, including our students, have demonstrated remarkably stable attitudes across critical domestic policy choices. However, foreign affairs judgment and related preferences have been more closely linked with an understanding of salient events and crises. It is also important to understand how course learning influences our students' policy connections and judgment as they gain new political information.

Relating Preferences

In recent decades, solid majorities of college students have consistently opposed increased military spending (Saenz et al. 2004). According to HERI, in 1992 only 18 percent of entering college freshmen nationwide agreed or strongly agreed that military spending should be increased, jumping to 45 percent in 2002 (after 9/11). Entering freshmen's support for military spending was down to 39 percent in 2003 and 34 percent in 2005, showing annual decreases in what HERI researchers suspect is tied to casualties and negative views of Iraq.

Figure 3.3 demonstrates how support to increase or greatly increase defense spending soared for SUNY Fredonia students beginning the US politics course in the direct aftermath of 9/11, dropping somewhat before increasing again as the nation braced for war in Iraq. But by fall 2003–fall 2005, student support for increased defense spending fell back to pre-9/11 levels.

There was far more stability across domestic policy preferences. At the end of our fall 2000 courses, 69 percent of students felt that there should be greater federal government involvement in environmental protection, a figure at 68 percent at the conclusion of our fall 2005 courses. At the completion of fall 2000, 70 percent of our US politics students favored increasing federal spending on health care, a number at 74 percent in fall

Figure 3.3   Trending Support for Increased Federal Spending

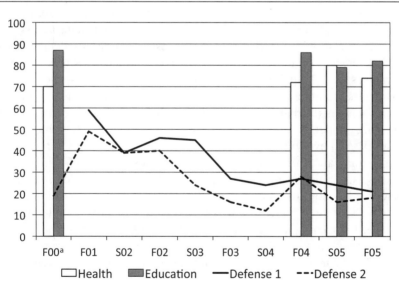

Notes: The solid line indicates the percentage of support by SUNY Fredonia students beginning the US politics course to "increase/greatly increase" defense spending. The dashed line indicates support by students completing the US politics course for defense spending increases. Bar graphs indicate the percentage of support by SUNY Fredonia students completing the US politics course to "increase/greatly increase" federal spending on health care and public education. The question wording is given in Appendix A.

a. Fall 2000 figures available only for students completing the US politics course at SUNY Fredonia.

2005. For these fall 2000 students, 87 percent supported increased federal spending on public education, holding steady at 82 percent in fall 2005.

Of 108 University of Wisconsin, River Falls (UWRF), students surveyed at the end of a spring 2001 US politics course, 84 percent supported increased federal spending on public education, 59 percent supported increased federal spending on health care, 62 percent favored greater federal involvement in environmental protection, and 23 percent supported increased defense spending. For 237 UCSB students surveyed at the end of the fall 2004 US politics course, 92 percent supported increased federal spending on public education, 75 percent supported increased federal spending on health care, 60 percent favored greater federal involvement in environmental protection, and 11 percent supported increased defense spending. Like the SUNY Fredonia and UWRF students, the UCSB students were more likely to prefer that defense spending stay the same, with 41 percent supporting that option. For SUNY Fredonia students completing the fall 2004 US politics course, 39 percent preferred that defense spending stay the same, a policy preference option averaging 41 percent for our students completing the course from fall 2001 to fall 2005.

Our US politics students' policy preferences on health care, public education, and environmental protection held very constant across the years, but also within each term. The largest variation in federal spending preferences on these issues was 4 points, and most terms saw minor increases of 2–3 points in favor of increased federal spending and involvement in these three areas. Our students' defense spending preferences demonstrated greater fluctuation, with double-digit decreases from entering students' preferences across the spring 2003–spring 2004 courses. And every change in defense spending preferences during each term from fall 2001 to fall 2005 reflected less support for increased defense spending. On average, 36 percent of our SUNY Fredonia students entering US politics courses, fall 2001–fall 2005, supported increased defense spending, which fell to 29 percent for students completing the course. It appears that our students' defense spending preferences were more responsive than other issue areas in an information environment and related discourse heavily focused on the war on terrorism and in Iraq.

Concern, Attention, and Preferences

The information environment, political debate, associated imagery, and information emanating from a war on terrorism to a war in Iraq provided a unique opportunity to assess how Millennials grappled with a salient and evolving political process. Our findings demonstrate further how attentiveness, interest, and perceived relevance relate not only to knowledge acquisition and learning but also to the reasoning process behind related policy preferences that define this cohort.

Understandably, our nation's college students, like most Americans, were shaken by the 9/11 attacks and turned their attention in the immediate aftermath to the issue of terrorism. In 2002, the Harvard IOP found that more than two-thirds of college students were greatly or somewhat concerned about an upcoming terrorist attack in the United States. Eighty percent reported being greatly or somewhat affected in their thinking about national issues following 9/11.

When we asked our SUNY Fredonia US politics students in fall 2002 how much concern US leaders should devote to future potential terrorist attacks on the United States, 73 percent answered that they should be a "somewhat more important concern," 17 percent considered future terrorist attacks to be the "single most important concern," and 10 percent responded that we "should be more concerned about other issues such as the economy and education." In spring 2003, the numbers were at 67 percent, 20 percent, and 13 percent, respectively. But by spring 2005, only 47 percent of our students felt that US leaders should make future terrorist attacks a somewhat more important concern, 11 percent the most important concern, and 42 percent now answered that these leaders should be more concerned about other issues such as the economy or education. In fall 2005, the numbers continued this trend, with 35 percent of our students feeling leaders should be more concerned about other issues, 53 percent feeling that terrorist attacks should be a somewhat more important concern, and 12 percent feeling these should be the most important concern.

Pew surveys in July–August 2003 found Millennials and Gen Xers less likely than older age groups to view military strength as the best way to ensure peace. In October 2002 the Harvard IOP reported that a strong majority of students (51 percent) felt the United States should take action against Iraq if UN inspections failed, but support dropped to 18 percent if the United States had to act alone. In fall 2002, 54 percent of our SUNY Fredonia US politics students responded that they would support a military invasion of Iraq only with UN support and only 12 percent without UN support, numbers very similar to national findings of college students. When surveyed in late January 2003 (two months before the war commenced) only 9 percent of our students agreed that we should invade Iraq without UN support, with 52 percent supporting such an intervention only with UN support. Twenty percent weren't sure and 17 percent were against the war at all costs.

However, like most Americans, college students rallied in the short term behind the Bush administration's decision to invade Iraq (Harvard

IOP 2005). When asked about the Bush administration's decision to go to war at the end of the same spring term in May 2003 (two months after the war had commenced), 32 percent of our SUNY Fredonia US politics students noted that they completely supported the decision, with 38 percent somewhat in support. Thus, about 70 percent exhibited some support for the war as it was launched during the spring 2003 term when they were enrolled in the introduction to US politics. What is not clear from our survey results is whether students understood that the UN Security Council had rejected the decision to go to war and voted to allow for more time for UN weapons inspectors.

Nationwide, the Harvard IOP reported in 2005 that the younger generation was actually the most supportive in the earliest stages of the war in Iraq. Pew Center surveys for 18- to 29-year-olds showed higher levels of support in July 2003 (66 percent), September 2004 (59 percent), and July 2005 (55 percent) on the question of whether "the United States made the right decision in using military force against Iraq." These levels were regularly higher than for other age categories as the war progressed over this two-year period, with the biggest gap opening up with those 65 years of age or older (12 points in 2003 and 18 points in 2005). However, younger people would also turn dramatically against the war as it continued, particularly as we approached the 2004 presidential election.

Importantly, this was clearly a salient current event with perceived relevance for Millennials, including our students. It provided an opportunity to stimulate related learning and to link new political information with an understanding of related policy. Figure 3.4 demonstrates the high level of attentiveness to the war in Iraq for our SUNY Fredonia students *entering* a US politics course, fall 2003–fall 2005, and this level of attentiveness generally increased by the end of the course. With political debate and related media coverage turning from relatively positive to increasingly negative on the war in Iraq (e.g., Lichter 2004), fall 2003– fall 2005 was also a period of great opinion change on the war, according to trends demonstrated in national polls. For example, in a December 2005 report by the Pew Research Center, national support that the war in Iraq was "the right decision" reportedly fell from nearly 70 percent in fall 2003 to under 50 percent in fall 2005. The Pew Center also reported that national support for "keeping troops in Iraq until stabilized" dropped from well over 60 percent in fall 2003 to below 50 percent in fall 2005.

Albeit with different question wording but with similar trends, our survey of fall 2003 SUNY Fredonia US politics students demonstrated solid support for the invasion of Iraq and even for the idea of a long-term occupation with substantial numbers of US troops. By fall 2004 and fall

Figure 3.4 Considering the War in Iraq upon Entering a US Politics Course

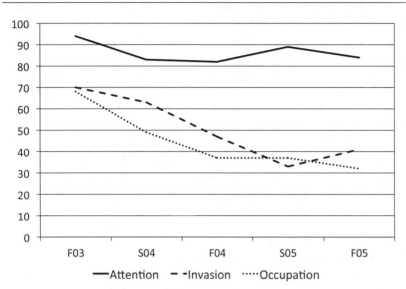

Notes: The dashed line indicates the percentage of SUNY Fredonia students beginning the US politics course who "somewhat/completely supported" the Bush administration's decision to invade Iraq. The dotted line indicates support for a long-term occupation of Iraq. The solid line indicates the percentage of students paying attention "sometimes/a lot" to the war in Iraq. The question wording is given in Appendix A.

2005, these levels of support had dropped dramatically like the trends in the national adult population. Our findings also mirrored those for college students across the country. For example, the Harvard IOP reported in nationwide polling that undergraduate support for the war in Iraq had dropped from over 60 percent in October 2003 to 47 percent in October 2004 and 43 percent in April 2005.

While general public opinion also shifted increasingly against the war in Iraq, the change was particularly pronounced for the Millennial Generation. This can be associated with the strong learning curve for this cohort, including our students, who gained increased awareness of related figures and facts through prolonged attentiveness to the event and course learning.

Information Impact

Attentiveness to events is strongly connected to the surveillance knowledge of our college-age students. There is also evidence that the higher education environment has a particularly strong impact on learning in what is traditionally the less familiar area of foreign affairs. For example, the Intercollegiate Studies Institute (ISI) found that knowledge of the Persian Gulf War of 1990–1991 was the top-ranked increase out of sixty questions from freshman to senior year in a survey measurement of civic knowledge across our nation's campuses in 2005. Students' knowledge of Saddam Hussein ranked seventh on the list. In general, the ISI study reported learning gains on matters of overseas conflict, events, and figures among the most substantial for our nation's college students.

With heightened attentiveness, our students entered US politics courses at SUNY Fredonia from fall 2003 to fall 2005 with a solid recognition of Saddam Hussein as the former leader of Iraq, and there was little change in this level of recall by the end of the course (see Table 3.1). There was greater change in geopolitical knowledge of the surrounding region, with our students' ability to name two countries bordering Iraq increasing by seven points.

Understanding related details in the region of a conflict is an important component of information and one that is not always absorbed simply by relying on information within the mediated political environment. For example, studies find that over ten years after the war in Vietnam ended, only 32 percent of US adults could locate Vietnam on a map (Delli Carpini and Keeter 1996). About one-quarter of Americans knew that Kuwait was a monarchy and one-fifth knew how their House representative or US senator had voted on the resolution to authorize the Persian Gulf War (Wilcox,

Table 3.1   Learning About US Politics, Political Figures, and War

Fall 2003 to Fall 2005 Knowledge of War in Iraq Political Figures/Facts	Pre	Post	Change
Secretary of state	38%	46%	+8
Secretary of defense	40%	46%	+6
Saddam Hussein	84%	85%	+1
1 country bordering Iraq	74%	78%	+4
2 countries bordering Iraq	38%	45%	+7
British prime minister	52%	55%	+3
Mean knowledge scale (0–6)	3.22	3.57	+.35*
Alpha reliability scale	.70	.70	

Notes: The column figures are based on the pooled data of 738 student respondents both entering (pre) and completing (post) US politics courses at SUNY Fredonia, fall 2003–fall 2005. Knowledge scales are constructed where correct answers = 1, 0 otherwise. Where two answers are possible, 2 = both answers correct, 1 = one answer correct, 0 otherwise. The question wording is given in Appendix A. * $p \leq .001$ for paired sample t-tests of pre and post mean knowledge scores.

Hewitt, and Alsop 1996). However, most people knew something about the personalities associated with the conflict (Bennett and Manheim 1993). And these differences can be particularly pronounced by age. According to a June 2004 Pew survey, 23 percent of 18- to 29-year-olds had heard a lot about the United States planning to hand over civilian authority to Iraqi leaders, compared with 45- to 64-year-olds at 52 percent.

As I previously noted, there were solid gains in open-ended recall of the secretaries of state and defense after a course in US politics during a time of heightened attentiveness on the part of our students. Furthermore, there were also substantial increases in surveillance knowledge of domestic figures and facts and on items of textbook knowledge for our students during a period of significant attentiveness to war in Iraq. Our students had added levels of political knowledge during a period in which emotion often permeated a national discourse rife with political and symbolic cues competing for Millennial attention.

Table 3.2 demonstrates how affective attitudes, including confidence in the president, trust in government, patriotism, and the enemy image of Iran all significantly influenced how our entering US politics students during the fall 2003–fall 2005 period formulated preferences on the invasion or occupation of Iraq. Those students with higher confidence in the president, more trust in government, higher degrees on the patriotism dimension of national identity, and the most negative perceptions of Iran were also the most likely to support the invasion and ongoing occupation of Iraq.

Our male students were also more likely to support the invasion of Iraq, consistent with other studies that find males are more likely to support military intervention, particularly in retrospective judgments of war decisions (Wilcox, Hewitt, and Alsop 1996). Once combat begins, gender differences have been found to diminish (Conover and Sapiro 1993), and our students also exhibited no significant gender differences on the topic of a long-term military occupation of Iraq.

On a salient topic, where attention to the issue was unusually high, partisan and ideological cues also merged with political predispositions in support of the war effort. Republicans and conservatives, cognitively linking policy judgment with attitudes concerning Republican president Bush, were significantly more likely to support the war (e.g., Gaines et al. 2007). In a highly salient issue environment such as the war in Iraq, these relationships may also demonstrate responsiveness to not only information levels but also the political discourse. One argument put forward by the Bush administration for the necessity of an ongoing occupation in Iraq is to counter the influence of Iran. Table 3.2 demonstrates significant relationships with regard to enemy images of Iran and support for the occu-

Table 3.2   Processing the Invasion and Occupation of Iraq

Support for:	Invade		Occupy	
	Pre	Post	Pre	Post
Political cues and predispositions				
Confidence in president	.375**	.203**	.483**	*.373**
Trust in government	.193**	.092+	.125+	.091+
Patriotism (low to high)	.035+	*.006*	.068**	*.013*
Liberal-conservative ideology	.103+	**.157***	.241**	*.170**
Party identification	.143**	*.141***	.162**	**.213***
Enemy images (Iran)	.045	.005	.159**	*.115**
Gender (male)	.289**	**.322***	.046	.055
Policy preference				
Increase defense spending	.021	**.354***	.233**	**.389***
Nagelkerke pseudo R-squared	.432	.420	.596	.585

Notes: The table figures represent probit coefficients, where ** $p \leq .001$, * $p \leq .01$, + $p \leq .05$. An ordered-probit analysis is utilized with the dependent variables coded 1–4, in which 4 indicates the strongest support for the invasion and occupation of Iraq. An increase in the strength of statistically significant relationships is shown in bold and a decrease is shown in italics. The table figures are based on the pooled data of 738 student respondents both entering (pre) and completing (post) US politics courses at SUNY Fredonia, fall 2003– fall 2005. The question wording is given in Appendix A.

pation but not with regard to the initial invasion. Fuller understanding of the ideological and partisan differences in line with increases in political learning may also be responsible for strengthening the impact of conservative ideology on our students' support for the invasion and stronger Republican support for the occupation. At the same time, dissension in the elite ranks of conservatives over the ongoing occupation could also have somewhat reduced ideological cues in such interpretations by our students.

With higher levels of political knowledge at the end of a US politics course, the impact of the emotive attitudes of national identity, trust in government, confidence in the president, and enemy images diminished for our students. With greater political information, our students were less dependent on emotion-based shortcuts. They could draw more from related information and policy reference when considering issues before them.

Studies find that those individuals with lower information are found to exhibit less consistent and more disorganized policy preferences, while the more politically informed tend to possess higher levels of constraint among related policy preferences (Converse 1964; Jennings 1992; Sulfaro 1996). For our students, the relative influence of policy preferences for defense spending increased as stronger preferences for defense spending were more likely in support of the war and occupation. With increased political knowledge and heightened constraint across related policy preferences, I argue that our students exhibited more coherent and reasoned policy choices when possessing fuller political information after a term of US politics.

Concerns and Connections

Understanding how to reason through and access relevant information about related policies will be important for these Millennial-age students as new crises, challenges, and concerns are bound to arise. Millennials have been developing views and perspectives that may impact future policy considerations and judgments as they shape this cohort's worldview from experience and learning at this critical juncture. In April 2005 the Harvard IOP reported that 57 percent of college students nationwide believed the United States would invade another country in the next five years and 80 percent believed an invasion would occur in the next ten years. When asked what country they thought the United States would invade, most of the respondents believed that country would be Iran, followed by North Korea and Syria. Nearly half (49 percent) in 2005 believed that another large-scale terrorist attack would occur in the United States within five years, and 76 percent in the next 10 years.

Millennials are developing a framework for evaluating policy choices based on a balance of emotion and knowledge garnered through an eventful period in their young lives. In April 2006 the Harvard IOP reported 32 percent of students felt that the United States should stop the development of nuclear weapons in Iran, even if it requires unilateral military action, while 29 percent opposed unilateral action against Iran. Thirty-seven percent were not sure. The students remained more cautious than adults, as 50 percent of adults agreed that the United States should use whatever means necessary to halt Iran's acquisition of nuclear weapons.

This is a generation that possesses a clear global perspective as it learns how to sift through the political environment and encounters new political information. SUNY Fredonia US politics students reflect a growing and stable multilateral perspective evident among Millennials. Surveyed at the end of the fall 2003 and spring 2004 US politics courses at SUNY Fredonia, about half of the students supported a US invasion of North Korea or Iran similar to that in Iraq, *only* with UN support. Ten percent in fall 2003 and 5 percent in spring 2004 responded that they would support the United States going it alone.

A 2005 Harvard IOP report labeled the nation's college students as a "Global Generation." The report reflected widespread support among the nation's students for UN and multilateral solutions. Sixty-one percent of students felt that the United States should be the largest contributor to humanitarian aid and 67 percent that the United States should commit troops to prevent acts of genocide or ethnic cleansing. However, 74 percent of the undergrads believed the United States should let the United Nations take the lead in solving international crises and conflicts.

Figure 3.5 demonstrates that our SUNY Fredonia students entering the US politics course consistently agreed with a welcoming and integrative concept of US national identity. A solid majority agreed with the statement that immigrants make the United States more open to new ideas and cultures. An even higher amount consistently rejected the notion that to be truly American, you need to be born in the United States. Furthermore, few agreed that the more the United States influences countries, the better off these countries are. UCSB US politics students held similar conceptions of these items of national identity when surveyed at the end of the spring 2003 and fall 2004 terms.

At the same time, our Millennial-age students also exhibit a traditional sense of and connection to local space even as they demonstrate a more global perspective on the role of the US and related policy. Despite views of positive immigrant impact on US culture, a slight majority of our students surveyed also felt that the number of immigrants to the United States nowadays should be "reduced a little" or "reduced a lot," with only single-digit support for increasing the number of immigrants. The remaining students preferred that immigrant levels "stay the same." Any sense of attachment to a broader global community in terms of feelings of closeness to the world (we are the world, so to speak) was still dwarfed by perceived closeness to the nation. Feelings of closeness to the world for our students completing US politics at SUNY Fredonia topped out at 30 percent who answered feeling close or very close just after the 9/11 attacks, falling to as low as 12 percent in spring 2004, and averaging 20 percent for fall 2001–fall 2005. Feelings of closeness to the nation topped out at 55 percent in fall 2001 for our students, but averaged 42 percent across the entire study period. However, even closeness to the nation was overshadowed by closeness to one's community. Closeness to one's community reached as high as 70 percent for our US politics students surveyed, never lower than 56 percent, and averaged 61 percent from fall 2001 to fall 2005.

A more global outlook with strong emotional ties to community makes sense for college-age students initially finding their way from home and onto campuses. And as I explore in later chapters, this provides both opportunities and challenges for translating national and global political interests into extended Millennial participation and engagement. Although sudden global events had been thrust upon Millennials as they completed high school and entered college, this is still a young generation, with their strongest ties to their community and age group above all else.

Fear Not for a New Millennial Future

Defining events have impacted the Millennial experience, and many of these more salient events could be described as threatening, if not frightening. This chapter demonstrates how threatening images, symbolic predispositions, and affective attitudes can be triggered by crisis events and a consideration of related policy choices. Millennials also appear to be a

Figure 3.5   Conceptions of US Identity

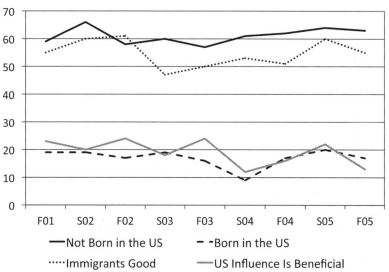

Notes: The solid black line indicates the percentage of SUNY Fredonia students entering US politics courses who "disagree/strongly disagree" that "to be truly American, you need to be born in America." The dashed line indicates the percentage of students who "agree/strongly agree" with this statement. The dotted line indicates students who "agree/strongly agree" that "immigrants make America more open to new ideas and cultures." The solid gray line indicates students who agree or strongly agree that "the more the US influences countries, the better off these countries are." The question wording is given in Appendix A.

cohort that has firmly established policy preferences that define its generation, yet they have adjusted their attitudes based on a perception of evolving current events and processes. New political information has been integrated coherently into policy judgment on even the most emotional of topics, war. Fear does not seem to be a defining characteristic in the judgment of Millennials, particularly when information is more available to make a reasoned assessment.

This is a cohort that came of age with the 9/11 attacks and war in Iraq, but according to the 2005 national College Student Survey, only 14 percent of students felt fearful about their safety because of world events (HERI 2005b). After all, this is a generation that has faced not just threats from abroad, but mediated threatening imagery connected even to the more localized school environment. Millennials were the first generation to enter college following the Columbine school shootings, which had garnered intense attention in April 1999. Nevertheless, 42 percent of SUNY Fredonia students completing our US politics courses in fall 2000 felt schools were "safe enough," compared with 32 percent who felt the schools were "not safe enough." Of UWRF students completing the spring 2001 US politics course, 51 percent felt schools were "safe enough," compared with 29 percent who felt the schools were "not safe enough."

Columbine, like the wars on terror and in Iraq, was a major media story and also a topical area covered in relatively visible films by controversial documentarian Michael Moore. Accepting the Best Documentary Oscar for *Bowling for Columbine* in March 2003, Moore announced to a live national TV audience: "We like nonfiction and we live in fictitious times. We live in a time where we have fictitious election results that elect a fictitious president. We live in a time where we have a man sending us to war for fictitious reasons . . . shame on you, Mr. Bush, shame on you." And Moore would follow up his outburst at the Academy Awards with the release of *Fahrenheit 911*, a highly critical view of Bush's handling of the presidency and the 9/11 attacks, generating buzz and controversy heading into the 2004 election.

Furthermore, according to Pew surveys in 2004, *Fahrenheit 911* was one of only three news stories young adults under 30 paid more attention to than seniors, along with the release of Mel Gibson's controversial *Passion of the Christ* and the Summer Olympics. On the other side of the spectrum, adults under 30 were far less likely than seniors in 2004 to pay attention when no WMDs were found in Iraq, or to pay attention to recent attacks on civilians and troops in Iraq or the Democratic vice presidential nomination (see Wattenberg 2008, 73–74).

Thus, what, how, and where one receives political information can be critical to interpretation, understanding, and policy reasoning. Michael Moore's films provided quite a different perspective and imagery related to Bush administration policies than, for example, *The O'Reilly Factor* on Fox News. The mediated political environment drives emotive constructs whether through dramatic perspectives by a documentarian, talk show hosts, bloggers, or even political rhetoric by the president and administration officials. This makes the impact of related political knowledge, including contemporary facts and figures, introduced and/or reinforced by enrollment in a US politics course, all the more important for our Millennial-age students in sorting through an often emotion-laden, mediated political environment.

Conclusion

It is important to recognize the types of mediated symbolic conceptions and affective attitudes our students bring into a US politics course and how these affect policy reasoning on the most salient issues before them. With limited real-life knowledge, in particular, of world affairs and past foreign conflicts, many of our Millennial college-age students may be susceptible to the symbolic rhetoric of leadership during a crisis event and media portrayal as such. This chapter has explored how a US politics course helps connect attentiveness to salient events and processes with greater cognitive awareness. It demonstrates how related political information and policy preferences can inform judgment on related issues, including war, even when students are bombarded by competing political cues and threatening images. Every bit of political knowledge helps to counteract what these young minds otherwise grab on to in order to fill in the blanks garnered from the mediated political environment.

It is important to have a foundational knowledge of long-standing democratic institutions and constitutional principles, to understand basic governmental responsibilities and potential limitations. However, the findings here demonstrate that Millennials also need to navigate a minefield of competing voices, to at least understand the critical players and actors. Much of political processing is a capacity for making sense of the political world as it emerges. Who was responsible for 9/11 and what are the relevant issue concerns? What is the geopolitical reality of the Middle East, and how does that relate to US policy considerations? These do not have easy textbook answers. This process demands a nimble capacity to survey events as they emerge and to critically reason through an array of information, reasoning that students as developing citizens can learn as they are introduced to US politics.

A sudden surge in trust and confidence without corresponding knowledge and thoughtful reflection can create an imbalance that provides too much authority to leadership and too little input from the citizenry. Conversely, a precipitous decline in such affective attitudes can lead to political disengagement when our students feel otherwise uninformed on the most pressing policy questions of their time. Trust in government and confidence in the president, like other affective attitudes, are best balanced with a healthy dose of political knowledge. This is an important lesson for our students learning about US politics and government.

Political information alters the dynamic in how our Millennial-age students may consider decisions such as war. With recent tensions over Iran's hardline crackdown of student protesters, the US strike to kill Osama bin Laden in Pakistan, new conflicts in the Middle East and North Africa, and so on, our students and their Millennial cohorts will continue to wrestle with emotion and cognition as they confront such new realities and policies. As I have discussed, fear and threat are not just symbolically associated with foreign affairs and figures. Strongly emotive images and language have been loudly associated with the political debate and policies addressing health care, the economy, jobs, and the environment, to name a few.

The findings show that Millennials are not driven or inherently responsive based on fear, having experienced a series of dramatic and shocking events in their young lives. And when infused with related political knowledge, the tendency to rely on emotive attitudes and threatening imagery is even less pronounced for our Millennial-age students. Furthermore, Millennials demonstrate quite stable predispositions and preferences that will help them to traverse many of the significant policy issues in front of them. How our students, as emerging citizens, receive this information both inside and outside of the classroom is a critical factor in how they will process it now and into the future. Once students leave the higher education setting, the wide-ranging media will be the likeliest source of information consumption updating an understanding of politics and policy. Consequently, how we integrate media sources into the US politics learning experience will be critical for how our students learn to work with the most relevant media sources within the classroom environment and beyond it.

4

Media Channels for Political Learning

Don't want to be an American idiot. One nation ruled by the media.
—*Lyrics from Green Day's "American Idiot," 2004*

We may laugh off the confusion facing our *Who Wants to Be a Millionaire* contestant discussed in Chapter 2 when it comes to his struggle with the most basic of constitutional questions one would find in any introductory US politics course. The fact is that the highly rated million-dollar televised game show figured that the average contestant's capacity to distinguish the most basic executive and legislative roles in our constitutional republic would be so lacking as to rank the question at the $64,000 prize level.

In the 2009 Oscar-winning movie *Slumdog Millionaire*, India's own version of *Who Wants to Be a Millionaire*, the show's South Asian equivalent of Regis Philbin is incredulous that this uneducated boy could struggle with a basic question of India's history but answer the most obscure and seemingly more difficult questions. In defense, the boy tries to explain how each of these answers had been imprinted through significant personal experiences critical to him at dramatic stages in his own life, whereas he just had not experienced the questions that most took for granted. While this premise may seem outlandish, it is not too different from our real-life contestant in *Who Wants to Be a Millionaire* who easily recalls the most decorated Grammy award winner, but cannot recall the most basic of constitutional facts. He recalled that which spoke most memorably to his own personal interests, life experience, media use, and surveillance.

77

Were this an isolated case of game show reality, we could drop the subject there. However, such confusion over the basic premises of the Constitution is widespread in the American public, with political and policy implications (Shenkman 2008). Just as our real-life *Millionaire* contestant learned to monitor musical artistic achievements and performance, a surveillance of political figures and policies also helps citizens to reach more informed decisions concerning the participating actors in the art of politics. Thus, how we learn to utilize and rely on media is just as important as how we learn to think about politics.

As we explored in Chapter 3, political knowledge is an important component of how our Millennial-age students can effectively sort through emotive cues and imagery connected to dramatic events and related coverage in the mediated political environment. Political knowledge is important not only for policy reasoning but also in how Millennials can learn from an increasingly pervasive media as they take part in a US politics course and when they have completed it. Political knowledge and understanding are critical to the quality of political judgments and the ability to make sense of political communication (Nie, Junn, and Stehlik-Barry 1996). Colby et al. (2007, 48) note, "without a strong foundation of institutional knowledge . . . it is far less likely that individuals can learn as much from media or political debates, assimilate new information about political issues, put international events in political context, or allow their opinions to be shaped by pertinent information." Consequently, learning how to connect political attentiveness, knowledge, and policy reasoning as one is introduced to US politics provides an important framework for furthering knowledge through media use as an engaged citizen.

Clearly, the media dynamic and resources are changing dramatically and pose challenges and opportunities in raising our Millennial students' attentiveness, interest, knowledge, and even engagement. Thus it is important to understand Millennial media consumption trends, use and learning impact, and how best to integrate emerging media resources as part of the educational experience as we strive to prepare our students to become informed citizens.

This chapter explores changes in Millennials' media attentiveness, use, and consumption habits. I examine national findings and those of our US politics students as part of the evolving media impact on Millennials' political awareness and understanding. As newspaper readership has declined markedly among this group, there is concern about how much these young adults can learn about politics and policy from TV news and the Internet (Bauerlein 2008; Niemi and Junn 1998). Macedo et al. (2005, 28), for example, observe that it doesn't appear that "either television or nontraditional sources such as the Internet have served to enhance the political knowledge of young Americans."

This chapter demonstrates how Millennials are learning through existing media channels, such as TV news, and emerging new media possibilities, including the far-reaching Internet, in which our students' attentiveness to these resources is a critical feature of knowledge gains. Moreover, it is important to recognize the particular connection between attentiveness to TV news and net news and surveillance knowledge. Internet use, in particular, has increased among this age group. Yet it is not clear that this is a distraction from the accumulation of political understanding, particularly for students taking a US politics course. It is not the case that Millennials will be consistently "tuned in" on the news of the day. However, attentiveness to political events can also increase general news attentiveness and knowledge. The key is establishing learning connections for salient events, media use, and related political information.

It is critical to work with and recognize the wide-ranging media sources available to this generation and understand how these translate into attentiveness, interest, and learning inside and outside of the classroom. For one, national findings show greater reliance on "soft news" sources and shows like *The Daily Show* and *The Colbert Report* for political information among the younger audience. Of course, there is debate on whether entertainment is at fault for declining news attention and a widening knowledge gap between those who follow entertainment and those who prefer news (Mindich 2005; Prior 2005). But there is also evidence that soft news can facilitate "incidental learning" in which "otherwise politically inattentive individuals are exposed to information about high-profile political issues, most prominently foreign policy crises, as an incidental byproduct of seeking entertainment" (Baum 2002, 91).

As I discuss in Chapters 2 and 3, our students' attention to salient political events is connected with higher levels of surveillance knowledge, which can also build other features of political knowledge. If a program like *The Daily Show* manages to encourage attentiveness to salient political events, it follows that it will also be related to higher levels of student surveillance knowledge based on earlier findings presented in this book. Furthermore, I explore an entertainment dimension to political interest among our Millennial-age students that connects interest in political music and film with attentiveness to *The Daily Show* and net news. This is not a soft news or a hard news question. It is a question of what facilitates attentiveness to and interest in political events by our Millennial-age students, which reinforce and/or increase understanding of related political figures and facts.

While any type of stimulating course method and resource is effective if it generates interest, awareness, and engagement, certain types of instructional devices may particularly reinforce contemporary media realities in line with political learning. Huerta and Jozwiak (2008), for example, examine the use of the *New York Times* as a supplemental reader to increase student engagement both inside and outside of political science courses. They assess the newspaper's effectiveness in three ways: making the class material more relevant, helping the students to stay abreast of the news, and improving their attitudes toward politics. Lopez et al. (2007) find that discussing media and utilizing media in the classroom makes students more likely to consume news and to have a more tolerant view of First Amendment issues, namely a free press.

Although several of our faculty assigned daily reading of the *New York Times*, we did not survey our students' attentiveness to print media. While I would assume that newspaper use is connected to political attentiveness, it is not a natural Millennial-age inclination to pick up a daily newspaper. We can require newspaper reading within a class, which is certainly beneficial to the immediate learning curve. It does not mean Millennials are likely to rely on a newspaper for political information outside of the course environment. On the other hand, there are other media channels that Millennials are more interested in and likely to engage.

This chapter also explores how instructional techniques that integrate multimedia sources (including TV news clips, Internet media, film, etc.) within the US politics classroom environment are connected to our students' attentiveness to salient political events and processes, political interest, and related surveillance knowledge. In an increasingly fragmented media environment with numerous options for Millennial minds, the US politics classroom is a critical opportunity to more fully integrate the most salient political events and our students' attentiveness to them as learning exercises.

This isn't to conclude that our students will not utilize outside media sources, including written material, to obtain information. One can argue that the burgeoning use of written online sources suggests otherwise, and is emerging as a critical mechanism for increasing Millennials' political information and avenues for engagement. An important factor in Millennial political information acquisition will have to do with the perceived relevance, connected interest, and inherent motivation. If there is an interest in the topic or issue, one could surmise that Millennials will find the most accessible and familiar media technology to engage it. Such sources could be introduced in the learning environment or be more widely available outside of the US politics classroom.

Tuning Out and Tuning In

Before we can assess the impact of media sources on our Millennial-age students, we must understand just how dramatically news media consumption and habits have changed as we have entered a new century. Such changes have created significant generational gaps that have sparked concern about how and what Millennials receive when it comes to political information. W. Lance Bennett (2007a, 19), for one, argues, "Young people are more tuned out than were their corresponding peers at any point in the last half century."

Concern emanates from the changing use of what have been more traditional news sources for political information. The most noticeable decline has been in newspaper readership among Millennials, particularly relative to older age groups. According to the NES, in 1960, 18- to 29-year-olds were the most likely to read newspapers about the presidential campaign (84 percent), compared with 30- to 44-year-olds (80 percent), 45- to 64-year-olds (81 percent) and those 65 years of age and older (74 percent). In 2000, 27 percent of 18- to 29-year-olds read newspapers about the campaign, and in 2004 it was 34 percent for this age group. In 1960, 18- to 29-year-olds were 10 points more likely to read newspapers about the campaign than those 65 years of age or older. By 2000 and 2004, they trailed this older age group by 29 and 27 points, respectively (see Wattenberg 2008, 19).

There has also been a dramatic decline in TV news viewership, particularly relative to political events and when compared with viewership by older age groups. In 1960, 79 percent of young adults under 30 watched the Kennedy-Nixon debates on television, 10 points higher than those over 65 years old, and about the same as the middle age groups. In 2000, 39 percent of those under 30 paid attention to the first Bush-Gore debate, compared with 67 percent of those 65 years old and over, according to the 2000 National Annenberg Election Study. In *Reaching Young Voters*, the Harvard IOP reported in 2004 that 23 percent of 18- to 29-year-olds relied on network news for campaign information, a figure at 39 percent for the 2000 presidential election.

In the emerging digital age, it is important to understand what role the Internet has played in perhaps redirecting Millennials to more accessible news sources for political information and replacing other more familiar news sources in the process. For purposes here, I am particularly interested in the different news sources for Millennial-age college students, including the young adults entering our US politics courses at SUNY Fredonia.

In fact, our findings revealed that our students still utilized television as a primary news source in far greater numbers than they did the Internet. In fall 2000, 71 percent identified television, 12 percent the Internet, and 9 percent newspapers as a primary news source. In fall 2001, it was 76 percent TV, 11 percent the Internet, and 6 percent newspapers. And in fall 2002, it was 66 percent TV, 18 percent newspapers, and 9 percent the Internet. In all semesters from fall 2000 to fall 2002, the Internet was never a primary news source for more than 12 percent of the students. Television remained the overwhelming choice for our students, hitting particularly high points close to dramatic events such as the Election 2000 recount and the 9/11 attacks.

Moreover, these numbers seem representative of Millennials nationwide during the first decade of the twenty-first century. In 2005, Pew reported that only 7 percent of 18- to 29-year-olds go online for political news. Even by 2006, CIRCLE reported in *The Civic Health of the Nation* that more 15- to 25-year-olds relied on TV (22 percent) than on the net (15 percent) for news and information.

What is clear from the findings is that our students—as representative of Millennials in general—have been increasingly unlikely to rely on newspapers as a primary news source. It does appear that the days of the printed press—particularly as a primary news source—are truly numbered for this generation. It is not clear that the Internet has emerged as the logical alternative, at least for now, when it comes to keeping abreast of the news and current events. The Millennial relationship with television news is a bit more complicated, however, particularly when one considers the pervasiveness of cable news networks.

As we reached the midpoint of the first decade of the new century, a majority of the nation's college population claimed to be following a variety of television news resources. In 2005, the Harvard IOP reported that 79 percent of undergrads watched network TV news channels regularly or sometimes, while 75 percent watched cable news channels regularly or sometimes. In the national adult population, 66 percent claimed to watch cable news sometimes or regularly. In 2008, the Harvard IOP found for 18- to 24-year-olds who are not on a college campus that cable television was the preferred medium for political news and information (35 percent as a top choice), followed by broadcast news at 31 percent. For those on a college campus, cable news (37 percent) was nearly tied with non-newspaper Internet sources (35 percent) such as Yahoo and CNN.com.

Over the course of the first decade of the new millennium, reliance on Internet news sources has been increasing, particularly among college students. However, TV news (cable, in particular) remains a significant source of news information for all Millennials, including those enrolled at our nation's campuses. What is particularly important are when and how our Millennial-age students' use of these media sources relates to political knowledge and learning.

Understanding Millennial Mediated Surveillance of Political Events

It is important to understand how our students gather mediated information in their understanding of the political world. We cannot assume as educators that Millennials entering our courses are paying consistent attention on a daily basis to the breadth of issues and events making the daily newspaper headlines, leading off the nightly evening news broadcasts, or even stored more accessibly across the Internet.

A daily digital Millennial alternative of print or broadcast news consumption has not automatically occurred in a new online environment. For example, a May 2004 Pew survey found only 7 percent of those under 30 years of age regularly read websites of major newspapers such as USAToday.com or NewYorkTimes.com. Nine percent in this age group used websites of local newspaper or TV stations regularly. Although the Internet opens up countless possibilities for political information, as I discuss here and throughout this book, it has not necessarily directed the digital generation to more traditional news sources even when available online. Bauerlein (2008, 33) goes so far as to suggest, "With so much intellectual matter circulating in the media and on the Internet, teachers, writers, journalists, and other 'knowledge workers' don't realize how thoroughly young adults and teens tune it out."

Surveys simply show that young adults follow political news stories at a lower rate than do older adults, and are less likely to be consumers of daily and evening news (Pew January 2007). Mindich (2005) describes a generational divide where 32 percent of 18- to 24-year-olds agree that they "need to get the news every day," compared with 62 percent of 55- to 64-year-olds.

Millennials are not automatically tuned in to the breaking news events that may grab the daily attention of older age groups—including US politics professors. Thus we must be particularly attuned to the salient events that do spark increased and sustained student attentiveness, thereby providing the ingredients for connecting political interest, learning, and engagement. It isn't so much what Millennials tune out as much as what they tune in that is critical to understanding how to connect our students' attentiveness to interest and learning. Attentiveness to a particular event can stimulate political attentiveness overall as students begin to understand more of the relevant connections when gathering related political information, similar to the cognitive process I discuss in Chapter 3.

For our SUNY Fredonia students entering the US politics course, fall 2001–fall 2005, attentiveness to the 9/11 attacks was clearly the high point of issue attentiveness. Eighty-six percent claimed to pay a lot of attention. And this appears to have translated into general attentiveness to TV news, with the highest mark for entering students set in fall 2001, just after the 9/11 attacks. Attentiveness to TV news also surged with students in line with attentiveness to the 2004 presidential election and the early stages of the war in Iraq. (See Figure 4.1.)

Increased interest and attention to a salient event can direct attentiveness to news in general (Prior 2002). While one is surveying the news for information related to the event, there is also exposure to other information within the broader newscast. Thus, salient events can lead to greater attentiveness and political learning overall. In a Pew survey report in November 2001, 66 percent of respondents nationwide said they were "more generally interested in the news" after the terrorist attacks than

Figure 4.1   Attention to TV and Internet News in US Politics Courses

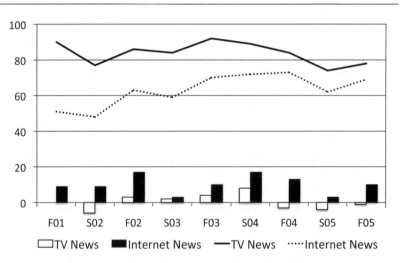

Notes: Trend lines indicate SUNY Fredonia students completing the US politics course who pay attention to TV news and Internet news media "sometimes/a lot." Bars indicate the percentage point change in attentiveness to TV news and Internet news media from the beginning of the US politics course. The question wording is given in Appendix A.

before. By 2005, the new century had featured a sustained period of high-profile news events, including the 9/11 attacks, the war in Iraq, the presidential election, and Hurricane Katrina. And in 2005 the Harvard IOP reported 68 percent of college students were following news about national politics somewhat or very closely, a number significantly higher for this age cohort than at the start of the new millennium.

Interest and attentiveness to salient new millennial events also generated increased use of Internet news media sources for our US politics students. While our students were still more likely to pay attention to TV news than to net news from fall 2001 to fall 2005, the attentiveness gap closed considerably between the media sources in each year. Attentiveness was essentially even between the two news sources by the midpoint of the first decade of the new century. Furthermore, news attentiveness gains during each course term were heavily slanted to the use of Internet news, and increase in attentiveness to Internet-based news was generally accompanied by a decrease in attentiveness to television news for our US politics students.

This could be a result of students' personal access to computers and smart phones in their dorm rooms and not necessarily to television. But beyond the college living environment, such behavior suggests an important shift in news consumption habits that is likely to continue after the college experience. Similar trends made lifelong newspaper readers and television news consumers out of earlier generations, who first read of Pearl Harbor in the headline news of the morning newspaper or remember where they were as they watched the assassination of JFK on CBS *Evening News with Walter Cronkite*. Similarly, this new generation of students has been accessing information from updates on the war in Iraq to breaking news on the presidential campaign from the comfort of their dorm room, laptop, or cell phone application.

Recognizing New Media Possibilities

A key element here is not necessarily the impact of old vs. new media technology but further understanding what drives our Millennial-age students to seek out particular media and related political information sources. While youth news consumption and interest in public events fell deeply and consistently over several decades, it can be argued that the big drop in news consumption occurred in the 1980s and into the 1990s—largely before the Internet (Levine 2007b, 125). In fact, it wasn't until 1994 that US Senator Diane Feinstein of California launched the first political website. Sites such as Hillary.com became a major presence as part of the 2000 US Senate campaign in New York, and by the 2002 election the vast majority of campaigns employed political websites (Howard 2006).

Among our SUNY Fredonia US politics students surveyed in fall 2000, 66 percent claimed to pay some or a lot of attention to nonpolitically oriented websites and 30 percent to politically oriented websites. But that number was likely inflated by the 2000 election finale and, in spring 2001, 19 percent of our students claimed to pay at least some attention to politically oriented websites and 65 percent to nonpolitical sites.

Millennial Internet use to retrieve political information has not suggested a level associated with older age groups or even past-generation young-adult use of more traditional media sources. Still, relatively higher Millennial generational comfort with this new Internet medium as a political information resource has been apparent from the beginning. According to Zukin et al.'s 2002 NCES survey, 28 percent of DotNets, compared with 24 percent of Boomers and 14 percent of Dutifuls, claimed to access news on the Internet three or more times a week. A Pew April 2007 report revealed that 28 percent of 18- to 29-year-olds accessed *most* of their information about the 2004 election from the Internet, up from 22 percent in 2000, and more than those in any other age group.

The use of the Internet as a resource has grown dramatically for Millennials and it has been evident across campuses. Between 60 and 70 percent of our entering US politics students at SUNY Fredonia claimed to use the Internet at least four to eight hours per week in fall 2001 and spring 2002, but by spring and fall 2005, it was about 90 percent. Entering the fall 2001 course, 22 percent claimed to use the net fifteen or more hours per week, a number at 28 percent in fall 2005. Net use particularly increased during the fall 2004 term, from 21 percent at fifteen or more hours per week to 41 percent by the end of the course, suggesting Internet activity related to the election. It was by far the biggest increase in high-level Internet use in the courses surveyed.

Since 2005, there has been an explosion of online social networking sites, including MySpace and Facebook, making daily Internet use as commonplace as text messaging on a cell phone for the younger generation. In a May 2006 Young Voter Strategies poll of 18- to 30-year-olds, 70 percent answered yes to using the Internet daily. According to the 2007 HERI survey, 86 percent of entering college freshmen had as high school seniors spent some time utilizing social networking sites such as Facebook and/or MySpace. In 2008, the Harvard IOP found that 86 percent of college students had access to Facebook.

Nevertheless, many observers remain unconvinced that increasing interaction and time on the Internet can be anything but a negative distraction for our Millennial-age students already struggling with information overload. For instance, Mark Bauerlein (2008, 37) fears that for Millennials, excessive time spent in social networking sites fixated on peer updates "harden[s] their minds to historical and civic facts despite more coursework, [shutting] out current events and political matters despite all the information streams."

Of our US politics students surveyed at SUNY Fredonia, fall 2001–fall 2005, those who spent more time online had *higher* levels of surveillance knowledge of facts and figures related to domestic politics and foreign policy. As Table 4.1 demonstrates, learning took place for all levels of net use. Those who were online generally began with a higher level of knowledge and retained this advantage over the term. The most significant differences between more frequent and less frequent net users at the beginning and end of the US politics course had to do with surveillance knowledge of domestic facts and figures. By the end of the US politics course there were also significant textbook knowledge differences. Higher levels of net use and knowledge were also connected when it came to understanding the basic principles and foundations of US politics. Apparently all of that time online was not getting in the way of learning the material, and it appeared to benefit it.

While students may go online to update Facebook sites, they may also be taking advantage of Internet sources to access relevant course

Table 4.1 Levels of Internet Use and Political Knowledge

Weekly Internet Use	Domestic Surveillance		Foreign Surveillance		Textbook	
	Pre *	Post *	Pre +	Post +	Pre	Post +
1–3 hours	2.3	3.1	1.9	2.2	1.7	2.0
9–14 hours	2.6	3.6	2.1	2.4	1.9	2.2
20+ hours	2.9	3.6	2.3	2.5	1.9	2.3

Notes: "Domestic Surveillance" indicates entering (pre) and exiting (post) mean levels of domestic surveillance knowledge, "Foreign Surveillance" indicates mean levels of foreign surveillance knowledge, and "Textbook" indicates mean levels of textbook knowledge, all as measured in Table 3.2, pooling fall 2001–fall 2005 surveys of SUNY Fredonia students in US politics courses. There were 886 students measured here who completed pre and post surveys and fell within three out of six possible categories of Internet use (1–3 hours, N = 309; 9–14 hours, N = 372; and 20+ hours, N = 205). The question wording of all categories is given in Appendix A. All pre-post mean increases, $p \le .001$ for paired sample t-tests of surveillance and textbook knowledge. One-way ANOVA was used to determine statistically significant differences (* $p \le .001$; + $p \le .01$) among the three levels of Internet use or pre and post tests.

information. According to the 2005 HERI College Student Survey, 84 percent of students utilized the Internet for research or homework, and 50 percent used the library. A 2005 Harvard IOP survey reported 34 percent of college students read online columns or blogs regularly or occasionally. And with our US politics surveys showing higher levels of political knowledge for heavier online users, one would think these individuals are not receiving all of their political information from the *World of Warcraft* or Perez Hilton's latest dish on celebrities.

It is important to recognize how available and seemingly accessible media sources can help connect and reinforce our students' attentiveness to salient events and processes with political learning as they encounter additional political information within the course learning experience. As students' familiarity increases with relevant political information, it can be reinforced and strengthened through news gathered from what is an increasingly familiar Internet realm for Millennials.

Table 4.2 demonstrates how students who paid a lot of attention to net-based news had higher levels of knowledge entering and exiting the US politics course. Textbook knowledge was slightly higher for students who paid more attention to TV or net news, but the most significant learning curve had to do with surveillance knowledge. Attentiveness to salient events drives both learning of related political figures and facts and the use of the most accessible media source to monitor related information. Thus it follows that our students' news attentiveness through the most accessible of media sources would also be strongly connected with surveillance knowledge gains.

Access to political information, in both the classroom and through the media, is an important aspect of the learning process for Millennial-age students seeking the most reliable tools with which to sort through the political world. As I discuss in Chapter 3, there can be a tendency to fall back on information shortcuts consisting of emotive attitudes and symbolic predispositions because they are convenient. However, such affective attitudes are also formulated through a perceived emotional attachment, trust, or confidence in related cues to rely on in guiding judgment.

Millennials are less familiar with traditional media sources and are thus seeking accessible sources as they are learning how to gather information about the political environment. It is important to recognize why these young adults may also rely on alternative sources of information rather than the traditional news channels. Therefore, it is critical to understand these access points and motivations in order to maximize related learning connections as part of the introduction to US politics experience.

The Daily Fix to Less-Than-Daily Media Attentiveness

Millennial-age students need to feel familiar, comfortable, and confident about political information sources. However, for many Millennials, the traditional media appears to be a less than reliable and accessible resource. For college students interviewed in 2006–2007 by CIRCLE in *Talking Politics*, the focus group participants complained about the quality of the media and that there are so many competing sources of news that it is difficult to know which sources provide the best information (25). Many students admitted to consequently filtering the media and were distrustful of the media as a resource. According to the GSS, confidence in the press declined from 32 percent in 1976 to 13 percent in 2004 among 18- to 25-year-olds.

For our students entering US politics courses at SUNY Fredonia, there was lower confidence in TV network media than in political institutions, which was also very low. Despite the rally around government institutions following 9/11, there was little boost in our students' confidence in the media in the aftermath of the attacks. In fall 2000 and spring 2001, confidence in TV network media was at 20 and 19 percent for students completing the US politics course. Just after the 9/11 attacks in fall

Table 4.2   News Attention and Political Knowledge

Attention to TV News	Surveillance Knowledge *	Surveillance Knowledge *	Textbook Knowledge	Textbook Knowledge
	Pre	Post	Pre	Post
None/rare	3.9	5.2	1.8	2.2
Some	4.5	5.8	1.8	2.2
A lot	5.2	6.3	1.9	2.2
Attention to Internet News	Surveillance Knowledge *	Surveillance Knowledge *	Textbook Knowledge *	Textbook Knowledge
	Pre	Post	Pre	Post
None/rare	4.1	5.4	1.7	2.1
Some	4.8	5.8	1.8	2.1
A lot	5.8	6.8	2.0	2.2

Notes: Mean levels of overall surveillance knowledge and textbook knowledge measured in Table 3.2, pooling fall 2001–fall 2005 surveys of 1,558 SUNY Fredonia students in US politics courses. The question wording is given in Appendix A. All pre-post mean increases, $p \le .001$ for paired sample t-tests of surveillance and textbook knowledge. One-way ANOVA was used to determine statistically significant differences (* $p \le .001$) among the three levels of TV and Internet news attentiveness for pre and post tests.

2001, confidence in TV network media jumped slightly to 29 percent for entering students and up to 31 percent by the end of the course. However, by the beginning of spring 2002 and fall 2002, our students' confidence in TV network media was at 22 percent for both courses. Confidence in Internet news media was even worse for entering students in the aftermath of 9/11, at 22 and 21 percent, respectively. By fall 2002, however, entering students' confidence in Internet news media, at 26 percent, had slightly surpassed confidence in TV network media.

With little confidence in news media sources, including new media options, it is important to recognize all possible avenues that our Millennial-age students may utilize in lieu of the daily newspaper, the evening news, and even an online news site with Twitter feeds. It isn't just about the technology but the perceived relevance and accessibility of the medium. And in a world with an endless supply of YouTube clips and Facebook updates, even the shrinking TV news sound bite is increasingly unlikely to counter the multitude of media options presented to Millennials on a daily basis.

For many Millennials, there is little incentive to seek out political information from media sources in which there is little inherent confidence and trust that knowledge gained will be relevant to one's concerns and interests. Political learning, particularly outside of the classroom, shouldn't be such an effort in the minds of Millennials. Our students will seek media sources that seem relevant and interesting and engaging, which can in many instances be classified as entertainment. David Mindich (2005, 39), for one, argues, "If we want to understand why many young people don't follow the news, we need to understand the lure of entertainment." But as I explore here, there is such a thing as entertaining news and learning while laughing.

Clearly, keeping your television attuned to the latest *Bachelor* or *Surreal World* episode will do little more than keep you up-to-date with the current exploits of fallen celebrities and individuals desperate to be in the public eye. And using YouTube to watch a squirrel water-ski will likely leave you less than informed about the matters of the day. Yet certain facets of entertainment can lead to political learning, intentional or not, as an incidental by-product of soft news. Likewise, political information and learning can actually be entertaining if presented in the proper way.

There is the potential learning impact of increasingly prevalent news entertainment programs, largely broadcast late at night, like *The Daily Show with Jon Stewart*. In order to understand how available media sources can inform our Millennial-age students, it is critical to recognize the significant generational reliance on such programs as a source of political information, whether intentional or incidental learning. It is clear that such late-night programs increasingly play a role for Millennials that we have traditionally associated with TV news programs. For example, a January 2004 Pew survey found that 61 percent of those under 30 said they sometimes learned something new from commentary on late-night comedy programs like *The Daily Show with Jon Stewart, Saturday Night Live,* or traditional late-night talk shows. Twenty-three percent said they regularly learned something from network newscasts.

Millennials who watch such soft news entertainment are also more likely to seek other sources of political information, which reinforces exposure to political information and can increase learning overall. For example, the 2005 Harvard IOP reported that 42 percent of college students regularly or sometimes watch *The Daily Show,* and 59 percent of those students who regularly watch *The Daily Show* follow national news in some other form.

Educators need to recognize the educational value of such programs in a media environment that has changed dramatically. Indeed, the increasing impact of *The Daily Show*'s comedy-styled coverage of news, coupled with the often questionable network nightly news and cable headline news coverage, has opened up a debate on which provides more substantive political information, particularly for younger Americans initially learning about politics and policy (Cao 2008; Cassino and Besin-Cassino 2009; Hollander 2005). While cable and network news media often seem distracted by the latest disaster, death, or downfall (Bennett 2007b), *The Daily Show* and now the *The Colbert Report* both review nightly news events and figures as well as interview significant political and societal figures, including relatively obscure scholars and activists. In fact, the TV Critics Association awarded outstanding news and information programming to Comedy Central's *Daily Show* over other cable and network news for the 2003–2004 season, a period involving the start of the war in Iraq and a presidential election.

There are a number of indicators that link more substantive actual news content and higher political knowledge with viewership of programs such as *The Daily Show,* particularly when compared with what we would consider more hard news sources. According to an April 2007 Pew report, 54 percent of regular viewers of *The Daily Show* and *The Colbert Report* were in the highest political knowledge level category. In comparison, 48 percent in the high knowledge category relied mostly on TV news websites, 43 percent on the daily newspaper, and 38 percent on the network evening news. As our Millennial-age students' media habits change and shift away from more familiar information resources, there are new opportunities to facilitate the US politics learning experience in line with generational interests and media use trends.

A US politics course can reinforce attentiveness to new media sources such as *The Daily Show*. For our entering US politics students at SUNY Fredonia, 43 percent in spring 2005 and 45 percent in fall 2005 paid some or a lot of attention to *The Daily Show*, numbers that increased to 50 and 53 percent at the completion of each course, respectively.

Moreover, attentiveness to *The Daily Show* did not signify an abandonment of other media information sources by our students. More of our students continued to pay more attention overall to TV news and net news even as their numbers increased for *Daily Show* attentiveness, demonstrating an increased interest in information acquisition overall.

US politics students paying a lot of attention to *The Daily Show* exhibited higher levels of political knowledge than did those who paid a lot of attention to TV news and net news, most notably with regard to foreign policy figures (see Table 4.3). As I have discussed, surveillance learning for our students is connected to an attentiveness to salient events that reinforces an awareness of related political facts and figures. Per-

Table 4.3 Daily Learning in US Politics

	Some TV	A Lot of TV	Some Internet	A Lot of Internet	Some of *The Daily Show*	A Lot of *The Daily Show*
Domestic political figures/facts						
Pre	3.0	3.7	3.1	4.0	3.1	4.0
Post	3.9	4.6	3.8	4.6	**3.9**	**4.8**
Foreign policy figures						
Pre	3.7	4.2	3.6	4.6	3.8	4.8
Post	4.0	4.6	3.7	4.8	**4.1**	**4.9**
Institutional process/foundation						
Pre	2.4	2.8	2.6	2.9	2.4	3.0
Post	3.0	3.2	3.0	3.2	3.0	**3.3**

Notes: The table contains mean knowledge levels for entering (pre) and exiting (post) SUNY Fredonia students in US politics courses, pooling 338 spring 2005 (N = 148) and fall 2005 (N = 190) surveys. The highest mean average for exiting knowledge for levels of attentiveness is shown in bold. Knowledge of domestic political and foreign policy figures (with the addition of Saddam Hussein) and textbook foundational knowledge (with the addition of the Electoral College) are drawn from the items in Table 3.2. Mean knowledge levels are organized according to student levels of attention to TV news, Internet news, and *The Daily Show*. The question wording is given in Appendix A. Independent sample t-tests indicate statistical significance at $p \leq .01$ for all comparisons of respondents with "some" and "a lot" of attentiveness to the three media sources in pre and post measures, except for independent sample t-tests in post measure group differences of textbook foundational knowledge, at $p \leq .05$.

ceived relevance and interest is another critical component of this learning curve. As we explored in Chapters 2 and 3, our students were particularly attentive to significant events associated with the war on terrorism and the war in Iraq, reinforcing knowledge gained through such attentiveness to media content on related media programming. In nightly programming, for years *The Daily Show* paid great attention to the war in Iraq, with its own news watch entitled "Mess-O' Potamia." As for the war on terrorism, Jon Stewart actually had tea with President Musharraf on the show, jokingly asking the Pakistani strongman, "Where is Osama bin Laden?" And as we have well established in our findings, bin Laden was at the top of recognizable political figures for our Millennial-age students first learning about US politics and considering related policies.

As I discussed in Chapter 3, our Millennial-age college students inevitably have paid the most attention to domestic politics at critical moments that are receiving heightened media attention, such as at the height of a presidential election. *The Daily Show* has established a nightly update on this topic titled "Indecision 2000, 2004, 2008." In August 2004, John Kerry became the first major party presidential nominee to appear on the show. In 2008, presidential candidate stops on *The Daily Show* and, increasingly, on *The Colbert Report* were viewed as necessities.

Heightened attentiveness to such salient political events and the media sources that feature related political figures and facts is bound to increase surveillance knowledge when it is reinforced and strengthened by exposure to related information in the US politics course. With an extended focus on the salient events of interest to our students and more in-depth reinforcement of related political figures, *Daily Show* attentiveness had a higher corresponding level of domestic surveillance knowledge than did TV news and net news attentiveness. Moreover, the gap in domestic surveillance knowledge between those students who watched *The Daily Show* a lot and those who watched somewhat was also higher than for those who claimed to pay a lot and those who paid some attention to TV or net news.

Students who were the most knowledgeable about US politics were also likely drawn to the entertaining yet informative content of a program like *The Daily Show,* but it is also clear from the findings that students' attentiveness to such a program also reinforced and increased their political knowledge. Importantly, the attentiveness and interest connected to salient current events and related surveillance knowledge also reinforced understanding and learning about enduring political processes and institutions. Students paying a lot of attention to *The Daily Show* also scored higher on textbook knowledge questions of institutional process and foundation by the end of the US politics course, as did students paying more attention to TV and net news.

The executive summary of the April 2008 Harvard IOP report *Youth Survey on Politics and Public Service* noted, "With overall name recognition of 84 percent, there is little doubt that Stewart and Colbert are playing some role in the political education/entertainment of this generation." But more than anything, Table 4.3 shows that students paying the most attention to some form of media dissemination of political information, whether *The Daily Show*, TV news, or Internet-based news, were the most politically knowledgeable entering and exiting our classes. Furthermore, these students continued to learn about politics in the US politics course as they relied on a variety of media sources. Such interest stretched beyond the hours within the classroom and into the mediated reality of politics where a general foundation and introduction to US politics will need to be continuously updated by surveillance and utilization of evolving information resources.

Entertained into Learning

One of the most critical elements discussed throughout this book is the importance of capturing our Millennial-age students' attention to salient political events as a gateway to learning. The findings demonstrate that students have been paying significant amounts of attention to particular salient events through hard *and* soft news sources. Even skeptics of Millennial news attentiveness would agree that however attentiveness to current events is derived is a positive. Wattenberg (2008, 60), for one, points out, "Young adults may not be paying attention to hard news shows or traditional political events, but they do like to be entertained. If soft news shows can provide entertaining coverage of political events, then they may well have the potential to save the day by making young people aware of at least some aspects of current events."

There is a significant capacity for information retention and related learning when entertainment is connected to perceived relevance and interests, as we considered in our *Who Wants to Be a Millionaire* example discussed in an earlier chapter. We can recite precise lines from movies, remember the exact lyrics to favorite songs, but can have a hard time recalling the political figures and events featured in last night's news broadcasts. However, as our *Daily Show* findings demonstrate, students' political learning can also be reinforced and stimulated as a process of more entertaining formats rather than through strictly hard news.

Film and music are other critical media vehicles that can entertain, inform, and connect with emotion and cognition, whether it is a film or song about the political plight of certain groups or about how to take action to confront injustice. Film and music can also draw young adults' attention to current events and political debates, triggering not only emotion and symbolism, but also a desire to learn more about the topic. For example, at the end of *The Deer Hunter* (the Best Picture winner in 1978) a soon-to-be-famous cast of characters, including Robert De Niro and Meryl Streep, spontaneously break into a rendition of "God Bless America." The movie and song symbolically closed out a decade of conflict over the war toward a national healing in the next decade and through Oliver Stone's own Vietnam film trilogy. Nearly thirty years later, Al Gore's Oscar-winning documentary *An Inconvenient Truth* brought the often-complex discussion (and debate) over global warming to a multiplex and DVD format accessible to a younger generation reared on such vehicles of communication and presentation.

The key is connecting these entertainment vehicles to salient political events and the attentiveness of a generational cohort, which relates to political learning. Music and performance informed and reinforced awareness and political understanding of the Baby Boom generation, from Martin Luther King's March on Washington to Woodstock. Generation X had mega–benefit concerts such as Live Aid and Farm Aid on foreign and domestic issues of concern. And into the 1990s, artists sang about the plight of Tibet, the rainforest, and so on. After 9/11 many of these voices joined together, young and old, from Neil Young to Wyclef Jean, for performance benefits to raise money for the victims of the terrorist attacks.

The 2004 election galvanized music and politics to an extent not seen since perhaps 1968. Old rockers like John Mellencamp and the Boss joined new rappers like Eminem and P. Diddy to challenge a generation to wake up, to mobilize. In the aftermath of a heated election, entertainers delivered political statements that were at times scripted and at other times off-script. Speaking alongside *Austin Powers*'s Mike Meyers, rapper Kanye West's off-the-cuff condemnation of President Bush's handling of the 2005 Katrina crisis would be played over and over again across the sound-bite cable-news environment and Internet chatter. Teaming up with world figures ranging from the economist Jeffrey Sachs to Microsoft's Bill Gates, to US and foreign presidents, and to U2's Bono and the *One* campaign has become a force for awareness about global poverty. The critically acclaimed alternative band Radiohead hosts a website that is as much a vehicle for political awareness as it is for music-listening pleasure.

For young adults first introduced to US politics, such media sources can also encourage attentiveness to salient political events and issues, thereby facilitating increased awareness of related political figures, processes, and facts. If student interest in politically oriented film and music is intertwined with heightened attentiveness to politics, it is as important to consider as the consumption of TV news sources when it comes to learning about US politics.

There is an entertainment dimension to political attentiveness and interest for our Millennial-age students. For 338 of our students polled entering the spring and fall 2005 US politics courses at SUNY Fredonia, there was a strong and significant correlation ($p \leq .001$) concerning interest in politically oriented music and interest in politically oriented film with attentiveness to *The Daily Show* (.25, .25). And these relationships only strengthened by the end of the term for our students (at .29 and .30, respectively). Importantly, our students' interest in politically oriented music and politically oriented film was not significantly related to attentiveness to TV news at the end of a US politics course. Despite the fact that *The Daily Show* and TV news are both broadcast on television, it was the perceived entertainment component of *The Daily Show* that connected it to political interests in music and film but not to what is conceived of as more traditional TV hard news. Equally important is the fact that *Daily Show* viewership is related to higher levels of political knowledge, which is another indicator of how our students can learn through what are considered entertainment channels. These are important considerations as we seek to understand and possibly integrate the most effective media resources for our Millennial-age students as they are introduced to the US politics learning experience.

Mediated Learning Impact
(Or Understanding Your Audience)

Within the introduction to US politics course, there is an opportunity to more fully understand the impact of media and its uses as part of the students' political learning process. Increasingly our Millennial-age students can draw from or ignore a vast array of media options, which also includes media featuring political content and major political events (Bauerlein 2008; Bennett 2007a; Wattenberg 2008). Attentiveness to salient political events is a critical part of how our students connect their own inherent political attentiveness, interest, and knowledge. This makes the integration of mediated current events more critical than ever for a

Millennial-age generation that might otherwise avoid the most significant of national political events. In this chapter, I explore how integrating a multimedia dimension of current political events into the US politics learning experience can cognitively stimulate the link among our students' attentiveness, interest, and learning.

Some researchers find that multimedia use of video and computer-enhanced visual presentation in political science enhance student interest and participation, yielding improvements in student learning as measured by both students' self-report and objective outcome testing (Luna and MacKenzie 1997; Pollock and Wilson 2002). Others find no significant differences between multimedia-driven classes and traditional class formats when it comes to student learning (Janda 1992; Mayer 2001). An ongoing debate over instructional impact may reflect an interaction between teaching styles and students' learning styles (Groth 2007). Students may learn and absorb political information in different ways (Gershkoff 2005). For example, Smith and Woody (2000) found that students who prefer visual input to verbal input will benefit more from multimediated instruction than those who are less visually oriented.

Our findings have demonstrated a connection among our students' attentiveness to TV news, to Internet news, and even to soft news sources with regard to political learning, particularly concerning surveillance knowledge. Furthermore, this conception of multimedia course methods includes the possible integration of "political entertainment" media resources, including politically oriented music, film, and clips from late-night programs such as *The Daily Show* and *The Colbert Report*. If instructional techniques were to more extensively integrate such news sources, related imagery, and information, I would expect these multimedia course methods also to be positively related to students' attentiveness, interest, and surveillance knowledge gains in US politics.

In order to assess multimedia impact, we were able to survey students who had extensive and integrated media exposure and those who did not as part of the introduction to US politics course. For 2,125 US politics students completing the course at SUNY Fredonia, fall 2000–fall 2005, slightly more than half responded that their US politics course instruction would "somewhat" or "regularly" utilize computer-generated presentations such as PowerPoint, computer-generated graphic imagery (e.g., photos, graphs, illustrations), and video imagery/audio support, including TV news, movie, or audio clips, as part of the course presentation (see Appendix A for the question wording). Consisting of ten different instructors across over fifty different US politics course sections, there was a relatively clear gap as well between those who used multimedia material "a lot" and those who simply "never did." Our students responded that 45 percent of instruction consisted of a lot of computer-generated presentation, whereas 40 percent responded that it never did. Thirty-nine percent of instruction consisted of a lot of computer graphic imagery, compared with 33 percent that never did. And 41 percent of the US politics instruction used a lot of video imagery, compared with 32 percent that never did.

The use of textbooks, readings, and assignments was relatively evenly represented across the US politics courses with little to no multimedia resources and for those courses that used some to a lot (see Appendix B). It wasn't that the more multimedia-integrated courses utilized readings and assignments that integrated more current events issues or vice versa. There were ample and diverse opportunities through the various course textbooks, lectures, course discussion, and assignments to direct students' attentiveness to current events. Instructors utilized a variety of methods to engage students' interest.

With over fifty course sections, ten different instructors, and about two thousand different students across five years, the objective was not to identify the numerous differences associated with particular course sections, instructors, or course material. The objective of this analysis was to examine the relative impact of multimedia vs. non-multimedia in order to shed more light on the role of media in our students' learning process inside and outside of the classroom. Thus, the most significant difference had to do with the integration (or not) of the media sources and how to most effectively illuminate current events. Multimedia sources could integrate news, political music, films, website information, and other assorted resources online where necessary to illuminate current events even as they were transpiring. The faculty who did not use these techniques could still certainly discuss current events as they were reported in the news or even in other venues.

Assigned textbooks and supplementary readings could cover relatively contemporary events and topics retrospectively and in close proximity to their occurrence, but the only way to directly tie in these events as they were occurring would be to integrate the latest news through multimedia techniques. This might include web-based news updates to retrieve information relevant to say, war in Iraq or the presidential election candidates. This could also explain why our students' net news use increased dramatically over these US politics courses.

In Figure 4.2, our findings demonstrate that the use of multimedia methods was particularly related to surveillance knowledge gains but not to textbook knowledge increases. In fact, the more traditional US politics instruction format resulted in slightly higher overall textbook political knowledge, possibly owing to a relatively higher instruction focus on enduring foundations, processes, and institutions, and less attention to an instructional surveillance of contemporary political figures and facts. On the other hand, the US politics courses utilizing multimedia had more substantial surveillance knowledge levels of both domestic and foreign figures and facts. Furthermore, those exposed to the multimedia methods had higher levels of interest in national politics and greater attentiveness to TV news.

It appears that the integration of media sources within the course served to enhance the cognitive connections with media sources outside of the classroom environment. With more visible connection to salient current events, this arguably facilitated student political interest critical to

Figure 4.2   Multimediated Instruction and Political Knowledge

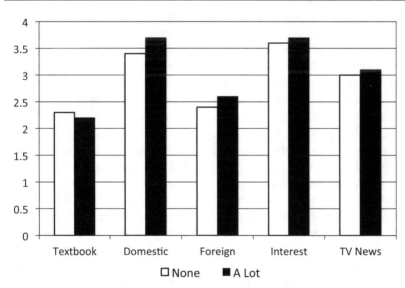

☐ None   ■ A Lot

Notes: This graph shows the mean level of textbook knowledge and domestic and foreign surveillance knowledge based on items listed in Table 3.2, as well as the mean level of interest in national politics and the mean level of attentiveness to TV news, for 2,125 students completing US politics courses at SUNY Fredonia, fall 2001–fall 2005. The left bar represents students who indicated "no real use" of multimedia presentation (e.g., computer-generated video imagery or audio support) in their US politics courses. The right bar represents students who indicated "a lot of use" of this type of multimedia presentation in their US politics courses. The question wording is given in Appendix A. There were statistically significant differences based on independent sample t-tests for textbook knowledge ($p \leq .01$) and domestic surveillance knowledge ($p \leq .001$). Foreign surveillance knowledge, interest in national politics, and attention to TV news had statistically significant differences, where $p \leq .05$.

gathering information on related political figures and facts. These are significant connections that can facilitate extended learning by our students within and outside of the introduction to US politics course.

Examining several of the more salient events that occurred during a US politics term, Table 4.4 shows a consistently higher level of surveillance knowledge, issue attentiveness, and related interest for our students who claimed that their course utilized video imagery such as news, film, or audio clips as part of the instruction. For example, students with a higher degree of stated exposure to such multimedia in their fall 2000 US politics course had higher levels of knowledge of the vice presidential candidates, greater attentiveness to the presidential election, and higher levels of interest in national politics. In fall 2001 and spring 2003, two terms in which wars in Afghanistan and in Iraq began during the course of the introduction to US politics course, students with higher levels of stated exposure to video imagery in their course instruction had much higher levels of knowledge of the secretaries of defense and state. Students exposed to multimedia course integration during the Hurricane Katrina crisis and aftermath had higher surveillance knowledge of the US senators from New York.

With higher levels of attentiveness reinforced with media sources of related current events and figures, these students were more likely to connect key political figures within the context of real political events and processes. On the other hand, multimedia exposure did not increase textbook knowledge of the Electoral College majority across any of the terms on a knowledge item that could just as easily be learned from the course reading. Finally, the students exposed to multimedia sources within the course also exhibited stronger interest in national politics across all of the events and terms, a critical component connecting attentiveness to an event with related knowledge gains. There were five terms in our US politics course in which some of the most salient events of the new century unfolded, including two highly contested presidential elections, the start of two wars, and the Katrina crisis. The students with higher stated exposure to in-class multimedia imagery always had higher levels of attentiveness and interest than those that did not and, with rare exception, had consistently higher levels of surveillance knowledge.

A key here is what captured students' attention and interest that motivated learning and what is likely to encourage political learning within and beyond the US politics course. It is important to understand how our students perceive the use of multimedia as a vehicle for building on the foundational knowledge inherent in an introduction to US politics course with a more fluid capacity to also introduce emerging political events and the cast of political figures involved in the process, policy, and debates.

Overall, 49 percent of our SUNY Fredonia US politics students surveyed in fall 2000–fall 2005 would prefer that the level of multimedia use increased, and 46 percent would prefer that it stayed the same. Only 4 percent would prefer that the US politics course use less multimedia in course instruction. Of those who reported their instructor never used computer-generated graphic imagery, 58 percent would prefer multimedia presentation, and of those who used it rarely, 63 percent would prefer more use. In no cases did more than 6 percent indicate a preference for less multimedia presentation among those who listed higher instructional levels of

Table 4.4 Multimediated Salient Events and Knowledge

Salient Events During the Term	Rare to None	Some to A Lot
2000 presidential election (F00)	N = 74	N = 158
Know Electoral College majority	.88	.88
Know vice presidential candidates +	1.9	**2.2**
Attention to presidential election *	3.3	**3.6**
Interest in national politics +	3.3	**3.6**
2001 war on terrorism (F01)	N = 127	N = 104
Know secretary of defense *	.22	**.35**
Know secretary of state *	.30	**.47**
Attention to war in Afghanistan +	3.3	**3.4**
Interest in world affairs	3.7	**3.8**
2003 launch of war in Iraq (S03)	N = 78	N = 108
Know secretary of defense *	.37	**.42**
Know secretary of state +	.48	**.52**
Attention to war in Iraq *	3.4	**3.6**
Interest in world affairs/national politics +	6.8	**7.1**
2004 presidential election (F04)	N = 76	N = 108
Know Electoral College majority +	**.83**	.76
Know vice presidential candidates	**1.7**	1.6
Attention to presidential election +	3.6	**3.8**
Interest in national politics +	3.8	**4.0**
2005 Katrina crisis (F05)	N = 139	N = 78
Know presidential appointment power	.77	.77
Know New York US senators +	1.1	**1.3**
Attentiveness to Katrina +	3.1	**3.3**
Interest in national politics +	3.7	**3.9**

Notes: Columns indicate the mean level of knowledge, attentiveness, and interest for related items for those with less or more multimedia instruction at the completion of US politics courses at SUNY Fredonia in respective terms. Bold indicates a higher mean level. The question wording is given in Appendix A. Independent sample t-tests of statistical significance (* $p \leq .01$; + $p \leq .05$).

multimedia use. And of those who rated their instructor's multimedia use as a lot, 62 percent would keep it the same. This was particularly pronounced for the lack of video imagery. Sixty-seven percent of students whose instructors never used video imagery would like more multimedia presentation, and 60 percent of those who had instructors who used it a lot preferred that such presentation stay the same.

In the UCSB US politics courses in spring 2003 and fall 2004, about 90 percent of students claimed the instructional use of computer-generated graphic imagery (e.g., photos, graphs, illustrations), but only 10 percent claimed video imagery/audio support (e.g., TV news clips, movie/audio clips). With this breakdown, half would prefer the same amount of multimedia presentation and the other half would prefer more in the US politics course. Almost none answered that they would prefer less multimedia.

Early on in the new millennium when we asked the question about desire for multimedia presentation, most students preferred more of it. Yet as "smart rooms" with technological capacity have proliferated on our campus and others, the learning impact of such techniques is at times affected by the commonality and unimaginative use of such resources. There is the mundane repetition of PowerPoint-generated slides, which do little except replace the reading of one's notes with the reading of one's computer-projected outline. This is not the type of learning environment that is any more apt to engage students in the US politics learning process than one without multimedia materials, and it can negatively impact learning and interest. The successful multimedia learning environment involves the fluid integration of technology, video, and/or computer-generated resources to bring the material to life, to integrate such things as current events that demonstrate how elections work, debates over the war on terrorism and in Iraq, examples of how a president is working with Congress to pass policy, contemporary democratic debates that address issue concerns, and so on.

When considering the overwhelming and consistent desire for integrated multimedia use in an introduction to US politics course by our students surveyed across years, across instruction, across course sections, and across campuses, a skeptic might conclude that these students simply want to be entertained through more visual stimulation. However, based on our findings, I would contend that students want strong course connection with the most relevant current events that drive their interest and attentiveness to politics. These students desire greater cognitive engagement with US politics in ways that they deem most relevant to the most significant political events transpiring in their lives. The proper use of multimedia sources can solidify these connections and facilitate related learning as part of the course experience.

Conclusion

In a media-saturated environment, our students' political knowledge and learning are very much connected to entertaining late-night programs such as *The Daily Show*, which features a nightly satirical (but apparently informative) rundown of political events. This supports the findings that the most influential media learning sources—including TV news and net news—help to connect our students' attentiveness to salient events with political interest and surveillance knowledge.

It is critical to understand what mediated political information our Millennial-age college students are accessing (or not) and how it relates to political knowledge and learning. This is important for our broader understanding of Millennials and how related media technology can facilitate political understanding and engagement within this age cohort. In a media-saturated world, our students are more familiar with accessing political information in TV news clips and YouTube-style links. New information bursts across YouTube from the most inane (winking chipmunks) to the most serious (war footage from Iraq) to everything in between. Much of what our students will learn about politics and government occurs outside of the assigned books, in news flashes and web bites. Therefore, it is all the more important that Millennial-age college students be exposed to political information in the classroom in a way that reinforces the desire to learn and engage US politics outside of it. This chapter demonstrates that a multimedia integrated learning environment can facilitate political attentiveness, interest, and learning for a generation reared on the visual, on the immediate, and on the transitory.

While it is true that we are probably more likely to see a younger adult on a smart phone than one huddled behind a newspaper, it doesn't mean they aren't absorbing information. Millennials just aren't gathering and using political information in traditional ways that make sense to an older generation reared on the daily paper and the evening news. In fact, the findings show that higher levels of online use are related to the highest levels of political knowledge for students entering and exiting our US politics courses.

The media is in a state of flux, raising great possibilities and challenges, optimism yet concern. On the other hand, this is nothing new. The World War II generation adjusted to life via the radio, the Boomers to broadcast television, and Generation X to cable news. And somehow democracy managed not only to survive but to thrive amid new ways of political communication and understanding. We face such a time again, a period of not only great transformation in political events and figures but also the technology that connects citizens with democracy.

For the Millennial Generation, there is a general inclination to just not consume the media, but be the media. Much of this activity is developed, disseminated, discussed, and debated online, whether on social networking sites like Facebook or uploaded as video clips on YouTube. But engagement doesn't need to end there and can be an entry point into additional sources of learning and other forms of action within and beyond the world of cyberspace. In the 2008 presidential election, this digital intersection was on full display as part of a historic mobilization by Millennials.

5

Connecting Political Interests and Engagement

It's okay to like somebody, but you don't have to vote for him.
—*Stephen Colbert, urging young-voter abstinence*
on The Colbert Report, *2008*

"We will remember that there is something happening in America, that we are not as divided as our politics suggests. We are one people, we are one nation, and together we will begin the next chapter." On February 2, 2008, musician will.i.am of the Black Eyed Peas released a music video montage entitled "Yes We Can" on YouTube and DipDive.com. The video integrated presidential candidate Barack Obama's words with those spoken by a host of celebrities in support of his campaign and quickly went viral across its postings, watched 22 million times by late February. The proliferation of new media sources including YouTube and social networking sites such as Facebook translated into an extensive network and mobilization of Millennial supporters for Barack Obama (Winograd and Hais 2008), and likely propelled him into front-runner status with a surprising win in the Iowa caucuses. Obama's concession speech following Hillary Clinton's comeback in the New Hampshire primary was quickly molded into the "Yes We Can" video montage. It immediately reached his energized young supporters, who not only watched and listened via YouTube and social networking sites, but acted by turning out at the polls while encouraging the same of many of their peers.

As Brian Stelter (2008) of the *New York Times* wrote, "Younger voters tend to be not just consumers of news and current events but conduits as well—sending out links and videos to friends and their social networks. And in turn, they rely on friends and online connection for news to come to them." This is a generation that views media as more than just a source of news information. Millennials are actively using media channels to receive and share information that can be connected to opportunities for political engagement and participation. Yet even with new media technology, Millennial-age students still need to make the cognitive connections that link their attentiveness to and interest in political events with related learning and engagement.

This book has explored how attentiveness to salient events connects to political learning. It examines how political learning connects to policy reasoning on the most salient of issues for our Millennial students. The findings demonstrate how the media plays a critical role in related political learning through various traditional and emerging sources with which to access political information, particularly on the most significant political events of interest to this age cohort. This chapter examines how and when political attentiveness, interest, knowledge, and media sources stimulate political engagement and participation among students of this age group.

An examination through the 2008 election and into the initial years of the Obama period provides for a fuller understanding of how political knowledge and attentiveness to the most salient of events relate to interest and engagement for these new Millennial minds. A lack of attention to news and current events and low levels of political knowledge are a significant factor in why many younger people don't participate more actively (Mindich 2005; Wattenberg 2008). Many young adults have not felt informed enough about politics to know how and when to participate. An attentiveness to salient events, which includes the Millennial excitement related to the historic 2008 election and Obama's transition into office, provides an important opportunity to explore how heightened attention and interest affected political knowledge and, consequently, engagement.

Zukin et al. (2006, 126) find political attentiveness and political knowledge key precursors of engagement. Political knowledge and understanding help convert opinions into meaningful political involvement and positively influence political participation (Althaus 1998; Popkin and Dimock 1999). As Macedo et al. (2005, 32) note, "People who know more about politics are more actively engaged in it: those with a higher level of political knowledge are more likely to engage in every type of political activity." In the assessment of Millennial college-age students here, I consider engagement to include participation in a range of political activities, including voting, public service, community activity with some political crossover, and even discussing and debating politics and policy outside of the classroom.

The centrality of political knowledge to political participation makes the learning experience in an introduction to US politics course a vital link for our students who may otherwise avoid engaging political life. Thus the course integration of salient political events is an essential component in connecting our students' learning with heightened engagement. Exposure to current events and debate is viewed as key to not only stimulating knowledge but sparking engagement. Youniss and Levine (2009, 6), for example, describe how "Current event discussions are linked to greater interest in politics, improved critical thinking, civic knowledge and more interest in discussing public affairs beyond the classroom."

Developing political understanding through attentiveness to political events can provide a gateway into learning and engagement for our students. It can foster confidence in other avenues of participation by building related knowledge as a component of political interest attached to political events. As Colby et al. (2007, 47) note, "Even those who avoid more demanding types of political engagement are exposed to political events." Thus, I argue that a course integration of salient political events is also an important instructional vehicle to encourage political participation and engagement. And this chapter explores how political knowledge and learning during the heightened attentiveness of the 2008 election and early Obama presidency, in particular, provided critical linkages to participation outlets for these Millennial-age students

In order to understand how to connect our students' learning with knowledge and action, it is important to understand how this cohort mentally organizes certain elements of political and civic life. The chapter examines, for example, how our students connect interests in local politics with public service, their interest in national politics with world affairs. It considers what aspects of political interest are most significantly related to media sources and new Millennial events. Moreover, it explores how to bridge the Millennial gap between the familiar act of community volunteerism and the less familiar concept of national political engagement. It is important to understand how our students organize attention, interests, and action. By doing so, we can better comprehend how to enhance connections across local interests and attentiveness to significant events. While Millennial interests are drawn in by dramatic moments and events, they also need to be more fully integrated with more comprehensive interests and sustained action.

Our students demonstrate consistently higher levels of interest in national politics and world affairs. Interests in local politics are more consistently integrated with interests in community activism. There is a prevalent interest in but individual disengagement from what I refer to as "distant politics." Students get excited and interested in the significant political events and moments of their time but can be unsure of how to connect such interests with action.

This chapter examines the nature of this disconnect and also considers how to close this gap. It explores how to further integrate new Millennial interests with action, highlighted by a most salient 2008 presidential election process. We also need to recognize how less salient events for Millennials, such as the midterm election of 2010, are thus less likely to encourage related interest and participation. Consequently, it is also important to identify salient nonelectoral events and processes that pique Millennials' attention and interest in order to facilitate more sustained opportunities for connecting learning and engagement.

Engaging in a Salient Political Event

The 2008 presidential election was a particularly salient political event and process for Millennial-age college students in which political attentiveness translated into engagement. Entering the US politics course, 80 percent of our SUNY Fredonia students claimed to pay at least "some" attention, with 40 percent paying "a lot" of attention to the 2008 presidential election. By the completion of the course, 93 percent claimed to have paid at least some attention (and 71 percent a lot of attention). For our US politics students entering the spring 2009 course, 93 percent also claimed to have paid at least some attention to the 2008 election.

The time frame of the 2008 election coincided with the increasing prevalence of social networking sites as a more significant media source for Millennials. Seventy-six percent of our 337 students entering US politics at SUNY Fredonia in fall 2008 claimed to pay "some" or "a lot" of attention to TV news. However, only 19 percent paid a lot of attention to TV news, compared with 49 percent who paid a lot of attention to social networking sites like Facebook. For sixty students completing a summer course on US politics at UCSB in September 2008, 50 percent claimed to pay a lot of attention to social networking sites whereas 18 percent paid a lot of attention to TV news. At the completion of the fall 2008 course at SUNY Fredonia, 55 percent claimed to pay a lot of attention to social networking sites (84 percent at least some attention), compared with 22 percent who paid a lot of attention to TV news.

There was evidence that Millennials nationwide were using social networking sites as a medium to learn about and engage in the 2008 election process. A 2007 MTV poll found that 25 percent of those who had been to social networking sites visited a page belonging to or associated with a political candidate. A spring 2008 Harvard IOP survey reported that 37 percent of college students utilized Facebook to promote a candidate or issue, up from 14 percent in 2006.

Millennials also translated heightened attentiveness to this political event and use of media sources into directed political participation, in terms of voter registration and turnout. Relative youth turnout in many of the 2008 caucuses and primaries soared beyond 2004. In New York, 18- to 24-year-olds made up 15 percent of voters, almost double their 8 percent share of the state's primary vote in 2004. And in Iowa, where Obama went from an inspiring long shot to a legitimate candidate for president across white America, 18- to 24-year-old turnout made up 22 percent of caucus goers compared with 17 percent in 2004. Furthermore, 57 percent of these young voters went for Obama and only 11 percent for Hillary Clinton.

In a fall 2008 Harvard IOP survey, 79 percent of 18- to 24-year-olds reported that they were registered to vote, which was a 10-point increase from fall 2007, and 63 percent claimed that they would "definitely" vote in the 2008 election. In September 2008, 83 percent of students completing the UCSB US politics course claimed that they would "definitely" be voting in the election and 81 percent claimed that they would be voting for Barack Obama. This wasn't too far off from the California exit poll, which reported 18- to 24-year-olds voting for Obama by a margin of 80 to 18 percent over McCain.

The New York exit poll showed a 73 to 23 percent advantage for Obama within this age group. For our SUNY Fredonia students completing the fall 2008 US politics course, 68 percent claimed to have voted, and 71 percent of that group claimed to have voted for Obama. For students entering the spring 2009 US politics course at SUNY Fredonia, reported voter turnout was at 73 percent, with 70 percent of them voting for Obama. In the nationwide exit poll, the 18- to 24-year-old margin was at 66 percent for Barack Obama and 32 percent for John McCain. In the fall 2009 Harvard IOP survey, 81 percent of college students said that they had voted in the 2008 general election, with a 56 to 35 percent margin in favor of Obama over McCain.

Based on US Census Bureau surveys, CIRCLE estimates that about 23 million people under the age of 30 voted in 2008, an increase of over 3 million from 2004 (Kirby and Kawashima-Ginsberg 2009). At 51 percent, it was a 2-point increase over 2004 and an 11-point increase in turnout over 2000 for the 18- to 29-year-old age group. For 18- to 24-year-olds as a group, 2008 voting turnout had increased to 49 percent from 47 percent in 2004 and from 36 percent in 2000.

Presidential elections provide an important vehicle for most young adults to first engage the political and democratic process. However, turnout for the younger generation had been trending downward since 18-year-olds were granted the right to vote with the twenty-sixth Amendment in 1971. From 1972 to 2000, voting turnout and registration had dropped by 13 and 14 points for 18- to 24-year-olds (Levine and Lopez 2002). In a 1999 nationwide survey report on the "New Millennium Generation," the National Association of Secretaries of State warned that America is "in danger of developing a permanent non-voting class."

An age voting gap was increasingly pronounced between the oldest voters who saw voting as a civic duty and a younger generation who increasingly viewed it as a choice, one that they often felt wasn't worth the effort. For example, in the 2000 election there was a 40-point turnout gap between those 65 years of age and older and those 18–20 years old. The gap for voters 25 years of age and older and those 18–24 years old was 27 and 26 points in the 2000 and 1996 presidential elections.

With the increasing reality that older people were much more likely to vote, a popular clothing line for the younger set, Urban Outfitters, was asked to pull a t-shirt stating "Voting is for Old People" after the Harvard Kennedy School of Government issued a public statement criticizing the message. Whether or not the t-shirt was meant to be tongue-in-cheek or meant to even urge youth turnout, the reality of the phrase was an increasing cause for concern. When interviewed for a 2000 MTV Choose or Lose program on the question of why he thought younger Americans didn't vote, a young man in his early 20s said: "I know it sounds bad, but we haven't had a war in a long time. . . . That would wake people up pretty quickly."

After a dramatic Election Night 2000, the 9/11 attacks, a war now firmly debated in Iraq, a highly polarizing president as a recognizable cue for pressing policy choices, high attentiveness to the election, and significant mobilization of the youth vote (Shea and Green 2007), the voting trends turned. In 2004, the 19-point gap between voters 25 years of age and older and 18- to 24-year-olds was the smallest since 1972, when there was a 16-point gap in the first presidential election in which 18- to 20-year-olds could vote. Despite the fact that New York was not a competitive state in the 2004 or 2008 elections, our students were highly mobilized and engaged in the electoral process as they had opportunities to discuss and debate, learn and inform. Such exposure increases knowledge, which increases participation.

Elections can be a galvanizing force, particularly for young Americans finding their way into the political process and their democratic role. These are very salient events and processes with accessible media sources, as well as opportunities for learning and participation through discussion, voter mobilization, and turnout. The 2000 and 2004 elections, in many ways, set a new Millennial table for youth awareness and mobilization that surged into the 2008 election and the related opportunities for a candidate like Barack Obama.

With the massive media attention to the 2000 Election Night drama, recount, and ensuing "overtime" battle for the presidency, attentiveness also soared among our US politics students at SUNY Fredonia. There were learning opportunities to consider constitutional implications related to the Electoral College and to consider the role of the courts and the media in politics, and so on, all while referencing the evolving contemporary political event by integrating related media information into the course. By the completion of the fall 2000 US politics courses, 92 percent of our students claimed to have paid at least some attention and 60 percent a lot of attention to the 2000 presidential election. In our fall 2004 US politics courses, there were extensive opportunities to integrate attentiveness to salient events, including the war in Iraq, with the presidential election. Highly watched presidential debates and media coverage unfolded inside and outside of the classroom, with 97 percent of our students paying at least some attention and 70 percent a lot of attention to the 2004 election during the fall semester. These were high numbers that would once again be reached in fall 2008.

Beyond the Vote

We can examine voter turnout trends as one measure of how attentiveness to a salient event, coupled with interest, translates into political participation. Moreover, we can *usually* depend on college student attentiveness as we approach the final months of a presidential election. However, we cannot be certain that attentiveness will always approach the unusually high interest and high Millennial participation demonstrated in recent presidential elections.

Voter turnout generally declines for each younger age cohort, and this gap increased dramatically from 1972 to 2000. On the other hand, higher youth attentiveness and turnout as part of the 2004 and 2008 election processes could be evidence of a more sustained commitment to the voting apparatus of representative democracy. Most likely, youth attentiveness and involvement in presidential elections will be contingent on context and the related salience of other political events that encouraged greater interest and engagement in 2004 and 2008.

When MTV Rock the Vote arrived on the scene in the 1992 presidential election there was a corresponding boost in youth turnout that helped elect 47-year-old Bill Clinton, the highest numbers for 18- to 24-year-old turnout since 1972. Beyond new forms of entertainment media utilized to reach out to the MTV generation, the economy was also a very salient issue for the college-age cohort. But with MTV Choose or Lose still actively involved in youth mobilization efforts in 1996 and 2000, turnout rates for 18- to 24-year-olds plunged once again, to say nothing of the paltry turnout in 1994 and 1998 among college-age voters. Nonpresidential election–year attentiveness and thus turnout particularly suffer among younger voters, with turnout rates of 21- to 24-year-olds halved from 1966 to 2002.

External mobilization efforts are not as effective when younger voters are not themselves inherently interested in and attentive to a political event or process, including a midterm election. And the same logic applies to related learning and engagement stemming from a US politics course. As I discuss in Chapter 3, our US politics students' attentiveness to the 2002 midterm election was significantly lower than attentiveness to the 2000 or 2008 elections. Despite attentiveness to 9/11, the war on terrorism, and rumblings about war in Iraq, there was little Millennial attentiveness to the midterm elections in which 2002 turnout level was less than 20 percent for 18- to 24-year-olds.

This has direct implications for the learning experience as we seek to integrate nonpresidential and midterm election events into the US politics course. If there is no genuine student attentiveness or interest extending beyond the classroom, there is less likelihood of connecting an in-class learning experience with knowledge gains and participation. As I contend throughout this book, it is most effective to integrate political events that are already salient to students in order to facilitate related learning and engagement.

For example, in an important special election to replace the deceased Senator Ted Kennedy, who was instrumental in Obama's early campaign and a key piece in the administration's efforts to pass health care reform, about 15 percent of 18- to 29-year-olds turned out to vote in Massachusetts. Voting turnout in the Massachusetts special election for those 30 and older was nearly 60 percent. By comparison, 48 percent of 18- to 29-year-olds had voted in Massachusetts in the presidential election, with 78 percent of them voting for Obama. Youth turnout in the 2009 Virginia and New Jersey gubernatorial races was also poor at 17 and 19 percent, all victories for an increasing Republican opposition to Obama's agenda. As CIRCLE director Peter Levine noted in January 2010, "Three state elections do not necessarily make a national trend, but there is clearly an issue right now with youth turnout and enthusiasm."

By spring 2010, students who were entering our US politics courses at SUNY Fredonia were generally too young to have participated in the 2008 election. In fact, only 28 percent claimed to have voted in the 2008 election, while 52 percent claimed not to be old enough at the time. Thus for these students who hadn't reached 18 by the 2008 election, the first opportunity to learn the habit of voting at a state and a national level would be the midterm elections. The problem is that younger Americans are much less likely to demonstrate interest and thus to turn out to vote in nonpresidential elections.

Of our students completing the spring 2010 US politics course, 31 percent said they "definitely" planned to vote in the fall 2010 elections. This was about 50 points lower than for students who claimed they would vote in the 2004 and 2008 elections. The spring 2010 Harvard IOP reported that 31 percent of 18- to 29-year-olds and 38 percent of college students claimed they would be voting in the fall 2010 elections. Thus, the learning opportunities, particularly connected to electoral engagement, have been much lower for the midterm elections than as part of the highly salient presidential elections of the first decade of the twenty-first century.

As Millennials are coming of age, they are connecting to and absorbing political information through the events of their time. It is not to say that they are "prisoners of the moment," but they are learning about politics in terms of connecting it to the most salient political events of interest in their minds. These are the features that stimulate learning and, in turn, political engagement on related concerns.

The presidential election provides one important vehicle for engaging our students through their own attentiveness and interest in a salient political event, but it cannot be the sole means. As Martin Wattenberg (2008, 113) points out, "Just tuning in to a particularly exciting Super Bowl doesn't make one a football fan; similarly, just participating in one especially hotly contested election doesn't make a group an integral part of the US political process." Yet, all too often, a younger American develops the habit of voting in a presidential election perhaps every four years as the *one* act of political participation carried on into adult life. Others who view presidential elections as the only mechanism for democratic participation, and who are not excited enough or don't feel informed enough about it, just stay away from political and civic engagement altogether, unaware of the various alternatives for participation as an active citizen. This is where it is vitally important to identify other areas of salience and political interest relevant to our students in order to stimulate other avenues of related learning and engagement.

Learning How to Participate

A CIRCLE study in 2007 utilizing focus groups on selected campuses around the nation revealed that many students perceive political involvement to be intimidating because it is complicated and they do not feel qualified or sufficiently well informed (26). For many younger Americans first confronting the political world, there can be a lack of confidence in their ability to competently participate. Consider a student surrounded by a group of friends perceived to better understand the latest Xbox moves. Perhaps feeling intimidated, that student will find a way to avoid such interaction for fear of not being up to this basic task of participation. Of course, that student would be more likely to participate if he or she felt armed with the requisite knowledge to properly contribute to the activity.

Political knowledge is a key component of political participation, even if that participation is only entering a voting booth in the presidential election. In 1999, the National Association of Secretaries of State revealed that many young people were not voting because of uncertainty about how to handle the mechanics of the process.

This makes the introduction to US politics course a particularly important conduit, at the most basic level, to political participation for our entering college students, even on the most common participatory act of presidential voting. You would assume that many entering college students were already gathering information about the historic 2008 election. However, an introduction to US politics provided many with one of the first real vehicles to consider the historic nature and implications of the election as the campaign events transpired during this period. For our SUNY Fredonia students entering US politics courses in late August 2008, 35 percent felt "pretty much" informed and 18 percent "very much" informed about the presidential candidates. By the completion of the course and election in early December 2008, 40 percent felt "pretty much" informed and 44 percent "very much" informed.

By the end of the course, students were paying much more attention to the 2008 presidential election, similar to the surge that was part of the 2004 election, and thus were in a more comfortable and confident position to participate. Our students' relationship between political learning and likely participation was still very much connected with their attentiveness to a salient political event in their own minds. For example, at the completion of the spring 2010 US politics course, only 16 percent felt "pretty much" informed and 5 percent "very informed" to make a decision about the candidates in the fall 2010 elections.

Furthermore, political knowledge is critical as one moves beyond the simple act of voting to a broader notion of political engagement and democratic participation. As we entered the new millennium, college students particularly expressed a need for "more practical information about politics before I can get involved." In spring 2000, the Harvard IOP found that 87 percent of students agreed with this statement, with 49 percent strongly agreeing. Even as the nation wrestled with 9/11, the war on terrorism, and a war in Iraq, well over 80 percent of college students continued to express this sentiment through fall 2003. It wasn't until fall 2004 at the tail end of the presidential election that this figure dropped substantially, with 65 percent agreeing that they needed more practical information and 26 percent agreeing strongly. However, the number would surge back to 87 percent in the near aftermath of Hurricane Katrina before settling back down into the 60s as we approached the fall 2008 election. When provided with a new option to neither disagree nor agree with the Harvard IOP spring 2010 survey statement "I feel like I need more practical information about politics before I can get involved," 56 percent of college students agreed while only 18 percent disagreed.

It appears that Millennial-age college students felt most informed and therefore able to get involved in politics as they entered the highly salient political context of the 2004 and 2008 presidential elections. Attentiveness, interest, and use of media sources surged at the height of these electoral events in which Millennials were more likely to gather more accessible related political information and facts. To facilitate greater participation beyond voting every four years also requires our students' political attention and understanding of related political figures, institutions, and processes beyond the height of the 2008 election and into the postelection Obama era.

Gathering Related Knowledge

In the early years of the Obama administration, students' textbook knowledge remained relatively unchanged from our survey of the fall 2000–2005 period, demonstrating the consistency of most foundational knowledge regardless of the changing political context. A strong majority of our students continued to enter the introduction to US politics course with a better grasp of certain textbook than surveillance knowledge, similar to national findings for high school seniors. For example, most entering the fall 2008, spring 2009, or spring 2010 US politics course were still comfortable selecting the Supreme Court as responsible for determining whether a law is unconstitutional, ranging from 66 to 76 percent. By the end of the course, the range was 80–84 percent. The ability to recall that the president is responsible for the appointment of federal judges grew from an average of 49 percent to an average of 74 percent by the completion of the fall 2008–spring 2010 courses.

There was, however, a substantial increase of 33 points over the fall 2008 course in our students' knowledge that the smallest Electoral College majority consists of 270 votes. This was far higher than the 16-point gain for spring 2009 and the 21-point gain for spring 2010 students. It represented the highest knowledge surge on the Electoral College question since fall 2004, suggesting the impact of attentiveness to this salient event on related knowledge.

There was a large surveillance learning curve on related items associated with the experience of taking the course during the 2008 election. Knowledge that the Democrats controlled the US House increased most dramatically in fall 2008, by 31 points to 75 percent, compared with a 9-point gain in spring 2009 and 21-point gain in spring 2010. Demonstrating the impact of heightened electoral attentiveness on political knowledge, a Pew Center survey conducted in December 2008 also reported that 82 percent of adults nationwide knew that the Democrats had the majority in the US House, compared with 53 percent in May 2008.

Certain aspects of political information are effectively reinforced as relevant knowledge for navigating and participating in the contemporary political environment when one is paying attention and interested in it. In late August 2008 on the eve of the Republican nominating convention, 31 percent of our entering students in US politics could list Joseph Biden as the Democratic vice presidential candidate. However, by the end of the fall 2008 course, 82 percent could name at least one of the two vice presidential candidates and 73 percent both candidates. Former Alaska governor Sarah Palin was launched from obscurity to late-night comedy within weeks, if not days, and has been a media mainstay ever since. And for our entering spring 2009 US politics students, 85 percent could recall both vice presidential candidates, a number much higher than for our entering fall 2005 students or for our fall 2001 students. Previous vice presidential candidates Joe Lieberman and John Edwards (at least before his own media sex scandal) did not penetrate our students' minds quite like Sarah Palin.

In a December 2008 Pew survey, 87 percent of Americans correctly selected Hillary Clinton as the nominee to US secretary of state; Clinton was already quite well-known in her various incarnations as first lady, US senator, and presidential candidate. Through it all, she had incredible amounts of attention on national news as well as late-night comedy programs. Thus she was one of those rare political figures who were particularly visible for our students, whether they were completing US politics in fall 2000 or entering the course in fall 2008.

In spring 2009, 66 percent of entering US politics students at SUNY Fredonia could identify Hillary Clinton either as resigning her position as US senator or beginning her appointment as secretary of state. But her resignation from the Senate and transition into secretary of state left many of our students dumbfounded as to her replacement, Kirsten Gillibrand. Entering the spring 2009 US politics course, 36 percent of students could name both US senators from New York, compared with 62 percent entering the course in fall 2008. And our students weren't alone. In spring 2010 statewide polls of New Yorkers, many claimed not to know enough about Gillibrand to form an opinion. And outside of the initial media glare one year later, 24 percent of entering US politics students in spring 2010 responded secretary of state as the position now held by Hillary Clinton.

Surveillance knowledge levels are a particularly important indicator of our students' attentiveness to and engagement in the contemporary political environment. If our students are paying enough attention to understand the political figures involved, they are exposed to some aspect of the role such political actors play in the process and within institutions. Our students continued to learn about political figures and facts in line with their attentiveness to related political events and consequently greatest perceived relevance to our students' lives.

For example, knowledge of vice presidential candidates and that of the Electoral College majority is at a high point just following a fall election, whereas other elements of textbook knowledge are relatively unaffected by the varying salience of political events. Likewise, related knowledge is lower when political attentiveness is lower. Political knowledge gained as part of the most salient points of the presidential election helps to connect the learning process with participation. Still, it is important to understand how to facilitate such connections beyond the quadrennial election cycle. There are other salient events to consider in the early years of the Obama administration and throughout the decade.

Connecting the Events on Millennial Minds

The initial period beyond the heightened attentiveness to a presidential election can serve as a teaching channel. It can bring politics and government to life through the integration of related current events in sync with students' awareness. The salience attached to the historic 2008 election and inauguration provided for critical learning opportunities to encourage participation beyond voting on Election Day. For our US politics students, there was a great deal of attention to the 2008 presidential election, to the post-election transition, and to Obama's first year as president. For example, 78 percent of our fall 2008 students paid at least "some" and 39 percent "a lot" of attention to the post-election transition. Eighty percent of students entering the spring 2009 US politics course paid at least some attention, with 47 percent paying a lot of attention to Obama's post-election transition. By the end of the spring 2009 course, 72 percent claimed to have paid at least some attention to Obama's first one hundred days in office.

Obama's first one hundred days in office also involved several crisis events and concerns that received a great deal of media coverage and thus the president's attention. By the end of the spring 2009 course, 82 percent of our students had paid at least some attention to the financial crisis and 61 percent at least some attention to the swine flu outbreak. As students entered the US politics course in spring 2010, 70 percent had paid at least some attention to Obama's first year as president. However, where 42 percent had paid a lot of attention to the 2008 election, 21 percent had paid a lot of attention to Obama's first year as president. There was clearly an attentiveness difference between the electoral event and the governing process, which proves a challenge for encouraging sustained learning and engagement.

It is important to identify ongoing political events and to survey the attentiveness of our students to these concerns and debates. A critical political and policy debate heading into Obama's second year was health care reform, which was making its way toward legislative approval and Obama's signature during the spring 2010 US politics courses. The Harvard IOP reported in fall 2009 that 43 percent of college students nationwide were closely following the discussion in Washington about health care reform. For our entering spring 2010 students, 41 percent were paying at least some attention to the health care debate. By the end of spring 2010, 57 percent of these students were paying at least some attention to the health care debate. There was increasing salience on the issue over the course of the term and a learning opportunity beyond the election.

Electoral and nonelectoral political events can pique our students' interest, connecting learning with engagement. Figure 5.1 demonstrates how, nationwide, college students' perceived relevance of politics has surged around significant events in the new millennium. This includes 9/11 in fall 2001, the launch of the war in Iraq in spring 2003, and the 2004 and 2008 presidential elections, according to surveys conducted by the Harvard Institute of Politics. In fall 2001 and fall 2004, students nationwide were in particularly strong disagreement with the statement that "politics is not relevant to my life right now." Spikes in perceived relevance also coincided with a heightened discussion by college students of current events, presumably related to events such as 9/11 and the 2004 election, for example.

This might explain why our entering and exiting SUNY Fredonia US politics students' attentiveness to TV news and net news media was signif-

Figure 5.1   Relevant Politics and Current Events Discussion

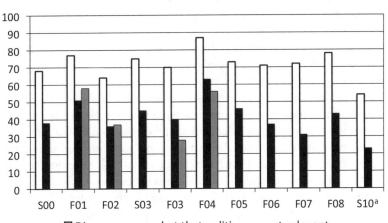

□ Disagree somewhat that politics are not relevant

■ Disagree strongly that politics are not relevant

▨ Discuss current events often

Notes: The white bar indicates the percentage of college students who disagreed somewhat with the statement "Politics is not relevant to my life right now." The black bar indicates the percentage who disagreed strongly with the statement. The gray bar indicates the percentage who discuss current events more than once a week, with data only available for fall 2001, fall 2002, fall 2003, and fall 2004. Compiled by the author with data from the Harvard Institute of Politics surveys of the nation's college students.

a. In spring 2010, students were provided the option to neither disagree nor agree.

icantly related to surveillance political knowledge but not to textbook knowledge during the fall 2001–fall 2005 period and also during fall 2008–spring 2010 (see Table 5.1). Attentiveness to events such as the presidential election and war in Iraq was also more significantly correlated with surveillance knowledge than with textbook knowledge for our students across the fall 2001–spring 2010 period. Students connected attentiveness to these unfolding events with their understanding of the contemporary political figures and facts associated with the political debate and process.

These relationships were even stronger in proximity to the events. While Table 5.1 shows how a general recollection of attention to 9/11 and the war on terrorism still maintained a significant connection with surveillance knowledge across the fall 2001–spring 2010 period, the strongest knowledge connections existed in proximity to related events. For example, the correlation between attentiveness to the 9/11 attacks and surveillance knowledge of foreign policy figures and facts was most significant at the end of the fall 2001 courses (.21, p ≤ .01). Similarly, Table 5.1 shows the strong connection between our students' political knowledge and more contemporary debates on the financial crisis (fall 2008 and spring 2009) and health care reform (spring 2010). In all cases, surveillance knowledge exhibited a stronger relationship than did textbook knowledge with attentiveness to these events and debates.

This is just another example of how our students who are learning the most about US politics are also paying the most attention to the contemporary mediated political environment. It also demonstrates how course learning reinforces these connections. The significant relationship between surveillance knowledge and attentiveness to these salient events is even stronger at the completion of a US politics course. Furthermore, as knowledge grew overall throughout the duration of the course, there was also a more significant relationship with textbook knowledge and attentiveness to the financial crisis and health care debate. This shows how attentiveness to salient political events can also connect with knowledge of related enduring foundations, institutions, and processes likely connected with these debates.

Those with more political knowledge are more likely to participate in politics because they feel more informed. For our US politics students who were surveyed in fall 2001–spring 2010, surveillance political knowledge was significantly correlated with expected or actual voting in the presidential election. Furthermore, surveillance (.36) and textbook knowledge (.11) were both significantly related to our students' belief that they were sufficiently informed to make a decision about the presidential candidates. This was particularly pronounced as part of the high atten-

Table 5.1 Political Knowledge and Attentiveness

Political Knowledge and Attentiveness to:	Textbook (0–3) 2001–2005		Surveillance (0–4) 2001–2005	
	Pre	Post	Pre	Post
Media sources				
TV news	.05	.03	.18**	.18**
Internet news media	.08**	.03	.20**	.18**
Millennial events				
Presidential elections	.18**	.19**	.35**	.32**
War in Iraq	.07*	.01	.18**	.09**
9/11, war on terror	.03	.03	.06*	.06**
Financial crisis				
Health care debate (S10)				
Modes of action				
Voting in presidential election	.08**	.12**	.22**	.22**
Informed to vote				
Mean	1.81	2.15	1.64	2.16

Political Knowledge and Attentiveness to:	Textbook (0–3) 2008–2010		Surveillance (0–4) 2008–2010	
	Pre	Post	Pre	Post
Media sources				
TV news	.02	.02	.12**	.09*
Internet news media	.09	.05	.12**	.12**
Millennial events				
Presidential elections	.17**	.07	.34**	.29**
War in Iraq	.14**	.09	.19**	.21**
9/11, war on terror	.02	.04	.03	.11**
Financial crisis	.14	.21**	.06	.24**
Health care debate (S10)	.07	.12**	.21**	.31**
Modes of action				
Voting in presidential election	.06	.04	.22**	.26**
Informed to vote	.20**	.11**	.31**	.36**
Mean	1.45	1.92	1.44	1.81

Notes: Figures are Spearman correlation coefficients, where ** $p \leq .01$ and * $p \leq .05$. Textbook knowledge is scaled 1–3 based on the closed-ended questions identifying Senate term length and whose responsibility it is to determine whether a law is unconstitutional, and the open-ended recall of whose responsibility it is to appoint federal judges. Surveillance knowledge is scaled 1–4 based on the closed-ended identification of party control of the US House and the open-ended recall of the two US senators from New York and the last names of the 2000, 2004, or 2008 vice presidential candidates in proximity to the relevant elections. Attentiveness measures are on a four-point scale, where 1 = no attention and 4 = a lot of attention. Voting in presidential election measures whether students "definitely" plan to vote or voted in a recent election. "How informed do you feel to make a decision about the presidential candidates" is scaled where 1 = not at all and 4 = very much. Empty cells indicate that the data were not available for the time period.

tiveness and participation surrounding the 2008 presidential election for students surveyed in fall 2008–spring 2010. Surveillance knowledge was significantly more related to these indicators of political participation and strengthened as part of the learning experience in US politics.

Connecting Interest and Participation

It is important to understand how to connect our students' political attentiveness, learning, and interest with modes for political engagement and participation. One particular disconnect has to do with the increasing volunteerism of our Millennial-age students and the question of broader political engagement. Findings are mixed with regard to how community service relates to political engagement (Ball 2005; Colby et al. 2007), with some asserting there is no relationship (NASS 1999; Hunter and Brisbin 2000), or even a negative dynamic (Galston 2001).

Political knowledge is a key connecting point to broader political engagement. On the other hand, our students have demonstrated no significant relationship between political knowledge and volunteerism. Perceived political knowledge appears to be less associated with Millennial volunteerism in the community than it is with engagement in politics. For example, in a 2002 Harvard IOP survey, 89 percent of college students said volunteering in the community is easier than volunteering in politics.

Furthermore, our entering college students are simply more accustomed to the act of volunteering in their communities. In 2005, the HERI US Freshman survey reported that 83 percent had volunteered at least occasionally during their high school senior year, the highest ever measured, and, in the 2006 HERI survey, an all-time high of 67.3 percent stated there is a good or some chance that they would continue to volunteer in college. For our students entering the US politics course at SUNY Fredonia, fall 2002–spring 2010, from 75 to 87 percent claimed to have volunteered at least a little during the previous twelve months. Lower levels of volunteerism generally were reported in the spring courses and the higher levels in the fall courses, with fall closer to high school graduation for many of these college freshmen.

Perhaps because of a greater familiarity with community volunteerism at younger age levels, Millennial-age students have tended to view this style of engagement as more directly relevant and impactful in their local lives. On the other hand, political engagement is viewed as a more distant participatory element connected with solving the bigger problems facing the nation. Since its inaugural survey in spring 2000, the

Harvard IOP consistently has found that college students perceive community volunteerism as a more effective way than political engagement to solve important issues facing the local community. Political engagement is viewed as a more effective tool than community volunteerism in solving the important issues facing the country.

Nevertheless, there is reason to believe that high rates of volunteerism can translate into high levels of political engagement as students move further into adulthood (Verba, Schlozman, and Brady 1995; Yates and Youniss 1998). Volunteers are more likely to engage in political activity and feel less alienated from public institutions. With the uptick in Millennials' political engagement starting around the middle of the first decade of the twenty-first century, it appears the earlier impact of community engagement may be translating into other forms of action (Macedo et al. 2005, 125).

The challenge is to bridge interests and access points as our students, with increasing levels of familiarity with community volunteerism and service, are also introduced to US politics. While our students' political interest relates to attentiveness to the most salient political events on a national and a global level, their own interest in public service is linked more to community activism and local politics. The big, salient political events connect to Millennial interest in national politics and world affairs. The bigger question is how to translate such interest into participation beyond voting every four years if our students are not more readily making those connections.

As Figure 5.2 demonstrates, interest in national politics and world affairs has been consistently higher for our students exiting our US politics courses than interest in local politics, community activism, and public service. Moreover, interest in such "distant politics" also appeared more responsive to the major events of the time, peaking upward in fall 2001 and fall 2004. A downward trend in interest in national politics and world affairs also appears more responsive (than interest in local politics) to disengagement from the political space, as many have become disenchanted with the partisan bickering in the early years of the Obama administration after a more hopeful view that things could change in Washington.

Our students have consistently connected their political knowledge both entering and exiting the US politics course with an interest in national politics and world affairs, with the most significant correlation between surveillance knowledge and interest in national politics (.37 pre, .33 post) for fall 2001–spring 2010. Considering just the fall 2008–spring 2010 period, the correlation is even higher (.41 pre, .43 post). Yet across

Figure 5.2   Levels of Political Interest upon Exiting a US Politics Course

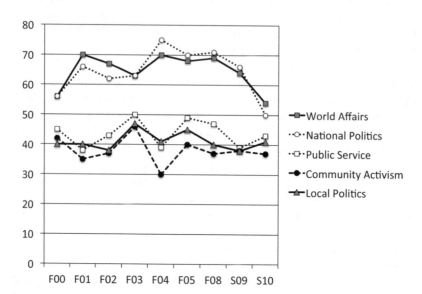

Notes: Trend lines indicate SUNY Fredonia students completing a US politics course who are "interested" or "very interested" in the given areas. The question wording is given in Appendix A.

the time periods, there is no significant correlation between political knowledge and interest in local politics, community activism, or public service. There are slightly significant relationships between surveillance knowledge and interest in political music/film for students completing the course.

These cognitive connections are so enduring and constrained in our students' minds that we can conceive of them as distinct indexes of interest in US politics. Table 5.2 shows how our students connect interests in public service and community activism with local politics, while connecting interest in national politics with an interest in world affairs. Furthermore, interests in local and national politics are also disconnected from our students' interests in politically tinged music and protest politics, which can be conceived as making up a third dimension of "expressive politics" that may not be as perceptually bound to a local or national space. And such connections were essentially unchanged for our students surveyed during the fall 2001–fall 2005 period and during the fall 2008– spring 2010 stretch. These connections remained similar for students entering and exiting a US politics course.

Table 5.2   Rotating Interest in US Politics

Interested or Very Interested in:	2001–2005 Pre	2008–2010 Pre	2001–2005 Pre	2008–2010 Pre	2001–2005 Pre	2008–2010 Pre
Local connections						
Community activism	.88	.88				
Public service	.83	.86				
Local politics	.68	.63				
Distant politics						
National politics			.85	.89		
World affairs			.84	.86		
Expressive politics						
Political music/film					.87	.88
Political protest					.74	.80
Variance explained	34	39	19	19	16	16
Eigenvalue	2.8	2.4	1.3	1.4	1.1	1.2
Alpha reliability	.69	.74	.73	.77	.65	.63

Interested or Very Interested in:	2001–2005 Post	2008–2010 Post	2001–2005 Post	2008–2010 Post	2001–2005 Post	2008–2010 Post
Local connections						
Community activism	.86	.89				
Public service	.84	.85				
Local politics	.72	.77				
Distant politics						
National politics			.88	.90		
World affairs			.87	.88		
Expressive politics						
Political music/film					.89	.85
Political protest					.74	.72
Variance explained	37	37	20	21	15	15
Eigenvalue	2.6	2.6	1.4	1.5	1.1	1.0
Alpha reliability	.75	.80	.74	.79	.66	.64

Notes: Coefficients shown are factor loadings higher than .20 based on principal components extraction with varimax rotation. Factors based on five-point scales, where 1 = not interested and 5 = very interested, for 1,558 respondents for fall 2001–2005 and 459 respondents for fall 2008–spring 2010 completing the questionnaire at both the beginning and end of the US politics course.

Table 5.3 also shows how our students' interest in what might be conceived of as more "distant politics" is also more strongly correlated than "local connections" with attentiveness to TV news and net news media as well as attentiveness to big events such as the presidential elections and the war in Iraq. This also holds true on more recent issues such as the financial crisis and health care debate. Despite the fact these students are more likely to view public service linked to local political interest, interest in local connections is less linked to attentiveness on these pressing issues. One exception was Hurricane Katrina, which apparently tied more directly into conceptions of local volunteer contributions and public service as an outlet of access and action for this younger generation. This provides one such example of how students can link their own participation and engagement with a significant and salient national, if not global, event with widespread mediated political coverage and perceived relevance to the times. That said, one could argue that these students also viewed such participation as more of an example of community activism and volunteerism at a local level than as an example of political engagement at a level of national interest. The challenge is to help bridge these connections in our students' minds to understand how to become more engaged at a local level on issues of salient national interest. It involves how to translate issues of local interest into political engagement at a national and a global level.

For students entering the courses in spring 2009 or spring 2010, there was a stronger relationship between the "local connections" index and attentiveness to Obama's transition into the presidency. However, this reduced slightly by the end of the course, as the "distant politics" interest index remained stronger and more constant with students' attentiveness to

Table 5.3 Connecting Interest and Attentiveness to US Politics

Interest in and Attentiveness to:	Local Connections	Distant Politics	Expressive Politics
Media sources			
TV news	.16**	.25**	.11**
Internet news media	.14**	.23**	.25**
Social networking (F08–S10)	.04	–.12**	.10*
Millennial events			
Presidential election	.11**	.34**	.20**
War in Iraq	.11**	.28**	.09**
9/11, war on terror	.10**	.11**	.01
Hurricane Katrina (F05)	.26**	.24**	.12**
Financial crisis (F08–S09)	.16**	.38**	.19**
Health care debate (S10)	.02	.45**	.12
Obama as president (S09–S10)	.10**	.35**	.23**

Notes: Figures are Spearman correlation coefficients, where ** $p \leq .01$ and * $p \leq .05$. Local connections, distant politics, and expressive politics indexes are each based on the factor analysis described in Table 6.2. Attentiveness measures are on a four-point scale, where 1 = no attention and 4 = a lot of attention. Respondents consist of SUNY Fredonia students completing the US politics courses, fall 2001–2005/fall 2008–spring 2010, unless otherwise indicated. For example, attentiveness to Hurricane Katrina only measured students completing the fall 2005 courses.

Obama's transition into the job. It appears that these Millennial-age students were mobilized to connect local politics, community activism, and public service with the former community organizer Obama's message of broad change. However, in the end, attentiveness to the presidency was once again more connected to students' perceived national and global interests.

Despite the explosion of social networking sites, there was no connection here as an outlet for interest in local politics and community activism. In fact, there was a slightly negative significant relationship between attentiveness to social networking sites and interest in distant politics. Only in the realm of "political expressions" was heightened attentiveness to such sites connected, as an outlet for interest in political music and film and perhaps a mechanism to register social and political protest. Albeit not as strong as the distant politics index, a political expressions index did strengthen on attentiveness measures related to the presidential election and on issues such as the financial crisis. A political expressions index was also linked more strongly with attentiveness to net news media than with TV news. It was the only interest index significantly connected with heightened net use, suggesting the connectedness of such expressive interests to a more fluid, virtual space rather than to a local or national location.

It is here that an integrated learning environment as part of the introduction to US politics course that draws in salient political events, media sources, and diverse examples of participation can help our students to link what can otherwise be disconnected areas of political interest and participation. With higher levels of political knowledge by the end of the US politics courses during the fall 2001–spring 2010 period, students significantly connected expressive interests with expected or actual voting. The relationship also strengthened slightly between interest in local connections and voting in presidential elections.

Nevertheless, those most interested in distant politics were also the most likely to vote for president. On the other hand, volunteer service was strongly correlated (.31) with the local connections interest index and weakly correlated with distant politics interest (.07). Our students connect volunteerism with interest in local connections. However, high levels of volunteerism have not translated into higher levels of interest in local politics, community activism, and public service. Interest in these areas lingers well below interest in national politics and world affairs for our students both entering and exiting the courses. Interest remains high in national politics and world affairs, particularly in line with attentiveness to salient events. However, our students have not been as likely to connect public service with their interest in such distant politics.

Directed Relevance

The findings here demonstrate how political learning provides a foundation upon which to reinforce and connect surveillance knowledge, interest, and engagement. It is about connecting what is relevant to our Millennial-age students and their interests to understanding the outlets for engagement. Learning about US politics can include an understanding of the opportunities available to more actively engage in politics and democratic life.

Although our US politics students have less comparative interest in local politics and community activism, this area of interest is most significantly connected to the most common form of engagement for this generation, that is, volunteerism. Meanwhile, higher levels of interest in national politics and world affairs find few recognizable participation outlets beyond voting in the presidential election for many students developing an understanding of US politics. As our students' knowledge levels grow, the evidence shows that the likelihood for participation increases. Understanding that our students may not yet grasp the direct avenues for engaging more actively on issues of national or global significance as an outlet for their interest is an opportunity to direct our students to participation possibilities connected to their areas of interest and in line with their attentiveness to contemporary political events and processes.

The opportunity to participate more directly in national-level politics can strengthen the connections between our students' political interests and learning. And in fall 2006 and spring and summer 2007, I surveyed 101 predominantly SUNY students who were interning in Washington, DC, for the semester or the ten-week summer program to better understand these connections. The students interned in various federal governmental offices, governmental agencies, and political and nongovernmental organizations, and they also participated together in a course that met once a week.

Out of 101 SUNY interns surveyed, 87 percent were interested in national politics (44 percent very interested). For our spring 2007 students, interest strengthened in national politics from the already high figure of 39 percent "very interested" to 55 percent "very interested" by the end of the semester. Interest in world affairs moved from 49 to 60 percent very interested. With an opportunity to connect these interests with related participation, interest in national politics and global affairs was also more significantly correlated with interest in public service than for our US politics students without such a direct frame of reference.

Political learning was even more directly affected by students' attentiveness to related political events and the perceived relevance of political figures and facts. Knowledge levels for the fall 2006–spring 2007 SUNY interns were dramatically higher than those for our introduction to US politics students, particularly when it came to surveillance knowledge. For example, 91 percent knew which party had House control, 71 percent could name both US senators from New York (and 97 percent at least one), 79 percent could identify Rehnquist as chief justice, 77 percent could name Condi Rice, and 73 percent could name Don Rumsfeld. Eighty-nine percent could name the British prime minister.

For these interns, there was an opportunity to experience events directly and to associate these political figures with the principles of governance. With proximity to the bastions of power in Washington, DC, our SUNY interns were able to hear from the experiences of officials, analysts, and policymakers firsthand, as they were also actively involved in the political process. After the spring 2007 semester, the SUNY interns noted a slight impact of the internship experience on trust in government (11 percent increased, 26 percent somewhat increased) and faith in political leaders (13 percent increased, 18 percent somewhat increased). However, they noted a larger impact on desired political participation (40 percent increased, 32 percent somewhat), desired political attention (40 percent increased, 29 percent somewhat), and particularly a desire to gain more political/policy information (58 percent increased, 26 percent somewhat), in which the internship experience had raised overall interest in politics and policy (58 percent increased, 24 percent somewhat).

These findings demonstrate how important it can be to find an outlet for related political interest in order to encourage a sustained level of participation and continued political learning. An internship can be an important vehicle to realize such connections for our Millennial-age students. It is also another example of how political interest and knowledge are stimulated and reinforced by the perceived relevance of the learning experience in our students' lives.

Clearly, many students will not have the opportunity to intern in Washington, DC, or to get directly involved in politics at a national or global level beyond their local community. Still, there are numerous opportunities to engage issues of national and global significance at a community level, and increasing numbers of campuses, including SUNY Fredonia, are encouraging student involvement in service learning and community engagement. With this in mind, the introduction to

US politics course can be a critical resource where students can begin to understand how to connect their attentiveness to political events and expanded political knowledge with related areas of political interest and engagement.

Engaging the Future

The salient events of an eventful first decade of the twenty-first century have provided critical learning opportunities contributing to the possibilities for engaging Millennials in an active democratic space. These students have been entering college and our US politics courses with points of political interest and attentiveness that we must understand in order to best facilitate related political learning and engagement. The 2008 HERI American Freshman survey reported that, after entering the new millennium with a record low 28.1 percent in 2000 who viewed it as "important" or "essential" to keep up-to-date on political affairs, freshmen in the post-9/11 era had shown increasing interest in political affairs, reaching 39.5 percent in 2008. By 2006, discussing politics for college freshmen was more prevalent than at any point in the forty-one-year history of the American Freshman survey, wherein 33 percent of freshmen reported they had discussed politics as a high school senior, compared with 25 percent in 2004.

Moreover, heightened interest in politics and attentiveness to such seminal events can translate into learning and engagement. Indeed, CIRCLE (October 2006, 14) reported in 2006 that "since 2000 the gap between service and politics appears to have narrowed for younger Americans. It may be that the compelling series of news events that began on September 11, 2001, captured young people's attention and motivated them to participate in large scale political affairs."

Our surveys also showed that after 9/11, US politics students' concerns peaked with the war in Iraq and mobilization, drawn out by the intensely divided feelings exacerbated in the United States leading up to the 2004 election. The Katrina crisis added one more important layer of related attention and desired action. And for many Millennials, these interests and experiences were crystallized in the 2008 election as part of an already tumultuous decade.

In fall 2008, the HERI survey reported that college freshmen were more politically engaged than at any point during the last forty years. With 35.6 percent of incoming freshmen discussing politics more recently, this surpassed the previous high-water mark of 33.6 percent recorded in 1968. Our surveys showed that interest in national politics for UCSB students completing the US politics course in summer 2008 was at 77 percent, with 23 percent of those very interested. Interest in national politics stood at 71 percent for our SUNY Fredonia students completing the US politics course in fall 2008, with 21 percent very interested. It was the highest number of those "very interested" that we surveyed besides those completing the fall 2004 semester (21 percent very interested) on the heels of the highly polarized 2004 election.

Millennials were more politically engaged because of their interest in and attentiveness to the events of the time. And this stretched into spring 2009 for our entering students in US politics as the historic inauguration of Barack Obama took place. Sixty-five percent expressed interest in national politics.

As significant salient events fade into the politics of policymaking, it is a greater challenge to sustain interest in politics and find the connecting points to engage a new group of Millennial-age cohorts finding their way into political life. For instance, the fall 2009 HERI survey reported that college freshmen were less likely to discuss politics frequently (33.1 percent) when compared with the election-year high of 35.6 percent in 2008. Freshmen nationwide were less likely to believe that keeping up-to-date with political affairs is "very important" or "essential," at 36 percent in 2009 compared with 39.5 percent in 2008. In the fall 2008 Harvard IOP survey, 78 percent of college students disagreed (43 percent strongly) with the statement that "politics is not relevant to my life right now." In spring 2010, 54 percent of college students now disagreed (23 percent strongly) with this statement. In our spring 2010 US politics course at SUNY Fredonia, interest in national politics for our entering students was at 40 percent. It was the lowest level since we began surveying students in 2000. By the completion of the course, it was at 50 percent, still the lowest.

Conclusion

The first new millennial decade had a steady trend of sustained interest in national politics. Historic events, wars, and elections populated the airwaves, whether CNN or Colbert, the Internet or iPods, Fox News or Facebook. This generation was introduced to US politics during quite an eventful start to a new century. But as the dust settled and the first African American president transitioned into the challenges of governance, many Millennials were not as clear about where to focus their attention and energy with regard to US politics and government. This is where a US politics course can help to identify our students' points of political attentiveness and related interest. With related political learning connected to perceived relevance, Millennials can recognize the political figures and processes through mediated sources.

The 2004 and 2008 elections provided critical opportunities for engagement. However, we cannot simply hope for the best every four years as we concern ourselves with the day-to-day realities of the democratic space. While taking advantage of the salience and interest attached to these quadrennial electoral events, it is also important to understand how to translate our students' interest and engagement beyond presidential elections. Thus, it is critical to recognize what types of events continue to trigger heightened Millennial interest and engagement and how to work with perceived outlets to link interest with participation.

There are opportunities to connect interests in public service with participation in local politics and community activism in line with our students' own construction of interest in politics. The findings demonstrate that Millennials are increasingly likely to volunteer in their communities. Still, students learning about US politics also need to recognize the possibilities to engage in activity connected to relatively higher interests in national politics and world affairs. The findings here show how more direct participation in political engagement outside of the classroom contributes to students' interest in politics, related knowledge, and desire for continued attentiveness, learning, and participation in the democratic process.

More direct participation in politics can be difficult for Millennial-age students who are just gaining the initial confidence that goes with learning foundational and surveillance knowledge for engagement in political life. Thus, there are other participation outlets that Millennials can utilize that work with the more accessible and familiar media sources that I discuss in Chapter 4. Our students and Millennials nationwide were able to combine their attentiveness to the 2008 election, in particular, to build on related knowledge and participation through new media sources, including social networking sites. Nevertheless, there are still challenges in linking Millennial use of these social networking tools more coherently with interests in national politics beyond political expression shared with their age cohort.

As a critical entry point in the learning environment, the introduction to US politics course can help spur our students' learning and engagement as salient political events grab Millennials' attention and interest. Students' understanding of political figures and facts helps these Millennials to feel more comfortable and confident in engaging in the political process and our democratic future. Moreover, there will continue to be ongoing and important policy debates that can be connected to Millennial attentiveness, interests, and learning.

While salient events and processes such as 9/11 and the 2008 election were historic opportunities to facilitate related student learning and engagement, our Millennial students also need to recognize that sustaining civic life cannot simply be about an emotional reaction to perceived villains or a short-term crush on a political celebrity. The learning curve as part of an introduction to US politics course can be critical for our Millennial-age students as they sort through an assortment of affective attitudes and predispositions triggered by the mediated political debate. They are learning to forge important policy choices and judgments through related political information. It is also critical for those learning about politics to understand the roles of participation and perseverance beyond fleeting events as Millennials find diverse outlets for sustained attentiveness, learning, and engagement beyond these dramatic moments. Millennial political learning and engagement will need to reflect the unique preferences, perspectives, and possibilities inherently central to this generation's developing and lasting relationship with its cohort and American democracy.

6

Democratic Directions for a New Millennial Generation

We are bound by ideals that move us beyond our backgrounds,
lift us above our interests and teach us what it means to be citizens. . . .
I ask you to be citizens. Citizens, not spectators. —*President George W. Bush
delivering his first inaugural address, January 20, 2001*

Ours is a history of renewal and reinvention, where each generation
finds a way to adapt, thrive, and push the nation forward with energy,
ingenuity, and optimism. That is your charge as graduates—our future is
in your hands. —*President Barack Obama's national message
to the high school and college graduates of 2010*

Nearly ten years after the historic 2000 election and approaching two years from his own historic election in 2008, President Barack Obama delivered a national message to high school and college graduating classes of 2010. Obama's message was more somber than the thanks he delivered to Millennials as part of his January 2009 inaugural night celebration with which we opened this book.

Barack Obama asked, as presidents will do in times of great transition and need, for this generation to face and not retreat from the challenges ahead. He noted, "There are generations of Americans who came of age during periods of peace and prosperity. When they graduated from high school or college, they entered a world of comfort and stability, where little was required of them beyond their obligations to themselves and their families. That is not the world you are about to inherit. You are growing up in a time of great challenge and sweeping change."

The graduating high school seniors of 2010 were in the heart of the Millennial experience, reared on the historic events and dramatic series of crises in the first decade of a new century. The 2010 college graduating class had helped to elect this young president while reshaping many of

135

the mechanisms by which to express and engage in political and civic life. Yet the question remained whether 2010 would be all that different from 2000 when it came to the forecasts for ongoing youth political participation as we entered another decade.

Recognizing the dip in the enthusiasm of this younger cohort that had rallied in force behind his campaign's slogan of "Change We Can Believe In," Obama continued, "At times like these, when the future seems unsettled and uncertain, it can be easy to lose heart. When you turn on the television or read newspapers or blogs, the voices of cynicism and pessimism always seem to be the loudest. Don't believe them."

The president was addressing a conflicted generation at perhaps a crucial turning point in US politics, if not history. This Millennial Generation had been reared for community service, voted in relatively high numbers in the past two presidential elections, and had learned to face great challenges through the experiences of the times. It is also a generation in which today's technology and perhaps a youthful mindset can focus extensively on the here and now and ask themselves, "How is any of this relevant to me?" If the status quo of politics once again seemed insurmountable to a younger cohort, or at least less than inspiring, it might be time to quickly flip the screen, view the latest clip, or move on to the next hit. President Obama called upon this generation to look beyond themselves and this moment to the evolving future and their role in it. He reminded these graduates, "While government plays a role in making a more prosperous and secure future possible for America, the final outcome ultimately depends on you and the choices you make from here on out."

Despite all of the enthusiasm generated among young Americans for change as embodied by Barack Obama, it seems unlikely that this generation will heed the call to service just because the president asks. This may have worked in 1960, but fifty years later and two generations removed, talking points must also recognize the instant messaging, instant gratification realities of perhaps the biggest generation of "choice" in US history (Bauerlein 2008; Twenge 2006). For Millennials, engagement is viewed as a choice, not as a duty as it was for earlier generations (Dalton 2007). These are decisions made by individuals concerning information they want to gather and a style of politics that they choose to engage (Zukin et al. 2006).

Throughout this book, findings show that the most effective way to engage Millennials in the US political process is by identifying what political events have their attention. It involves connecting attentiveness to related interests with Millennial perspectives. In the end, Millennials will be the ones to choose how they engage (or do not) in our democratic future.

We cannot simply ascribe past generational expectations onto this emerging cohort. Millennials' grandparents might have been more comfortable expressing political acts by voting, joining unions, and political parties. Millennials' parents perhaps involved themselves in political life by physically turning out to support causes and issues through rallies, marches, and sit-ins. We need to be cognizant of how events and technology contribute to the Millennial perspective and how best to utilize related elements to connect our students to the US political process. In order to help our Millennial-age students translate knowledge and interest into engagement, it is just as important to recognize what forms of participation may appeal to this age cohort, in which new media technologies continue to play an expanding role.

This concluding chapter examines how Millennials exhibit a mindset with consumer tendencies yet support government involvement with both individualistic and civic traits. It explores the relationship that Millennials have with media technology, the marketplace, government and political leaders, and how it translates into engagement on the issues of importance to this age cohort. Salient political events have drawn Millennials into closer attentiveness to political figures and have shaped affective attitudes toward institutions and political leaders such as the president. At the same time, lower confidence levels in the president and low trust in government result in a tenuous Millennial relationship with US politics at times. The president provides an important entry point to US politics for our Millennial-age students. However, it is just as important to move our students' interest and engagement on related policy beyond an evaluation of the president's handling of—and the political partisan bickering on—issues important to this generation.

With increased political knowledge as part of the US politics course, our students are able to rely more on political information than on affective attitudes in policy judgments. In turn, I argue that this can build confidence in a perceived ability to engage the political and policy environment. Furthermore, increasing the avenues of perceived and direct Millennial engagement in politics can develop a higher sense of political efficacy.

Millennials need to believe that the government and its related leaders will be responsive to their interests and actions in order to build enduring confidence in democracy and thus a desire to engage more actively in it. This chapter demonstrates how Millennial-age students support a healthy questioning of government, vigorous debate, and the right to protest that would appear in line with teaching techniques that integrate discussion and debate on the most salient of issues, including war. As part of the learning experience, this helps our Millennial-age students to more significantly link their own actions, such as political efficacy, with the country's direction and confidence in American democracy itself.

This chapter considers important Millennial attitudes and perceptions—as knowledge is gained as part of the US politics course—when it comes to the role they see for themselves and their views about where we are headed as a country. Confidence in democracy can be critical in determining how our Millennial-age students engage politics into the future. When it comes to our Millennial students' perceptions of their generation's prospects, they are very much connected to the closeness they feel to this age cohort. Thus our students need to understand how they can participate in US politics to forge change and to positively impact their generation's future.

For entering college students with inherently stronger connections to their community as an accessible place, learning as part of a US politics course can help to build a stronger sense of familiarity and attachment to the national political space and confidence in American democracy. It can also help our students to understand the challenges facing their generation and the role they can play in impacting government and policy as they learn more about related processes, institutions, and politics.

Millennials have continued to exhibit unique and consistent preferences that are shaping a group identity and reflect how they are likely to engage in US politics. And for educators, it is critical to understand such Millennial characteristics and perspectives to most effectively link related political events of interest to facilitate learning and engagement. Our students' attentiveness to salient political events is linked not only to learning and interest, but, I argue, to confidence in American democracy. As our students' own knowledge of related figures and facts on events of interest increases, their sense of confidence in the democratic process as a whole also increases, as does the likelihood that these Millennials will be active participants.

Choice, Challenges, and Citizenship

It is vital to recognize generational perspectives and attributes of Millennial-age students in order to most effectively introduce US politics that extends learning and engagement beyond the classroom. As W. Lance Bennett notes (2007a, 14), "The challenge for civic education and engagement is to recognize the profound generational shift in citizenship styles," wherein "young people are far less willing to subscribe to the notion held by earlier generations that citizenship is a matter of duty and obligation." There is "a diminished sense of governmental obligation, a higher sense of individual purpose; voting is less meaningful than personally defined acts such as consumerism, community volunteering, transnational activism; and a mistrust of media and politicians is reinforced by a negative mass media environment."

This is an age cohort that has been reared with more hours of community service than any previous generation. It has also come of age in a 24/7 cable news, Twitter, and YouTube world. There can be great focus on individual expressions and actions while providing the choice to turn to something else in a nanosecond when the novelty wears off. Millennials can mobilize quickly to action, as witnessed during the 2008 election and, just as quickly, turn away, as surveys found in the aftermath of the election.

Reflecting on findings of the 2008 American Freshman Survey, HERI director Sylvia Hurtado optimistically noted, "I think this last election, and the need to attend to the nation's problems, [have] captured the hope and the imagination of college students who will be committed to helping to devise solutions." Yet less than two years later in his assessment of spring 2010 survey findings for our nation's undergraduates, John Della Volpe, director of polling for Harvard's IOP, worried, "millions of young people are losing faith in government, politics, and in many cases—the American dream."

This is what makes identifying Millennials' own attentiveness to salient political events, interest in politics, use of media sources, preferences, and attitude toward government and politics critical to the learning impact in the classroom and beyond. Political knowledge and engagement need to build off of the genuine interests and perspectives of Millennials. We must be aware of the times and perspectives in which this age cohort is learning about the political world and how they are making their way into adult life.

The puzzle for many observers is how to engage a generation that demonstrates a renewed interest in public affairs and a desire for change through government while possessing many individualistic traits adopted as a product of their times and technological resources. Macedo et al. (2005, 51) go so far as to suggest, "a form of individualism centered on unfettered choice has become a dominant cultural norm." It can be hard to teach citizen engagement when, as consumer activist Ralph Nader often notes, we are "growing up corporate." All around us there are signs of commercialism and consumerism. The once-public spaces or ballparks, such as a veterans' field or memorial auditorium, have given way to corporate monikers, even on many college campuses. Big-time college athletics has been a conduit for Nike swooshes, which scream corporate sponsorship but say little about civic engagement. This is a generation that has been marketed to since birth (Twenge 2006), which has only intensified because of the size and potential consumption of their cohort (Howe and Straus 2000). Cassino and Besen-Cassino (2009) argue that for Millennials, politics is one more thing to be consumed.

Millennial traits, however, provide opportunities to connect national political attentiveness and consumer behaviors with tangible opportunities for community activism and new forms of political participation, which can strengthen political learning and engagement. In a 2005 Harvard IOP survey, half of college students defined themselves as politically active. However, it is a definition that differs from earlier notions of political engagement, including new technological abilities such as writing e-mails in support of political causes (30 percent) and signing petitions online (36 percent). Seventy-nine percent of students described wearing a t-shirt to reflect political or social opinion as a political activity and 70 percent described wearing a wristband in support of a political cause as a political activity. T-shirts and wristbands had become the new yard sign for a relatively mobile younger generation. Furthermore, 57 percent viewed attending a concert or buying music specifically because of a political or social belief as a political activity, and 74 percent viewed boycotting a company with social or political values one disagrees with as a political act.

Zukin et al. (2006, 60) find "buycotting" to be the most common nonelectoral activity for this younger age group, and 90 percent of these DotNets who engaged in consumer activism saw it as an individual activity rather than an organized campaign. For the younger generation, Dalton (2007) argues that such nonelectoral activities, which include buying products for political reasons and the willingness to act on principles, are examples of a new kind of "engaged citizenship." Individual choice and related consumer activities make up a new spectrum of participation in line with the unique characteristics of the Millennial Generation.

Making Money and Making Government Work

Consumer choice is increasingly merged with political expression for Millennials, which makes financial consideration a necessary part of this "democratic" equation. Moreover, the rising cost of college itself and the poor state of the economy and employment in recent years have also arguably placed greater emphasis on the financial aspects of a college experience. Despite the fact that the 1970s has often been referred to as the "Me Decade," with swinging bell-bottoms and disco nights at Studio 54, only 50 percent felt money was a very important reason to go to college in 1976. Sixty-six percent felt increasing one's earning power was a very important reason in 2006. A record 78.1 percent of incoming freshmen identified "being well-off financially" as a very important objective in the fall 2009 HERI survey, compared with 45 percent of college freshmen in 1967. John Pryor, lead author of the report, noted that concern about money "just really permeated everything," with numerous indicators of a student population increasingly anxious about the economy and their own future prospects.

In our survey of UCSB students completing a US politics course in summer 2008, 80 percent were interested in "making a lot of money," with 42 percent "very interested." This compares with 47 percent who were interested and 10 percent very interested in public service. At SUNY Fredonia, 71 percent of students completing a US politics course in fall 2008 were interested and 44 percent very interested in making lots of money. In comparison, 47 percent were interested in public service, with 11 percent very interested. At the end of the spring 2010 courses, 76 percent were interested in making lots of money and 49 percent very interested, compared with 43 percent interested and 8 percent very interested in public service.

Such interest distinctions do not mean that our Millennial-age students are inherently wed to the wonders of the marketplace over government, nor do they put inherent faith in the corporation over community solutions. In fact, the findings once again show a generation that recognizes the influence and power of the marketplace but also favors significant government involvement on what this age cohort identifies as some of the most important policy concerns.

Zukin et al. (2006) found in 2002 that while 70 percent of DotNets would consider working for a large corporation and 56 percent for government, 51 percent trusted government while only 19 percent trusted corporations. In spring 2010, the Harvard IOP reported that while only 36 percent of college students nationwide trusted the federal government most or all of the time, trust of Wall Street executives was at 12 percent. While a majority of Americans agree with the statement, "When something is run by the government, it is usually inefficient and wasteful," these younger Gen Nexters reject this idea, according to a Pew Center report in 2007. Millennials are less critical of government regulation of business but also less critical of business itself, the most likely of any generation to support privatization of the Social Security system.

Therefore, it would appear that this is a generation that is open to the possibilities of the marketplace and role of the consumer but also supportive of the role of government on the most salient and important policy issues. There are important debates before Millennials that address deeply held convictions about the government's role and provide opportunities for learning and engagement beyond the drama of war and the height of a presidential election. As in our discussion in Chapters 3 and 4, such debates provide an opportunity to build related learning connected to attentiveness as well as to integrate media sources into and beyond the US politics learning experience.

On the day Barack Obama signed health care reform into law, gaffe-prone Vice President Joe Biden leaned over and whispered to the president that this is a "big F***ing deal," as the microphone and the instantaneous YouTube reality picked up and played the comment again and again. But even before health care legislation became a major feature of Obama's first year in office, Harvard IOP surveys reported 64 percent of college students in spring 2007 and 60 percent in spring 2008 felt basic health care should be a right for all people and, if someone has no means to pay for it, the government should provide it. And in spring 2007 and spring 2008, well before the BP oil spill crisis, 70 percent and 66 percent of students, respectively, agreed that "protecting the environment should be as high a priority for government as protecting jobs."

In the annual HERI survey, the number of college freshmen who believe that a national health care plan is needed to cover everybody's costs has been hovering around 70 percent, with around 80 percent believing that the federal government is not doing enough to control environmental pollution. For our SUNY Fredonia students both entering and exiting our courses in US politics, the number agreeing that federal involvement or spending on health care should be increased or greatly increased was near 70 percent in fall 2000 and spring 2010, and lingered around the mid-70s in fall 2004–2005 and fall 2008 to spring 2009. Our students' support for increased or greatly increased federal involvement in environmental protection hovered in the high 60s from fall 2000 to spring 2010, and similar support was registered by students surveyed in US politics courses at UCSB in spring 2003, fall 2004, and summer 2008.

On the other hand, our students continued to express little support for increased defense spending across the decade. It was at 20 percent for those completing the fall 2000 and the spring 2010 US politics course. And fatigue over the war on terrorism and war in Iraq likely translated into low levels of support for the ongoing occupation in Iraq (26 percent in fall 2008, 27 percent in spring 2009) and in Afghanistan (38 percent in spring 2009, 38 percent in spring 2010). According to the spring 2009 Harvard IOP survey, two-thirds of college students and 18- to 24-year-olds nationwide opposed the decision by Obama to send more US troops to Afghanistan.

Millennials have consistent and unique perspectives about the role of government in their lives, which also impact the roles they feel they should play with regard to US politics and policy. Dalton (2007) describes such weak Millennial support for defense spending coupled with strong support for federal government involvement on health care and the environment as a generational attribute of a new type of "engaged citizenship" made up of independent, assertive citizens concerned with others. According to Dalton, the World War II generation favors more spending on defense and less on social programs, whereas Millennials, less bound by traditional notions of "civic duty," are nonetheless driven to act in multiple ways on issues of perceived importance.

An introduction to US politics course is not bound to an imposed civic concept that our Millennial-age students should be interested and/or active in particular events, with regard to certain issues, and in more traditionally expected modes of participation. There are policy issues that Millennials deem to be important and that necessitate a government role (or not) in their minds. There are evolving modes of participation in line with Millennial experiences saturated with media and consumer choices for information and participation. The successful introduction to US politics course relates learning and engagement to the policy issues prominent in our students' minds and allows Millennials opportunities to identify the appropriate channels available to further engage political understanding and participation.

Beyond the President and the Politics of Disappointment

Our entering and exiting US politics students, fall 2000–spring 2010, have retained remarkably similar and stable attitudes with regard to the federal government's role in education, environment, and health care. There is a stable Millennial commitment to the government's role in these areas, one that appears not to be shaped by the political debate or partisan bickering of "distant politics." The views on foreign policy decisions with regard to Iraq and Afghanistan, on the other hand, have trended consistently downward since the commencement of the wars. Such views appear far more responsive to the information environment and perceived direction of these efforts.

As one of the most accessible entry points to US politics, our students' views on policy tend to also be reflected in attitudes toward the president. Although he entered office with high hopes and solid approval among this younger cohort, President Obama's approval of his handling of health care and Afghanistan both dipped below 50 percent in fall 2009 and spring 2010, according to Harvard IOP surveys of our nation's college students. This despite the fact Obama still had overall presidential approval of 57 percent in fall 2009 and 60 percent in spring 2010 among students nationwide.

According to the spring and fall 2008 Harvard IOP surveys of college students, Obama was viewed as the best candidate to bring change to Washington by a margin of 30-some points over McCain. For our SUNY Fredonia students completing US politics courses in fall 2008, 68 percent approved of Obama's post-election transition. Sixty-eight percent of our entering US politics students in spring 2009 also approved of Obama's post-election transition and 63 percent approved of his performance as president at the end of spring 2009.

By contrast, for our entering students in fall 2008 and spring 2009, approval for outgoing president Bush was at 12 and 15 percent, respectively. President Bush's approval had fallen dramatically since 9/11 and the surge around the war on terrorism, hitting divisive levels around the 2004 election, before a consistent decline on the heels of Katrina and negative opinions on the war in Iraq. For college students nationwide, "trust in the president to do the right thing" most or all of the time never broke 33 percent in fall 2006, 2007, and 2008 surveys by the Harvard IOP. But in spring 2010, it was up at 51 percent.

For our SUNY Fredonia students completing the US politics course, "confidence in the president" surged from 44 percent in fall 2008 to 70 percent in spring 2009, settling back to 55 percent in spring 2010. As Obama's numbers settled back to earth and his administration was caught up in the rough-and-tumble politics of Washington, there was concern that this younger age cohort may wrap too much of their own political stakes in how they view the president's handling of and performance on pressing issues. This is where political learning in US politics can be critical, with less reliance on presidential cues and increasing reliance on related knowledge when it comes to policy judgment.

We need to continue to engage our Millennial-age students on the issues and resist the temptation to frame the policy debate in terms more familiar to the modern cable-news environment, pitting side against side in a zero-sum dynamic. Our findings demonstrate that Millennials hold consistent and deeply held views on certain salient policy issues that they believe demand policy solutions. However, it is key that this generation, including our students being introduced for the first time to the topic of US politics, feel invested in the debate and can link it to a recognizable outcome.

Winograd and Hais (2008, 5) argue that "endless arguments over ideas and values turn off a generation of activist doers" when they describe a "civic, unified Millennial generation with its penchant for win-win, group-oriented solutions to the country's challenges" (253). Younger Americans are experiencing continued frustration that those in the corridors of power aren't doing a better job of working out solutions. In an October 2006 Harvard IOP survey as we neared the midterm elections, 80 percent of college students agreed that "politics has become too partisan," a number at 77 percent in fall 2007. Seventy-two percent in fall 2006 felt that "the political tone in Washington is too negative." When presented with the option in a spring 2010 survey to either agree or disagree that politics has become too partisan, 50 percent agreed that politics was still too partisan and only 10 percent disagreed.

Unlike those of the early 1960s, when younger Americans sought to engage public service at a national level and viewed the federal government as a broad unified force for positive change, today's college-age youth continue to view government leadership with caution. Even though Barack Obama's early presidency triggered a nearly 20-point boost in college students' trust in the president, there was little impact on trust of the federal government. It was at 35 percent in spring 2010, compared with 31 percent in fall 2006, 30 percent in fall 2007, and 29 percent in fall 2008, according to Harvard IOP surveys. Similarly, for our students completing the introduction to US politics course at SUNY Fredonia, trust in the government in Washington, DC, to do the right thing "most of the time" or "almost always" was at 27 percent in fall 2008, 34 percent in spring 2009, and 26 percent in spring 2010. At the end of the decade, after a spike in trust following 9/11 and the early war on terrorism, trust in government was similar to where it started for our students in fall 2000 (see Figure 6.1).

Tapscott (2008, 246) argues, "The Net Generation does not put much trust in politicians and political institutions—not because they're uninterested, but rather because political systems have failed to engage them in a manner that fits their digital and ethical upbringing." This is where the US politics course can be critical in linking an introductory learning process with political interests, media sources, policy concerns, and participation channels connected to our Millennial-age students. It is important to integrate an understanding of real-life politics into a US politics course, but also for our students to recognize that politicians do not shape

Figure 6.1   Trust in Federal Government and Confidence in the President

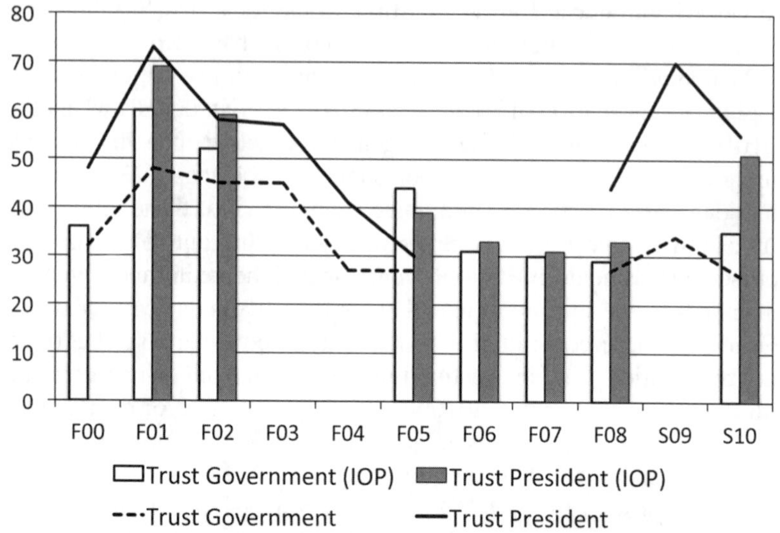

Notes: Trend lines indicate SUNY Fredonia students completing the US politics course who think that the federal government can be trusted to do what is right "most of the time" or "just about always" and who are "confident" or "very confident" in the president. Bars indicate students nationwide who were surveyed by the Harvard Institute of Politics who trust (1) the federal government and (2) the president to do the right thing "most of the time" or "all of the time."

Millennials' own capacity for political engagement. People can feel helpless when they are not informed enough to function without government cues, but they do not want to depend on institutions that they find untrustworthy. This creates a cycle that can encourage disengagement from political and thus civic life. Salient and current policy debates can and should be integrated into the US politics learning environment in line with our students' attentiveness and interest. However, we should recognize why these issues are important to Millennials to further stimulate related learning and engagement, rather than discourage it.

Encouraging Efficacy

The younger generation is less likely to engage in politics if they feel it is not responsive to their views and/or they lack understanding of how to engage in it. External efficacy, the belief that elected officials and government are responsive to an individual's concerns, has been consistently low for decades, especially among younger Americans. Twenge (2006, 156) argues that for Millennials there has been "a trend toward externality, believing things are out of control—choosing cynicism as their armor of choice . . . as opposed to an internal feeling of control that you can change your fate."

For our students completing the US politics course, fall 2000–spring 2010, only a small percentage, usually hovering around the 20s, disagreed with the statement that "public officials/political leaders don't care much about what people like me think" (see Figure 6.2). External efficacy was noticeably highest for our students at the end of the fall 2004 and 2008 courses that coincided with high youth voter turnout in those two presidential elections. Engaging in the electoral process as part of two very salient political events provided our students with the opportunity to connect heightened political attentiveness and interest with tangible political participation.

Figure 6.2   Political Involvement, Perceived Impact, and Efficacy

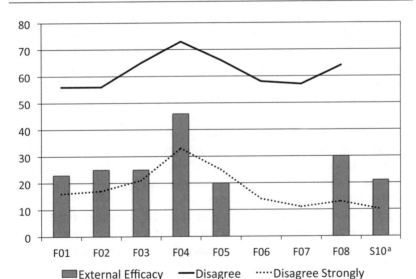

Notes: The solid line indicates the percentage of college students nationwide surveyed by the Harvard Institute of Politics who disagreed with the statement, "Political involvement rarely leads to tangible results." The dotted line indicates the percentage of students who strongly disagreed with the statement. Bars indicate the percentage of students completing the US politics course at SUNY Fredonia who disagreed or strongly disagreed that "public officials/political leaders don't care much about what people like me think." The national student data are from the Harvard Institute of Politics surveys and the SUNY Fredonia data are compiled by the author.

a. In spring 2010, the Harvard IOP survey provided the option to neither disagree nor agree.

However, a sense of external efficacy can be too focused on these quadrennial events. In spring 2009, external efficacy would move up into the mid-30s before dropping back into the low 20s as we completed the spring 2010 course. Despite Obama's "Change We Can Believe In" slogan, which led to widespread support across our courses and among students nationwide, external efficacy in our students had dropped significantly as Obama finished a tough first year and particularly rough debate over health care. In fact, it was below the higher external efficacy mark of 32 percent for our students completing the fall 2000 US politics course. For students nationwide, external efficacy had spiked back up during the 2008 election but had also plummeted as we headed into the spring of Obama's second year in office. For example, a fall 2008 Harvard IOP survey reported that 59 percent of college students disagreed that "people like me don't have any say in what the government does." In a spring 2010 IOP survey, it was down to 37 percent.

Consequently, it is important that Millennial-age students be introduced to other mechanisms beyond voting every four years to build a more enduring sense of political efficacy in order to foster more sustained engagement. For our 101 SUNY students completing the Washington, DC, internship program in 2006–2007, external political efficacy moved significantly from 30 percent to 51 percent as students experienced their own participation and responses from government, related agencies, and/or nongovernmental organizations. Moreover, the students' sense of internal political efficacy at the completion of the Washington, DC, internship program was particularly high. Eighty-five percent agreed or strongly agreed that "my participation and/or expression can make an impact on the political/policy process." The higher levels of external and, particularly, internal political efficacy for our SUNY interns demonstrate how engaging in politics as part of the learning experience can contribute to how students perceive their role within the broader political and democratic process.

It is admittedly more difficult to re-create such directly engaged opportunities across US politics classrooms. Still, the learning experience can be engaging for students if it effectively integrates salient political events and concerns. For students completing our US politics courses at SUNY Fredonia, 52 percent agreed with the "internal political efficacy" statement in fall 2008, 51 percent in spring 2009, and 44 percent in spring 2010. With no outlets for direct participation in government, our students' sense of internal political efficacy corresponded most significantly with the 2008 election cycle.

Figure 6.2 shows how college students nationwide related their own sense of internal efficacy most strongly with the fall 2004 and fall 2008 elections. Internal efficacy declined between elections even as other dramatic issues and events, ranging from war in Iraq to Katrina to health care, demanded resolution. For example, the Harvard IOP reported that 33 percent of students disagreed strongly that "political involvement rarely leads to tangible results" in fall 2008, a number that had dropped to 10 percent in spring 2010.

Understanding that political involvement stretches beyond the election cycle is a key hurdle to more extensively engaging Millennials in politics. College-age youth can be mobilized to feel motivated and be engaged in high-profile elections when the general electorate is similarly motivated. It is just as important to keep Millennials engaged and mobilized between these quadrennial electoral events.

Engaging Opportunities

Findings throughout this book show how salient nonelectoral events in this historic decade have engaged Millennials. From fall 2000 to spring 2010, multiple high-profile current events sparked debate and interest. Attentiveness to salient events and related discussion can bring politics to life while providing ownership for these emerging citizens. Exposure to politics in line with ongoing current events cannot only stimulate the learning experience, but can pique interest in political participation and future engagement for students who might otherwise be disinterested in what they deem to be irrelevant to their lives (Hess 2009). Engaging Millennials in salient political events and debates as part of an introduction to US politics course can increase a sense of efficacy when students are exposed to related political information and various types of participation opportunities.

By opening up current events discussions on even controversial policy topics, students can develop deeper understanding of and commitment to democratic values while enhancing their sense of political efficacy (Gimpel, Lay, and Schuknecht 2003). In fact, the Millennial Generation is quite comfortable with democratic debate, dissent, and taking a stand for a cause. In the 2006 HERI survey, 63 percent of US college freshmen believed that "dissent is a critical component of the democratic process." Harvard IOP trends show the percentage of students attending a political rally or demonstration rising each fall from 20 percent in 2002 to 36 percent in 2005, before leveling back off to the high 20s in ensuing years. As an example of new media avenues of participation, college students who had signed an online petition increased from 36 percent in fall 2005 to 56 percent in fall 2006 and 58 percent in fall 2007.

Figure 6.3 shows how our students entered a US politics course with a high level of support for protest and questioning of government. Whether or not they would personally engage in protest, our students were overwhelmingly and consistently supportive of the right to protest war in Iraq, even during the earlier heated months of the war. In general, support for questioning government even increased after a term of US politics, but it did decline slightly during the fall 2004 and fall 2008 elections, and most noticeably during spring 2010 when the health care debate was plastered across the airwaves.

Based on national surveys of Millennial college students during the decade, there is tolerance and support of dissent and debate but an appar-

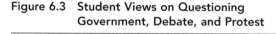

Figure 6.3   Student Views on Questioning Government, Debate, and Protest

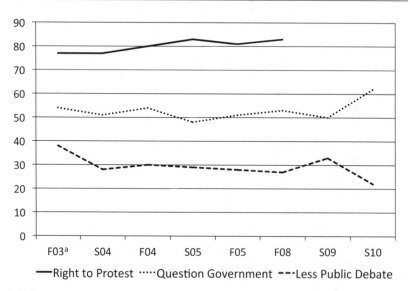

Notes: The solid line indicates the percentage of SUNY Fredonia students entering the US politics course who completely support the views of the protesters against the war in Iraq or support the right to protest but not the protesters' views. The dotted line indicates the percentage of students who feel it is more important than ever to extensively question our government's policies. The dashed line indicates the percentage who feel that we should support our government's policies with less debate.

a. Fall 2003 only included the question for students completing the course.

ent distaste for the rancorous partisanship and political gamesmanship that dominate much of what the media reports on Washington, particularly with regard to presidential elections and critical policy issues (CIRCLE 2007b). As Tapscott (2008, 248) observes, "University students are hungry for political conversation, but it's got to be free of spin." The Harvard IOP consistently has found that over two-thirds of college students feel that "politics has become too partisan" and that "elected officials don't have the same priorities as I have." And as the glow of the Obama victory morphed into partisan battles on the hill, numerous indicators of Millennial interest and engagement in US politics began a retreat to numbers that concerned scholars as we entered this new century. For our US politics students at SUNY Fredonia, it was a noticeable drop in national political interest from 66 percent in spring 2009 to 50 percent in spring 2010.

Building on New Millennial Connections

When views on national political figures and institutions are diminished, with less reliance on traditional national news sources and with shifting generational dynamics that make choice rather than a sense of national civic duty key elements of how Millennials chooses to engage in politics, it is increasingly challenging to connect this age cohort to the national political space beyond the most salient of political moments. In fact, the September 11 attacks, the ensuing wars in Afghanistan and Iraq, and national crises like Katrina likely triggered a temporary surge in national attachment that has otherwise been steadily diminishing for Millennials relative to previous generations (Rahn and Rudolph 2001).

When we asked our students how close they felt to the nation, the highest point was 58 percent, who felt "close" or "very close" when surveyed in the near aftermath of 9/11 as part of the fall 2001 US politics courses. By fall 2005 this number was at 36 percent, and also at 36 percent for students completing the fall 2008 courses. For students completing the spring 2010 courses, it was at 31 percent, the lowest number we had measured since fall 2000 when it stood at 27 percent. On the other hand, our US politics students' feelings of closeness to their community remained relatively similar to findings from fall 2000–fall 2005, with measures of 59 percent for students completing the course in fall 2008 and spring 2010.

However, our US politics students' sense of closeness to their age group continued to be a stronger and consistent attachment than were nation and community as we confronted 9/11, wars, Katrina, and a catastrophic oil spill beyond the Clinton and Bush eras and into the Obama administration. Our students' feeling of closeness to their own age group never dropped below 70 percent, while averaging 76 percent across the decade. It was at 77 percent as students completed the spring 2009 and 2010 US politics courses.

Approaching the turn of the millennium, Howe and Strauss (2000) had praised the emerging generation as optimistic team players who believe in their own collective power. Even as events disrupted calm and economic times turned tougher, Zukin and his collaborators (2006, 39) still found this to be a generation that exhibited a particularly profound self-identification as unique at a level beyond other cohorts. Similarly, a 2007 Pew Center survey reported that 68 percent of Gen Nexters viewed their generation as unique and distinct, a number higher than the other three major generational cohorts.

Hard times and social and economic challenges can forge a generational bond in a way that the best of times may not. Consider the World War II generation and the Boomers' ongoing identification with Vietnam and the civil rights struggle. This, after all, is a Millennial cohort that pulled together after 9/11, sent many of their cohorts to war, elected the first African American president, and presided over the explosion of new media technology and its application across society, government, and politics. Indeed, a January 2010 Pew survey found that while the World War II generation ranked their shared experience of the Depression and World War II at the top of what makes their generation unique, Millennials listed technology at the top of their own open-ended responses to the question. Whether we view this cohort as a narcissistically self-indulgent and self-entitled Generation Me or as an important demographic force that will use new technology they have largely developed as part of a millennial makeover, the consensus of such analyses is that this is an age group that is bound together through a unique sense of generational identification shaped by their times.

Thus, it is critical to understand how unique Millennial experiences, not a long-standing connection to the national space as evidenced in earlier generations, provide a gateway to political interest, learning, and engagement. It is generational identity and a perceived closeness to it, rather than any deeply held attachment to the nation, that open up the channels for Millennial political participation. This is not to say that Millennials cannot develop an attachment to the national political space by connecting generational concerns and perspectives with interest and participation in national politics. What it means is that it is important for US politics courses to integrate Millennial experiences to help identify and forge such connections.

For 2,019 students surveyed entering and exiting the US politics courses at SUNY Fredonia, fall 2001–spring 2010, closeness to their age group was more significantly correlated with closeness to their community (.44 pre, .46 post) than it was with closeness to the nation (.19 pre, .23 post). Dalton (2007), likewise, also expressed concern about the community as a part of the engaged citizenship cluster for this younger age cohort. For our students, closeness to their age group was also significantly correlated with interest in local politics (.12 pre, .13 post), community activism (.14 pre, .18 post), and public service (.18 pre, .16 post), but not with interest in national politics. Closeness to community was even more strongly correlated with interest in local politics, community activism, and public service, whereas closeness to the nation was most significantly correlated with interest in national politics.

All three measures of closeness were positively and significantly correlated with attention to TV news, external efficacy, and voting, with national closeness exhibiting the strongest relationship at .19 for TV news and .23 for external efficacy for students completing the US politics courses. Thus, while the strength of generational identification is driving elements of political and cognitive engagement for our Millennial students, national closeness still plays a more significant role when it comes to what we might consider national-level components of engagement. This makes it all the more important to integrate national-level salient political events, related media sources, and channels for participation to demonstrate such connections for Millennials more familiar with activity in their own community and connected to the concerns of their age cohort.

With national closeness weakening overall, we might anticipate lower levels of engagement for these younger cohorts at a national level but heightened connections to more accessible local and community opportunities for action. As interest in national politics has been more susceptible to changing events and related media coverage, our students' interest in local politics and community activism, albeit lower, has remained more consistent. The community itself provides a more natural closeness and accessibility, but for a generation accustomed to crossing geographic boundaries through virtual space, social networking sites provide another profound connection to generational identity, peers, and age group.

Our entering students in US politics courses were increasingly likely to pay "a lot" of attention to social networking sites, at 54 percent in spring 2009 and up to 63 percent in spring 2010, at the same time that other levels of media attention remained relatively static. This was also reflected in the gradual increase in the amount of time spent online, from 10 percent at 20 hours or more in fall 2008 to 16 percent in spring 2010. Twenty-six percent were spending at least 15 hours online in fall 2008, a number at 35 percent in spring 2010. Furthermore, our entering and exiting US politics students' closeness to their age group was significantly correlated with their use of social networking sites, whereas there was no such significant connection with closeness to the nation or the community.

It appears that social networking sites reinforce a sense of connectedness among Millennial cohorts. And there are profound possibilities to connect these more familiar new media resources with political participation revolving around particularly salient events like the 2008 election. The net and social networking sites provide numerous opportunities to mobilize members of this generation around numerous causes, events, and issues. On the other hand, it remains to be seen whether social networking sites can generate sustained Millennial engagement and participation in US politics and democracy beyond the connections it forges among this age cohort.

Whatever one's perspective on Millennial use of new media, we cannot ignore the prevalence of this technology as a channel for engaging our students in US politics. Findings in Chapter 3 show how high levels of Internet use are related to higher political knowledge, which facilitates participation. Social networking tools are just another media source that can be introduced in a US politics course as a more familiar and accessible Millennial resource with which to engage issues of interest to this age cohort.

New Millennial Direction

Millennials have come of age during a decade that saw the explosion of information technology that birthed MySpace, Facebook, YouTube, Twitter, and the like. These new technologies have opened up boundless opportunities that Millennials will utilize to positively transform or jeopardize our democratic future, depending on the argument. Therefore, it is important to understand how Millennials developing political attitudes, preferences, knowledge, and engagement relate to perceptions of this country's direction and their generation's prospects in it. Findings throughout this book reveal a generation that is driven to learn about and engage in US politics related to the most salient of events, processes, and issues deemed to be of importance and relevance to them. And the economy and related jobs have been a very salient concern for these recent or soon-to-be college graduates.

As Figure 6.4 demonstrates, two-thirds of our SUNY Fredonia students completing US politics courses in fall 2000 believed that the country was heading in the right direction even after a highly debated and controversial finish to the presidential election. After a tremendous rally around the nation and its institutions, over 60 percent of students completing the fall 2001 US politics course also believed the country was heading in the right direction. Furthermore, our students' expressed confidence in democracy soared over 20 points from fall 2000, a period in which a divided and bitterly polarized electorate in the aftermath of Bush vs. Gore would be symbolically united after the September 11 attacks. However, as the 9/11 rally wore off and debate heated up over homeland security, war in Iraq, and the economy, fewer and fewer of our students perceived the country to be moving in the right direction.

Figure 6.4 Direction of the Country and Confidence in American Democracy

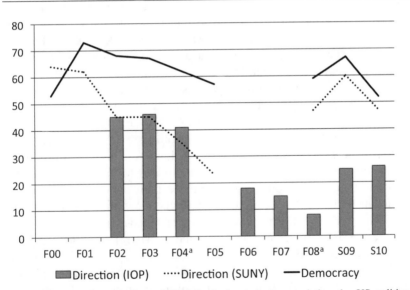

Notes: Trend lines indicate SUNY Fredonia students completing the US politics courses who are "confident/very confident" in American democracy and who feel that the country is heading in "somewhat/very much the right direction." Bars represent the percentage of students nationwide surveyed by the Harvard Institute of Politics who believe that things in the nation are "generally headed in the right direction."

a. Harvard IOP surveys were completed in October before the 2004 and 2008 elections. SUNY surveys were completed in December following the elections.

In fall 2000, 79 percent of our students completing the US politics course approved of President Clinton's handling of the economy and 32 percent strongly approved. But by the end of our fall 2002 courses, 61 percent of our students evaluated the national economy as "somewhat bad" or "very bad." And by the end of fall 2004, it was at 69 percent "bad."

Views on the direction of the country also evidenced the downturn in opinion on war in Iraq, particularly among college students. As confidence in the president dropped, so did the perceived direction of the country. The Harvard IOP, for example, noted an almost identical downward trend in the perceived direction of the country and presidential approval. By 2006, one-third of students approved of the job President Bush was doing, a low at that point for his presidency and a 14-point drop from a spring 2005 IOP survey. Similarly, only 30 percent of those polled in 2006 believed the country to be heading in the right direction, a drop from 41 percent in spring 2005.

For our students, confidence in American democracy followed a similar trend but never dropped below 50 percent, even as confidence in the president and positive views of the nation's direction plummeted into the 20s. With the election of Barack Obama, our students' views on the country's direction and confidence in democracy surged back up. But as the economic crisis continued and battles ensued over policies from Afghanistan to health care, our students' confidence in American democracy and views on the nation's direction dropped again as we approached the end of the decade, albeit nowhere as low as during the second Bush term.

When the spring 2010 Harvard IOP asked college students, "What national issue concerns you most," health care (at 21 percent) and national security (8 percent) were well below the economy (46 percent). The economy can be a very salient issue for our Millennial-age students and one that can be connected directly to their own lives, linking the national space with local communities. Furthermore, the state of the economy also connects directly to our Millennial students' perceived opportunities for their future as they make their way from college campuses into the working world.

Despite very bad economic perceptions, Millennials maintained a more positive outlook about the future of the country than did other age groups. According to a January 2010 Pew survey, 41 percent of 18- to 29-year-old Millennials said they are satisfied with the way things are going in the country, compared with just 26 percent of those ages 30 and older. Pew reported that "whatever toll a recession, a housing crisis, a financial meltdown, and a pair of wars may have taken on the national psyche in the past few years, it appears to have hit the old harder than the young."

By fall 2008–spring 2010, our students' evaluations of the national economy were almost universally bad, even as other issues swirled on the political scene. Still, our students held a much more positive view of the country's direction than they had in the second term of the Bush administration. There was a relatively higher degree of confidence in the president and perhaps a more enduring positive perspective that Millennials had developed from extensive involvement in the 2008 presidential election.

Our US politics students who voted in the 2008 presidential election were significantly more likely to hold a more positive perception of their generation's prospects. Moreover, the more closely connected our students felt to the Millennial age cohort, the more positive they felt about their generation's prospects. Those with the highest levels of internal political efficacy were also most significantly connected to this age cohort, suggesting a strongly perceived concept of Millennials' ability to effect change as a generational group. (See Table 6.1.)

Table 6.1   Perceived Direction of Country and Generation's Prospects

	US Direction Fall 2000	US Direction Fall 2008	Generational Future Fall 2000	Generational Future Fall 2008	Generational Future Fall 2008[a]
Trust in government	.38**	.05	.20+	.09	.08
Confidence in president	.19+	.16*	.06	.04	.07
Confidence in democracy	.13	.03	.22*	.14	.08
Closeness to nation	.07	.04	.05	.14	.13
Closeness to age group	.39**	.13	.21*	.25**	.25**
Attentiveness to news	.12	.03	.10	.03	.02
Informed about candidates	.04	.15	.01	.01	.03
Voted in presidential election	.12	.01	.16	.39*	.34+
Surveillance knowledge	.04	.04	.01	.03	.02
Textbook knowledge	−.05	−.04	.03	.03	.02
Democratic or Republican Party identification	−.04	−.23**	.01	.08	.08
Liberal or conservative ideology	.10	.02	−.09	−.27*	−.24*
Gender (male)	.01	.19	.02	.04	.03
External political efficacy	.21*	.17+	.09	.01	.04
Internal political efficacy					.18+
Pseudo R-squared	.34	.24	.34	.19	.22

Notes: An ordered-probit analysis is utilized for SUNY Fredonia students surveyed completing the US politics course in fall 2000 (N = 221) and in fall 2008 (N = 257). The dependent variables are coded 1–5. Perceived country direction is measured on an ordinal scale, where 1 = very much the wrong direction and 5 = very much the right direction. Perceived generational prospects is measured on an ordinal scale, where 1 = very pessimistic and 5 = very optimistic. Textbook and surveillance knowledge scales are based on items described in Table 2.2. The question wording for independent variables is given in Appendix A. ** $p \leq .001$; * $p \leq .01$; + $p \leq .05$.

a. This column includes the variable "internal political efficacy."

Eventful times can forge an enduring bond with generational cohorts, based on the experience and characteristics of Millennials discussed throughout this book. Recognizing our students' generational hopes and concerns can be an important component of how the US politics course integrates related policy debates and issues into the learning experience. And learning how Millennial challenges and possibilities stretch beyond the campus and community to the national space helps to forge our students' learning experiences into a more enduring connection with the direction of the country and with American democracy.

For two thousand students completing US politics courses at SUNY Fredonia, fall 2001–fall 2005 and fall 2008–spring 2010, Table 6.2 shows how identified closeness with their age group and perceived closeness to the nation are significantly related to perceived direction of the country, as part of an ordered-probit analysis. It demonstrates the importance of feeling connected to a cohort moving through the same experience as well as a connection to the national space in an evaluation of the country's direction. However, it also shows the even more significant relationship involving the trust placed in our government and confidence in the president when it comes to the perceived direction of the country. With this connection, it is not surprising the importance our students attach to voting in presidential elections as one of their most likely entry points into political participation. Yet perceived direction of the country is also significantly attached to the external political efficacy felt by our students, demonstrating the perspective that the most positive direction of the nation is one that is responsive to their needs and interests. With higher levels of surveillance knowledge about the related political figures and facts, students felt even more connected and positive about the country's direction, as more informed participants in it.

Our students' surveillance knowledge was even more significantly related to their confidence in American democracy, demonstrating how related learning of political figures and facts connects our Millennial-age students through relevant knowledge to democratic space. With a more significant relationship between surveillance knowledge and textbook knowledge when it comes to confidence in democracy, it is another indication of how our students' cognitive engagement in the contemporary political environment is a critical channel into the democratic process.

Nevertheless, trust in government and confidence in the president are also significantly related to our students' confidence in American democracy. But rather than simply entrust democracy to government and its elected leaders, confidence in democracy is also influenced by our students' sense of political efficacy, in which they feel that their political engagement impacts governmental decisionmaking.

**Table 6.2   Perceived Direction of Country and Confidence
in American Democracy**

	Direction	Democracy 1	Democracy 2[a]
Trust in government	.20**	.21**	.25**
Confidence in president	.46**	.33**	.34**
Closeness to nation	.08*	.27**	.25**
Closeness to community	.01	.01	.02
Closeness to age group	.09*	.06+	.08*
Political efficacy	.14**	.14**	.13**
Surveillance knowledge	.05+	.11**	.09**
Textbook knowledge	.03	.06	.07+
Democratic or Republican Party identification	−.01	.03	.04
Liberal or conservative ideology	.04	.03	.05
Gender (male)	.09	.09	.07
Attentiveness to TV news	.03	.09*	.07
Attentiveness to Internet news	.01	.02	.03
Attentiveness to war on terror			.08+
Attentiveness to presidential elections			.09*
Pseudo R-squared	.39	.40	.41

Notes: An ordered-probit analysis is utilized pooling the surveys of 2,000 SUNY Fredonia students completing the US politics course, fall 2001–fall 2005 and fall 2008–spring 2010. The students utilized in this analysis had completed both pre- and post-surveys. The dependent variables are coded 1–5. Perceived country direction is measured on an ordinal scale, where 1 = very much the wrong direction and 5 = very much the right direction. Perceived generational prospects is measured on an ordinal scale, where 1 = very pessimistic and 5 = very optimistic. Textbook and surveillance knowledge scales are based on items described in Table 2.2. The question wording for independent variables is given in Appendix A. ** $p \leq .001$; * $p \leq .01$; + $p \leq .05$.

a. This column includes the variables "attentiveness to war on terror" and "attentiveness to presidential elections."

Despite the partisan and ideological debate raging in Washington and across the airwaves, our students' confidence in democracy is not determined by partisan, ideological, or even gender differences. Reflecting earlier findings in this book that Millennials are less likely to view the democratic challenges facing the country in partisan and ideological terms, it also demonstrates how attentiveness to TV news media and salient events does provide these students with a positive connection to the democratic sphere.

Millennials connect the national space with the broader questions facing the country and democracy. Forging greater attachment with national-level issues provides an important connecting point with democratic engagement in the US politics learning experience. Although our students feel closer to their community than to the nation, it is a sense of greater cognitive attachment to the nation that relates to confidence in democracy, wherein our students feel they are a part of the larger democratic process rather than removed from it.

Despite the shift in Millennials' attention to new media sources and social networking, television news still provides a vehicle to broadly disseminate to the US public the most significant events that grip the national consciousness. It is the dissemination of these salient events to our students, rather than the media channel that delivers it, that is of greatest significance. With more specific attentiveness to critical new millennial events such as the presidential elections, the 9/11 attacks, and the war on terrorism, the significance of general attention to TV news is diminished and the influence of perceived closeness to this age cohort increases.

Beyond the Introduction to US Politics Course

VH1 has been fond of breaking down decades into pop music–encapsulated history segments entitled "I love the 70s," "I love the 90s," and now "I love the New Millennium" for the first decade of the twenty-first century. But however trivial the premise of easily encapsulating a decade and what it means to a generation, there is the reality that it is hard to understand exactly how significant certain moments and experiences can be unless one has lived through them at the critical moment of one's own coming of age. It is the firsthand experience that is a part not only of the learning experience but of the ownership of what it means that binds and empowers that cohort.

As we began this new century, there was much concern about the younger generation's understanding of and commitment to political participation and civic life and thus about the future of American democracy (e.g., Putnam 2000). For Millennials, the twenty-first century began with general disengagement from politics but a hopeful view for the generation's future prospects. In between, apathy turned to anxiety and anger translated into action, as younger Americans rallied around the country during times of significant crisis and then stormed the voting booth in consecutive elections determined to bring change to Washington and the nation.

This book has explored what drives Millennial political interests and attitudes and how to connect attentiveness to salient events in the learning environment. Rather than simply bemoan the levels of student civic knowledge or, even worse, ridicule it, this book seeks to recognize how to work with a better understanding of Millennials' own political awareness and what it means for policy reasoning, heightened interest, sustained learning, and engagement for college-age members of this generation. This is particularly pressing as reports continue to demonstrate that our students are not graduating from high school with a desirable level of civic knowledge (NAEP 2010). For students who go on to a four-year college, there is little evidence of civic learning over these college years (ISI 2006). As Colby et al. (2007, 14) have noted, "American higher education pays relatively little attention to undergraduate students' political learning."

An introduction to US politics course may be the most extensive opportunity for many Millennials to learn and think about US politics and government as they seek to understand and engage the pressing issues and transpiring events relevant to their own lives. And as I argue throughout this book, the most effective introduction to US politics includes the integration of salient political events relevant to the age cohort in question. This is key to piquing interest and directing the relevance necessary to learning and engagement. Learning about US politics and government, even at the most introductory level, can be a critical conduit to political participation and civic engagement.

The remarkable events of the new millennium have provided a unique opportunity to strengthen related knowledge and to connect student learning with related points of interest, action, and lifelong engagement. As the findings demonstrate, the educational impact is most effective when the topics learned and the practice of politics are more tangible and accessible for students, which includes the practical integration of relevant political events and processes. Most college freshmen have finally reached the voting age, and many are beginning to ponder significantly for the first time their own political and policy views outside of familiar family surroundings and with new and diverse peers. Millennials have been actively involved in the events of the time, whether through service in Afghanistan and Iraq, volunteer efforts following Katrina, or as part of a historic youth voter mobilization. At this age, they are better positioned than ever before to actually learn about and more actively engage in US politics.

Deepening surveillance knowledge of relevant political facts and figures is particularly important with regard to political interest and engagement. Entering students particularly lack surveillance knowledge of US politics and government, which relies on an interest in national politics and learning that is connected to attentiveness to political events and processes. An introduction to US politics course can provide a basic foundation and knowledge base for future citizens and a tool for retrieving and processing related political information on pressing policy debates and emerging events. Political learning provides a dose of confidence that comes with understanding how the process and system work and how one can engage. As students are increasingly comfortable with avenues for political participation, there is a greater likelihood they will pursue opportunities to gain firsthand experience in political life and the civic space through internships, campus dialogue, public service, and other means of engagement.

It will continue to be critical to recognize the most relevant connecting points for Millennial-age students to inspire sustained political learning and engagement. There will be significant new Millennial events that transpire, some very unpredictable, but those like the presidential election cycle far more predictable. An introduction to US politics course can be positioned to integrate our students' attentiveness to these salient events and processes within the learning environment in order to stimulate higher levels of political knowledge and engagement.

There are media sources to work with that can build on Millennial attentiveness to emerging salient events, sources that are already familiar to Millennials, including Internet news media, TV news programs, and even soft news—"entertainment-style" late-night programs—that provide surveillance of relevant political figures, processes, and facts that reinforce learning within the classroom. Such media sources can be integrated effectively as learning devices to quickly illustrate and demonstrate those surveillance points that students are familiar with to strengthen connections to their own identified political interest and related knowledge.

Clearly, new modes of technology will play a critical role in how Millennials understand and contribute to US politics and democratic life, but concerns remain as to how technology will be used to engage in or disengage from democratic dialogue and the civic space. Many opportunities are available across the social-networking sites, which we witnessed in full force during the 2008 election. However, there are few connections between the use of such sites and our students' broader interest in local or national politics. At the same time, social networking does connect with our students' interest in expressive politics, including music and film, and can thus be integrated into this type of participatory dynamic and debate. How educators integrate new media technology in a responsible and accessible manner can help to connect Millennial-age students with the related political facts, figures, and processes necessary to properly understand and engage in related policy debate and political participation.

Studies demonstrate what students don't know (or what they do), but there is no real examination of how to work with the type of information they are most likely to acquire in the evolving media-saturated environment. We must recognize that Millennials operate in an environment bombarded with information and images, and the classroom is just a minor reprieve from what is a 24/7 onslaught. No amount of classroom information can truly counteract that.

Civic knowledge is an outgrowth of the multifaceted learning experience, which includes what happens inside and outside of the classroom. Our students will learn about politics and government through accessing and absorbing information in diverse ways. This includes instructional lessons, but also a perusal of diverse information sources. This book has identified multiple and integrative learning routes to political knowledge, interest, and engagement. However, it is not about advocating for a particular instructional style. It is about utilizing the most appropriate instructional resources available to connect our students' interests with relevant Millennial events and to further integrate this learning and interest with action. It is to connect our students' higher interest in and attentiveness to what is too often perceived as distant politics at the national level with an understanding of how to more actively engage in related politics and issues. Conversely, it is important to connect our students' increasing familiarity with community engagement as another participatory outlet for the national and global issues of importance on their minds, and of generational interest.

The 2008 presidential election provided one such point connecting local participation with national-level interest for Millennials. Still, we need to do more to integrate salient events into the US politics experience, to build relevant connections between such truly historic events and processes. After a remarkable decade in which political interest and engagement for college students and Millennials nationwide surged around a series of historic events, in many ways sparking with 9/11 and war and cresting as Barack Obama settled into the presidency, many indicators settled back to 2000 levels. Nevertheless, emerging crises, such as the BP oil spill, closed out an eventful decade and will likely stretch into the next. And sudden and shocking events that we cannot even contemplate will continue to emerge to directly impact the younger generation's view of US politics and government and their role in it, thereby providing new opportunities and challenges for political learning and civic engagement.

Millennials will also need to navigate an increasingly emotion-laden political environment that encourages reliance on accessible political cues and symbolic predispositions, particularly when related political information is most lacking. In this case, political awareness and understanding can all too often center on celebrity figures, perceived heroes or villains, as featured in the media and in political banter. While a surveillance of related political information is a critical element of Millennial understanding and engagement, it will also be important for them not to be overly captive to the political tenor of any given moment and to instead establish their own self-sustaining generational tone.

With views on government and its leaders again turning sour, it is critical that Millennial interest, policy reasoning, and engagement be forged through the stronger connection of their cohort's own knowledge and interests in identified and relevant realms of US politics. There will be critical choices facing this generation and the nation that, for a cohort that demonstrates particularly unique and stable preferences on a host of critical policies involving the role of the government, the marketplace, and the consumer-citizen, will need to be negotiated. Political learning in the introduction to US politics course will help Millennials encountering these pressing issues to wade more effectively through the symbolic saturation across burgeoning media sources and to better access the most relevant political information and policy preferences related to the most serious of emerging policy choices. Millennials will be better suited to take ownership of their own learning and interests and to be less dependent on fluctuating affective attitudes toward political leaders and government. In the end, this will be critical in building a stronger and lasting relationship among this age cohort's confidence in American democracy, the perceived direction of the country, and the Millennial role in it.

The integration of the most salient Millennial events is key to Millennial attentiveness, interest in politics, media resources, and forms of engagement in which political knowledge and learning serve as the key to these "new Millennial connections." In an introduction to US politics course, we can facilitate critical learning connections that link attentiveness, interest, political attitudes, policy choices, media use, and engagement. However, in the end, it is up to each emerging generation, including Millennials, to sustain these connections. This is a cohort whose members are tightly bound to one another by their unique coming-of-age experiences. It is a generation that has the resources to pay greater attention and to mobilize more quickly than any other in history, if it so chooses. It has experienced the most profound of events in the new millennium and has demonstrated what it can do when engaged by an issue and as part of the evolving democratic process. Following an eventful introduction to US politics in the first decade of the twenty-first century, the experience and knowledge they gained during this learning period will undoubtedly shape the future of American democracy, one way or another, new Millennial–style.

Appendix A

Student Survey Respondents
from Four Universities, 2000–2010

Student survey data were collected by pencil-and-paper administration, December 2000 to May 2010, from undergraduates enrolled in the Introduction to American Politics course at the State University of New York (SUNY) at Fredonia, the Introduction to American Politics course at the University of California at Santa Barbara (UCSB), the Introduction to American Politics course at the University of Wisconsin at River Falls, and the Introduction to Politics course at Northumbria University in Newcastle, England, as well as from students enrolled in a required course while interning in Washington, DC, as part of the SUNY Washington Internship Program. Surveys were collected from a total of 3,221 students who were beginning their respective courses, and from 3,208 students who were completing the respective courses, for a total of 6,429 surveys.

SUNY Fredonia students were initially surveyed at the end of their US politics courses for the fall 2000 and spring 2001 semesters. Survey data were collected at the beginning and end of the US politics courses for fall 2001–fall 2005, fall 2008, and spring 2009 and 2010. Overall, 2,752 students were surveyed at the beginning of US politics courses at SUNY Fredonia. A total of 2,664 students were surveyed at the completion of US politics courses for fall 2000–fall 2005, fall 2008, and spring 2009 and 2010. A total of 2,019 students completed surveys at both the beginning and end of the US politics course for fall 2001–fall 2005, fall 2008, and spring 2009 and 2010. A unique identifying code was utilized to match pre- and post-surveys of individual respondents in related courses and terms.

On average, US politics course sections at SUNY Fredonia enroll 40–50 students, but the fall 2000, fall 2004, and fall 2008 terms each had one section with 100–120 students enrolled. With the exception of fall 2003 and spring 2004, three different instructors in each semester would distribute the questionnaires to their US politics course sections. Overall, ten different political science instructors distributed surveys to their respective classes at SUNY Fredonia, fall 2000–spring 2010. The following table lists the SUNY Fredonia students surveyed entering (pre) and completing (post) the US politics course, with students who completed both the pre- and post-surveys listed in italics.

	F00	S01	F01	S02	F02	S03	F03
Pre			241	197	332	219	87
Post	243	109	235	178	325	185	88
Both			*197*	*165*	*264*	*170*	*83*

	S04	F04	S05	F05	F08	S09	S10	Total
Pre	87	320	171	334	337	239	188	2,752
Post	88	297	162	215	260	137	142	2,664
Both	*81*	*260*	*148*	*190*	*235*	*105*	*121*	2,019

A total of 398 students were also surveyed at the end of the introduction to US politics course at UCSB at the completion of the spring 2003 quarter (N = 101), the fall 2004 quarter (N = 237), and the summer 2008 quarter (N = 60). A total of 108 students were surveyed at the end of the introduction to US politics course in the spring 2001 semester at the University of Wisconsin at River Falls. At Northumbria University in Newcastle, England, a total of 369 students beginning the introduction to politics course were surveyed at the start of the fall 2003 term (N = 112), and the spring 2004 (N = 78), spring 2005 (N = 45), and fall 2005 (N = 134) terms. A total of 100 SUNY students participating in the SUNY Washington Internship Program were also surveyed as part of the required course in the fall 2006 term (N = 26), spring 2007 term (N = 48) and summer 2007 term (N = 26). A total of 38 SUNY Washington intern students also completed a survey at the end of the spring 2007 term.

The Questionnaire

On average, students were asked to respond to 75–80 questions assessing political interest, attentiveness, attitudes, preferences, behavior, and knowledge. The questions included below were part of the fall 2000–spring 2010 pre- and post-surveys unless otherwise noted in italics and parentheses to the right of the question. For example, *(F04)* indicates questions included as part of the fall 2004 survey, (*S05*) indicates questions included as part of the spring 2005 survey, and (*F01–S05*) indicates questions included throughout the fall 2001–spring 2005 time period. There were also minor changes reflective of the survey populations. For example, UCSB students were asked to recall the name of the US senators from California rather than those from New York, and Northumbria students were asked their approval of the British prime minister rather than approval of the US president. Otherwise, the questions were identical for student groups when administered in the same time frame. Only questions that were asked across multiple surveys in the pre- and post-course data collection are included in the detailing of questions below. A few questions were asked as part of a single survey, such as attentiveness to London terrorist bombings in 2005, and the related details, where necessary, are discussed in the text of this book.

The following demonstrates the questionnaire design and layout presented to students, although the order of related questions did vary. All survey respondents were prompted by the following statement: "Please answer the questions to the best of your ability and honestly. If you are uncomfortable with the survey or a question, you are not obligated to answer. There are no right and wrong answers for most of the questions. The survey is part of a research project on political attitudes and interest. By choosing to complete this survey you are providing your consent to have the findings shared and published. Your responses are anonymous. Please do not write your name on the paper. When you are done, please place your paper face down and return as requested. Thank you."

* * *

Circle the appropriate number directly on the paper provided and fill in blanks.

On a scale of 1–5, where 1 = not interested at all, 2 = rarely interested, 3 = neutral, 4 = interested, and 5 = very interested, how interested are you in the following areas?

    National politics 1 2 3 4 5
    World affairs 1 2 3 4 5
    Local politics 1 2 3 4 5
    Community activism 1 2 3 4 5
    Public service 1 2 3 4 5
    Religion 1 2 3 4 5

Politically oriented film   1   2   3   4   5
Politically oriented music   1   2   3   4   5
Political/social protest   1   2   3   4   5
Making a lot of money   1   2   3   4   5   *(F00–S01, F08–S10)*

How much confidence do you have in the following, where 1 = no confidence at all, 2 = some confidence, 3 = neutral, 4 = somewhat confident, and 5 = very confident?

US Congress   1   2   3   4   5
The president   1   2   3   4   5
American democracy   1   2   3   4   5
US military leaders   1   2   3   4   5
TV network media   1   2   3   4   5   *(F00–F02)*
Internet news media   1   2   3   4   5   *(F00–F02)*
The electoral process   1   2   3   4   5   *(F00–S01, F04, F08–S10)*
News media   1   2   3   4   5   *(F08–S10)*

How close do you feel to the following, where 1 = not close at all, 2 = not very close, 3 = neutral, 4 = close, and 5 = very close?

The nation   1   2   3   4   5
Your community   1   2   3   4   5
Your age group   1   2   3   4   5
Your religion   1   2   3   4   5
The world   1   2   3   4   5   *(F01–S05)*

How much attention do or did you pay to the following, where 1 = none, 2 = rarely, 3 = sometimes, 4 = a lot?

TV news   1   2   3   4
Internet news media   1   2   3   4
September 11th terrorist attacks   1   2   3   4   *(F01–S09)*
The war in Iraq   1   2   3   4   *(S03–S10)*
War in Afghanistan   1   2   3   4   *(S02–F02)*
The 2000 presidential election   1   2   3   4   *(F00–F03)*
The 2004 presidential election   1   2   3   4   *(S04–S07)*
The 2008 presidential election   1   2   3   4   *(F08–S10)*
The 2002 elections   1   2   3   4   *(F02–S04)*
The 2006 elections   1   2   3   4   *(F06–S07)*
Hurricane Katrina and aftermath   1   2   3   4   *(F05, F08)*
The Daily Show with Jon Stewart   1   2   3   4   *(S05–S10)*
The Colbert Report   1   2   3   4   *(F08–S10)*
MySpace/Facebook–type sites   1   2   3   4   *(F08–S10)*

Rate yourself on a scale where federal spending/involvement in the following areas should be 1 = greatly decreased, 2 = decreased, 3 = stay about the same, 4 = increased, and 5 = greatly increased.

    Defense spending   1   2   3   4   5

    Social welfare   1   2   3   4   5   *(F00–S01, F04–S10)*

    Public education   1   2   3   4   5   *(F00–S01, F04–S10)*

    Health care   1   2   3   4   5   *(F00–S01, F04–S10)*

    Environmental protection   1   2   3   4   5   *(F00–S01, F04–S10)*

Place yourself on the 1–5 scale, where 1 = strongly agree, 2 = agree, 3 = neutral, 4 = disagree, 5 = strongly disagree *(all asked F01–S10)*.

    Immigrants make America more open to new ideas and cultures.
       1   2   3   4   5

    The American flag fills me with pride.   1   2   3   4   5

    I would rather be a citizen of America than any other country.
       1   2   3   4   5

    There is nothing particularly wonderful about American culture.
       1   2   3   4   5

    To be truly American, you need to be born in America.   1   2   3   4   5

    The more the US influences countries, the better off these countries are.
       1   2   3   4   5

On a scale in which 1 = very negative, 3 = neutral, and 5 = very positive, what is your view of the following countries?

    Iran   1   2   3   4   5   *(F03–S10)*

    Great Britain   1   2   3   4   5   *(F03–S09)*

    Saudi Arabia   1   2   3   4   5   *(F03–S09)*

    Canada   1   2   3   4   5   *(F03–S07)*

    China   1   2   3   4   5   *(F08–S10)*

How much of the time do you think you can trust the government in Washington, DC, to do what is right?

    1 = never, 2 = some of the time, 3 = neutral/don't know, 4 = most of the time, 5 = just about always

How would you rate the current state of America's economy?

    1 = excellent, 2 = somewhat good, 3 = somewhat bad, 4 = very bad, 5 = don't know

In general, do you think that the country is heading in the right direction or wrong direction?

1 = very much the right direction, 2 = somewhat the right direction, 3 = neutral, 4 = somewhat the wrong direction, 5 = very much the wrong direction

Public officials/political leaders don't care much about what people like me think.
1 = strongly agree, 2 = agree, 3 = neutral, 4 = disagree, 5 = strongly disagree

Approximately how much time do you spend using the Internet per week?
1 = not at all, 2 = 1–3 hours, 3 = 4–8 hours, 4 = 9–14 hours, 5 = 15–19 hours, 6 = 20+ hours

Generally speaking, do you think of yourself as:
1 = Democrat, 2 = Democrat leaning Independent, 3 = Independent, 4 = Republican leaning Independent, 5 = Republican, 6 = other

Generally speaking, do you think of yourself as:
1 = very liberal, 2 = somewhat liberal, 3 = moderate, 4 = somewhat conservative, 5 = very conservative

Do you approve or disapprove of President Clinton's/Bush's/Obama's handling of his job as president?
1 = strongly approve, 2 = approve, 3 = neutral, 4 = disapprove, 5 = strongly disapprove

Do you plan to vote in the 2000/2004/2008 presidential election?
1 = definitely, 2 = maybe, 3 = no, 4 = won't be eligible

Did you vote in the 2000/2004/2008 presidential election?
1 = yes, 2 = no, 3 = wasn't eligible

If you voted in the 2000/2004/2008 presidential election, which candidate did you vote for?

Have you done any volunteer work for any organization, group, or community in the past twelve months? *(pre-surveys only)*
1 = a lot, 2 = some, 3 = very little, 4 = none

If any, approximately how many hours in an average month have you spent volunteering? *(pre-surveys only)*

Overall, what is your primary source of news and/or political information? *(F00–S02)*
    1 = television, 2 = radio, 3 = newspaper, 4 = newsmagazine, 5 = the Internet, 6 = other

How much concern should American leaders devote to potential future terrorist attacks on the US? *(S03–S09)*
    1 = the single most important concern, 2 = somewhat more important concern, 3 = should be more concerned about other issues such as the economy/education, 4 = much less concern

Do you support the (Bush administration's) decision to go to war in Iraq? *(S03–S10)*
    1 = completely support, 2 = somewhat support, 3 = did not really support, 4 = did not support at all

Do you support the current policy of maintaining significant numbers of American soldiers in Iraq? *(F03–S10)*
    1 = completely support, 2 = somewhat support, 3 = do not really support, 4 = do not support at all

The number of immigrants to the United States nowadays should be *(F01–S04)*:
    1 = reduced a lot, 2 = reduced a little, 3 = stay the same, 4 = increased a little, 5 = increased a lot

With regard to our government's policies, it is more important than ever to *(F03–S10)*:
    1 = completely support them without question, 2 = generally support them with less public debate, 3 = more extensively question them, 4 = allow for more public rejection of our government's policies

What are your views of anti-war protests in America against the war in Iraq? *(F03–S09)*
    1 = completely support the views of the protesters, 2 = support the right to protest but not the views, 3 = they should not be allowed to protest the war, 4 = don't know

Are you generally more optimistic or pessimistic about the future prospects for your generation? *(F00–S01, S09–S10)*
    1 = very optimistic, 2 = optimistic, 3 = mixed feelings, 4 = pessimistic, 5 = very pessimistic

My participation and/or expression can make an impact on the political/policy process *(F06–S10):*
 1 = agree, 2 = somewhat agree, 3 = neutral, 4 = somewhat disagree,
 5 = disagree

How informed do/did you feel to make a decision about the presidential candidates? *(F00–S01, F08–S10)*
 1 = not at all, 2 = slightly, 3 = pretty much, 4 = very much

Do you happen to know which party currently has control of the US House of Representatives?
 1 = Democrats, 2 = Republicans, 3 = not sure

How long is a US Senate term?
 1 = two years, 2 = four years, 3 = six years, 4 = life tenure

Whose responsibility is it to determine if a law is unconstitutional or not?
 1 = the president, 2 = Congress, 3 = the Supreme Court

Dennis Hastert/Nancy Pelosi is *(F01–S04, S07–S10):*
 1 = US Attorney General, 2 = Speaker of the House, 3 = Senate Majority Leader, 4 = US Senator from New York

The smallest Electoral College majority consists of how many electoral votes? *(F00–S03, F04–S05, F08–S10)*
 1 = 170   2 = 200   3 = 250   4 = 270   5 = 300

How many members are there in the US House of Representatives? *(F00–F01)*
 1 = 100   2 = 235   3 = 270   4 = 435   5 = 585

Do you know the last names of the Democratic and Republican vice-presidential candidates of the 2000/2004/2008 presidential election? Proper spelling not critical.
 _____ _____ Don't know

List the last names of the current US Senators from New York:
 _____ _____ Don't know

Whose responsibility is it to appoint federal judges and justices?
 _____ Don't know

What job or political office is now held by William Rehnquist? *(F00–F05)*
_____ Don't know

List the last name of the chief justice of the US Supreme Court: *(F08–S10)*
_____ Don't know

What job or political office is held by Colin Powell/Condoleezza Rice/Hillary Clinton? (*F01–S10*)
_____ Don't know

What job or political office is held by Donald Rumsfeld/Robert Gates? *(F01–S10)*
_____ Don't know

The last name of the primary suspect in the World Trade Center terrorist attack is *(F01–S10):*
_____ Don't know

The US has been at war with the former ruling group of Afghanistan, known as *(F01–S10):*
_____ Don't know

The first and/or last name of the former leader/dictator of Iraq is *(F02–S10):*
_____ Don't know

Name any two countries that share a border with Iraq *(S03–S10):*
_____ _____ Don't know

The last name of the current British prime minister is *(F03–S10):*
_____ Don't know

Are you a political science major?
1 = yes, 2 = considering PS major, 3 = PS minor, 4 = no

Your year in college:
1 = freshman, 2 = sophomore, 3 = junior, 4 = senior, 5 = other

Approximate overall GPA: _____

Gender: 1 = female, 2 = male

(The questions below were included in post-surveys only for students completing the US politics course.)

Rate the extent of the instructor's use of the following types, if any, of multimedia presentation to illustrate the course material, where 1 = never, 2 = rarely, 3 = sometimes, and 4 = a lot.

Computer-generated presentation (e.g., PowerPoint slides to outline lectures) 1   2   3   4

Computer-generated imagery (e.g., photos, graphs, illustrations) 1   2   3   4

Video imagery (e.g., TV news clips, movie clips) 1   2   3   4

On a 1–5 scale, where 1 = much less and 5 = much more, would you prefer less or more multimedia use of the type described above in your courses? 1   2   3   4   5

Appendix B
Teaching US Politics at SUNY Fredonia

On average, US politics course sections at SUNY Fredonia enroll 40–50 students, but the fall 2000, fall 2004, and fall 2008 terms each had one section with 100–120 students enrolled. With the exception of fall 2003 and spring 2004, three different instructors in each semester would distribute the student surveys to their course sections (see Appendix A). Overall, ten different political science instructors distributed surveys to their respective classes, totaling more than sixty different course sections of the US politics course at SUNY Fredonia, fall 2000 to spring 2010. Typically, each instructor teaches two different course sections of the US politics course when scheduled to teach it in any given semester, and these course sections were held back-to-back in the same classroom.

In a survey of the faculty syllabi over these years, there was remarkable similarity in course expectations, core textbooks, and exam requirements. Course textbooks utilized were the most updated editions of familiar US politics textbook titles, including: *The American Democracy* (Patterson), *American Government* (Wilson), *American Government* (Wilson and DiIulio), *American Government, Continuity and Change* (O'Connor and Sabato), *American Government and Politics Today* (Bardes et al.), *American Government: Political Development and Institutional Change* (Jilson), *The Challenge of Democracy* (Janda et al.), *Dynamics of Democracy* (Squire et al.), *The Logic of American Politics* (Kernell and Jacobson), *The New American Democracy* (Fiorina and Peterson), and *We the People: An Introduction to American Politics* (Ginsberg, Lowi, and Weir). Generally, the instructors remained with the most updated versions of these textbook titles for several years, if not the entire survey period.

Although each of these textbooks has a slightly different style, approach, and organization, the books covered the same basic topical areas in an introduction to US politics. In varying orders, titles, and combinations, chapter topics typically included: democracy, the Constitution, political parties, media, interest groups, Congress, presidency, bureaucracy, courts, civil liberties and civil rights, and public opinion. A couple of faculty utilized more extended textbook versions including public policy chapters, but most used textbook versions without the policy chapters. Thus there was nothing extraordinary in the core textbooks utilized, and I would argue that they were quite representative of the vast majority of textbooks utilized across the typical introductory US politics courses at the college level.

About half of the faculty just assigned the textbook as required reading, while the other half assigned supplemental course reading. Supplemental course readings included: *Perspectives on American Government: Readings in Political Development and Institutional Change* (Jilson and Robertson), *Points of View* (DiClerico and Hammock), and *Taking Sides: Clashing Views on Political Issues* (McKenna and Feingold), wherein an instructional objective of this assigned reading was to stimulate related discussion and debate concerning the course material. Other supplemental reading included more contemporary debates, concerns, and issues, including: *American Government in a Changing World: The Effects of September 11, 2011* (Peterson et al. 2002), *We've Got Issues: The Get Real, No B.S., Guilt Free Guide to What Really Matters* (Bagby 2000), *Culture War: The Myth of a Polarized America* (Fiorina 2006), *A Divider, Not a Uniter: George W. Bush and American Politics* (Jacobson 2007), and *Hardball* (Matthews 1999).

All of the courses had three exams testing knowledge of the core textbook material that made up the bulk of the course grade. A couple of faculty also utilized quizzes throughout the semester to test knowledge on the textbook reading. One faculty member regularly assigned homework in the book *American Government Using MicroCase* (Norrander and Corbett) in order to expose students to basic statistical understanding and analysis of US government and politics.

Most of the courses also assigned a brief writing assignment that asked students to discuss a particular debate, issue, and/or current affair and to relate their analysis to material within the course. And one faculty member did set up in-class student debates on related supplemental readings as part of several of the course sections. Thus, varied instructional techniques were utilized across the course sections to encourage student engagement, debate, and discussion concerning US government and politics.

Diverse methods were also utilized to incorporate current events into the course learning experience. For the supplemental reading assignment, three faculty members required students to read the *New York Times* or another major daily newspaper to stay abreast of major political news. Two instructors also assigned a newspaper clippings assignment, asking students to track a particular issue/debate in newspaper coverage over the semester. As our survey findings in Chapter 5 discuss in greater detail, about half of the faculty also extensively integrated TV news clips, film clips, and Internet media resources into the course to assimilate historical, recent, and current events and political processes. The course description in the syllabi would also occasionally tie the significance of recent events and processes, such as the 2000 recount and 9/11, to US government and politics. However, there were no course assignments that asked the US politics students to engage, beyond a perusal of media sources, outside of the classroom (i.e., service learning) as part of the course requirements.

All students across the courses were asked to consider how the US politics course material related at some level to the contemporary political and policy debate, while some integrated contemporary events more extensively than others. However, we have no measure for this difference other than our students' described attentiveness to particular events, measuring students' attentiveness both outside and within the classroom. It was not meant to separate out individual course impact, but rather to focus on the influence of attentiveness to events overall no matter the source of that attention. Indeed, I had as much interest in the survey on incoming attentiveness to events as in the survey on outgoing attentiveness, and the surveys typically demonstrated little change in our students' attentiveness unless critical elements of the event and related process themselves changed, for example, the vote in a presidential election. Thus, I would not conclude that the course itself generated event salience for our students but that the findings demonstrate that more effectively integrating salient events into the course learning experience should only strengthen related knowledge, interest, and engagement, based on the survey results and analysis.

Despite instructional differences, there are key characteristics that we can expect and observe when Millennial-age students enter an introduction to US politics course. Within that dynamic there are a number of research objectives: to identify the relationships between political attentiveness, interest, policy preferences, knowledge, and engagement in light of salient political events and the US politics learning experience. For example, it was not the purpose of the study to assess the instructional impact of varied assignments, but to assess how attentiveness to salient events connects with critical features of political knowledge, interest, and engagement. I would argue that any technique that draws student attentiveness to political issues of concern, thus increasing interest and perceived relevance, is preferable, and there are findings to demonstrate how and why throughout this book.

The only significant instructional differences we actively measured through the student survey had to do with the integration (or not) of multimedia sources into the course. I anticipate media sources to be a significant source of political information that Millennials receive and will continue to receive. And I argue that certain media sources and use relate to political attentiveness that connects to interest and learning. However, we did not survey attentiveness to daily newspapers, as students were required to read a daily newspaper in several course sections. The objective was to measure what our students themselves determined to be salient based on entering surveys and how that was reinforced with learning and related attentiveness during the course. It was not to measure "constructed" salience through assigned readings, but how particular media sources identified with higher levels of entering student use related to other variables of interest at the beginning and end of a given term.

References

Almond, Gabriel. 1960. *The American People and Foreign Policy.* New York: Harcourt.

Almond, Gabriel, and Sidney Verba. 1963. *The Civic Culture.* Boston: Little, Brown.

Althaus, Scott. 1998. "Information Effects in Collective Preferences." *American Political Science Review* 92: 545–558.

Alvarez, R. Michael. 1997. *Information and Elections.* Ann Arbor: University of Michigan Press.

Anderson, David. 2004. *Youth 04: Young Voters, the Internet, and Political Power.* New York: W. W. Norton.

Ball, William. 2005. "From Community Engagement to Political Engagement." *PS: Political Science and Politics* 38: 287–291.

Bartels, Larry. 1996. "Uninformed Votes: Information Effects in Presidential Elections." *American Journal of Political Science* 40: 194–230.

Bauerlein, Mark. 2008. *The Dumbest Generation: How the Digital Age Stupefies Young Americans and Jeopardizes Our Future.* New York: Jeremy P. Tarcher/Penguin.

Baum, Matthew. 2002. "Sex, Lies, and War: How Soft News Brings Foreign Policy to the Inattentive Public." *American Political Science Review* 96: 91–109.

———. 2003. *Soft News Goes to War: Public Opinion and American Foreign Policy in the New Media Age.* Princeton: Princeton University Press.

Baumgartner, Jody, and Jonathan Morris. 2008. "Jon Stewart Comes to Class: The Learning Effects of *America* (*The Book*) in Introduction to American Government Courses." *Journal of Political Science Education* 4: 169–186.

Beaumont, Elizabeth, Anne Colby, Thomas Ehrlich, and Judith Torney-Purta. 2006. "Promoting Political Competence and Engagement in College Students: An Empirical Study." *Journal of Political Science Education* 2: 249–270.

Bennett, Stephen. 1994. "The Persian Gulf War's Impact on Americans' Political Information." *Political Behavior* 16: 179–201.

———. 1997. "Why Young Americans Hate Politics and What We Should Do About It." *PS: Political Science and Politics* 30: 47–52.

Bennett, Stephen, and Eric Rademacher. 1997. "The Age of Indifference Revisited: Patterns of Political Interest, Media Exposure, and Knowledge Among Generation X." In *After the Boom: The Politics of Generation X*. Edited by Stephen Craig and Stephen Bennett. Lanham, MD: Rowman and Littlefield, 21–42.

Bennett, W. Lance, ed. 2007a. *Civic Life Online: Learning How Digital Media Can Engage Youth*. Cambridge: MIT Press.

———. 2007b. *News: The Politics of Illusion*. 7th ed. New York: Longman.

Bennett, W. Lance, and Jarol Manheim. 1993. "Taking the Public by Storm: Information Cueing and Democratic Process in Gulf Conflict." *Political Communication* 10: 331–351.

Berelson, Bernard, Paul Lazarfeld, and William McPhee. 1954. *Voting*. New York: Free Press.

Berent, Matthew, and Jon Krosnick. 1995. "The Relation Between Political Attitude Importance and Knowledge Organization." In *Political Judgment: Structure and Process*. Edited by Kathleen McGraw and Milton Lodge. Ann Arbor: University of Michigan Press, 91–110.

Bernstein, Jeffrey. 2008. "Cultivating Civic Competence: Simulations and Skill Building in an Introductory Government Class." *Journal of Political Science Education* 1: 1–20.

Bixby, Janet, and Judith Pace, eds. 2008. *Educating Democratic Citizens in Troubled Times*. Albany: SUNY Press.

Boettcher, William, and Michael Cobb. 2006. "Echoes of Vietnam? Casualty Framing and Public Perceptions of Success and Failure in Iraq." *Journal of Conflict Resolution* 50: 831–854.

Boyte, Harry. 2005. *Everyday Politics: Reconnecting Citizens and Public Life*. Philadelphia: University of Pennsylvania Press.

Brewer, Paul, Kimberly Gross, Sean Aday, and Lars Willnat. 2004. "International Trust and Public Opinion About World Affairs." *American Journal of Political Science* 48: 93–109.

Bringle, Robert, Richard Games, and Edward Malloy, eds. 1999. *Colleges and Universities as Citizens*. Boston: Allyn and Bacon.

Brody, Richard. 1991. *Assessing the President: The Media, Elite Opinion, and Public Support.* Stanford: Stanford University Press.

Brokaw, Tom. 1998. *The Greatest Generation.* New York: Random House.

Buckingham, David, ed. 2007. *Youth, Identity, and Digital Media.* Cambridge: MIT Press.

Campbell, David. 2006. *Why We Vote: How Schools and Communities Shape Our Civic Life.* Princeton: Princeton University Press.

Cao, Xiaoxia. 2008. "Political Comedy Shows and Knowledge About Primary Campaigns: The Moderating Effects of Age and Education." *Mass Communication and Society* 11: 43–61.

Caputo, David. 2005. "A Campus View: Civic Engagement and the Higher Education Community." *National Civic Review* 94: 3–9.

Cassino, Dan, and Yasemin Besen-Cassino. 2009. *Consuming Politics: Jon Stewart, Branding, and the Youth Vote in America.* Madison, NJ: Farleigh Dickinson Press.

CIRCLE (Center for Information and Research on Civic Learning and Engagement). 2002. *The Civic and Political Health of the Nation: National Youth Survey of Civic Engagement.* College Park: University of Maryland.

————. 2006. "The Civic and Political Health of the Nation: National Youth Survey of Civic Engagement." October. College Park: University of Maryland.

————. 2007a. "Millennials Talk Politics: A Study of College Student Political Engagement." College Park: University of Maryland.

————. 2007b. "Dissonant Discourse Turning Off College Students to Formal Politics." November. College Park: University of Maryland.

————. 2008. "Young Voters in the 2008 Presidential Election." December 18. College Park: University of Maryland.

Colby, Anne, Thomas Ehrlich, Elizabeth Beaumont, and Jason Stephens. 2003. *Educating Citizens: Preparing America's Undergraduates for Lives of Moral and Civic Responsibility.* San Francisco: Jossey-Bass.

————. 2007. *Educating for Democracy: Preparing Undergraduates for Responsible Political Engagement.* San Francisco: Jossey-Bass.

Conover, Pamela, and Virgina Sapiro. 1993. "Gender, Feminist Consciousness and War." *American Journal of Political Science* 37: 1079–1099.

Converse, Philip. 1964. "The Nature of Belief Systems in Mass Publics." In *Ideology and Discontent.* Edited by D. Apter. New York: Free Press, 206–261.

Corbett, Michael. 1991. *American Public Opinion.* New York: Longman.

Craig, Stephen, and Stephen Bennett, eds. 1997. *After the Boom: The Politics of Generation X.* Lanham, MD: Rowman and Littlefield.

Dalgren, Peter, ed. 2008. *Young Citizens and New Media: Learning and Civic Engagement.* New York: Routledge.

Dalton, Russell. 2008. *The Good Citizen: How a Younger Generation Is Reshaping American Politics.* Washington, DC: CQ Press.

Dalton, Russell, Paul Beck, and Robert Huckfeldt. 1998. "Partisan Cues and the Media: Information Flows in the 1992 Presidential Election." *American Political Science Review* 92: 111–126.

Delli Carpini, Michael. 1989. "Generations and Sociopolitical Change." In *Political Learning in Adulthood.* Edited by Roberta Sigel. Chicago: University of Chicago Press.

———. 2000. "Gen.com: Youth, Civic Engagement, and the New Information Environment." *Political Communication* 17: 341–349.

Delli Carpini, Michael, and Scott Keeter. 1991. "Stability and Change in the US Public's Knowledge of Politics." *Public Opinion Quarterly* 55: 583–612.

———. 1996. *What Americans Know About Politics and Why It Matters.* New Haven: Yale University Press.

Dewey, John. *Democracy and Education.* 1916. New York: The Macmillan Company.

Dolan, Kathleen, and Thomas Holbrook. 2001. "Knowledge Versus Caring: The Role of Affect and Cognition in Political Perceptions." *Political Psychology* 22: 27–44.

Downs, Anthony. 1957. *An Economic Theory of Democracy.* New York: Harper.

Duncan, Lauren. 2005. "Personal Political Salience as a Self-Schema: Consequences for Political Information Processing." *Political Psychology* 26: 965–976.

Ehrlich, Thomas, ed. 1999. *Civic Responsibility and Higher Education.* Phoenix, AZ: Oryx Press.

Erikson, Robert, and Kent Tedin. 1995. *American Public Opinion.* 5th ed. Boston: Allyn and Bacon.

———. 2007. *American Public Opinion.* 7th ed. New York: Longman.

Gaines, Brian J., James H. Kuklinski, Paul J. Quirk, Buddy Peyton, and Jay Verkuilen. 2007. "Same Facts, Different Interpretations: Partisan Motivation and Opinion on Iraq." *Journal of Politics* 69: 957–974.

Galston, William. 2001. "Political Knowledge, Political Engagement, and Civic Education." *Annual Review of Political Science* 4: 217–234.

———. 2004. "Civic Education and Political Participation." *PS: Political Science and Politics* 37: 263–266.

———. 2007. "Civic Knowledge, Civic Education, and Civic Engagement:

A Summary of Recent Research." *International Journal of Public Administration* 30: 623–642.

Gerber, Alan, Donald Green, and Ron Shachar. 2003. "Voting May Be Habit Forming: Evidence from a Randomized Field Experiment." *American Journal of Political Science* 47: 540–550.

Gershkoff, Amy. 2005. "Multiple Methods, More Success: How to Help Students of All Learning Styles Succeed in Quantitative Political Analysis Courses." *PS: Political Science and Politics* 30: 299–304.

Gilens, Martin. 2001. "Political Ignorance and Collective Policy Preferences." *American Political Science Review* 95: 379–396.

Gimpel, James, J. Celeste Lay, and Jason Schuknecht. 2003. *Cultivating Democracy: Civic Environments and Political Socialization in America.* Washington, DC: Brookings Institution Press.

Gordiner, Jeff. 2008. *X Saves the World: How Generation X Got the Shaft but Can Still Keep Everything from Sucking.* New York: Viking.

Graber, Doris. 1988. *Processing the News: How People Tame the Information Tide.* New York: Longman.

———. 2001. *Processing Politics: Learning from Television in the Internet Age.* Chicago: University of Chicago Press.

Green, Donald, and Alan Gerber. 2004. *Get Out the Vote: How to Increase Voter Turnout.* Washington, DC: Brookings Institution Press.

Greenberg, Eric, and Karl Weber. 2008. *Generation We: How Millennial Youth Are Taking Over America and Changing Our World Forever.* Emeryville, CA: Pachatusan.

Groth, Miles. 2007. "Smart Classrooms Cannot Replace Smart Professors." The NEA Higher Education Journal, *Thought and Action* 23: 39–45.

Hamann, Kerstin, and Bruce Wilson. 2002. "Evaluating the Impact of Internet Teaching: Preliminary Evidence from American National Government Classes." *PS: Political Science and Politics* 35: 61–66.

Harvard Institute of Politics. 2000. "Attitudes Toward Politics and Public Service: A National Survey of College Undergraduates." *Executive Summary.* April. Cambridge, MA: Harvard University.

———. 2002. "A National Survey of College Undergraduates." *Executive Summary.* October. Cambridge, MA: Harvard University.

———. 2003. "U.S. College Students: Politically Untapped." *Executive Summary.* October. Cambridge, MA: Harvard University.

———. 2004. "The Political Awakening of a Generation." *Executive Summary.* October. Cambridge, MA: Harvard University.

———. 2005. "The Global Generation." *Executive Summary.* April. Cambridge, MA: Harvard University.

———. 2006. "Youth Survey on Politics and Public Service." *Executive Summary*. April. Cambridge, MA: Harvard University.

———. 2007. "Youth Survey on Politics and Public Service." *Executive Summary*. April. Cambridge, MA: Harvard University.

———. 2008. "Youth Survey on Politics and Public Service." *Executive Summary*. October. Cambridge, MA: Harvard University.

———. 2010. "Youth Survey on Politics and Public Service." *Executive Summary*. April. Cambridge, MA: Harvard University.

Hedges, Chris. 1999. "35% of High School Seniors Fail National Civics Test." *New York Times*, November 12, Sec. 1, p. 17.

HERI (Higher Education Research Institute). 2004. "Political Interest on the Rebound Among the Nation's Freshmen." *The American Freshman: National Norms for Fall 2003*. Los Angeles: HERI.

———. 2005a. *The American Freshman: National Norms for 2005*. Los Angeles: HERI.

———. 2005b. *The College Student Survey*. Los Angeles: HERI.

———. 2006. *The American Freshman: National Norms for 2006*. Los Angeles: HERI.

———. 2007. "More College Freshmen Show Interest in Politics." *The American Freshman: National Norms for Fall 2006*. Los Angeles: HERI.

———. 2008. *The American Freshman: National Norms for 2008*. Los Angeles: HERI.

———. 2009. *The American Freshman: National Norms for 2009*. Los Angeles: HERI.

Hess, Diane. 2009. "Principles That Promote Discussion of Controversial Political Issues in the Curriculum." In *Engaging Young People in Civic Life*. Edited by James Youniss and Peter Levine. Nashville: Vanderbilt University Press, 59–77.

Hetherington, Mark. 1996. "The Political Relevance of Political Trust." *American Political Science Review* 92: 791–808.

———. 2005. *Why Trust Matters: Political Trust and the Demise of American Liberalism*. Princeton: Princeton University Press.

Hetherington, Mark, and Suzanne Globetti. 2002. "Political Trust and Racial Policy Preferences." *American Journal of Political Science* 46: 253–276.

Hollander, Barry. 2005. "Late-Night Learning: Do Entertainment Programs Increase Political Campaign Knowledge for Young Viewers?" *Journal of Broadcasting & Electronic Media* 49: 402–415.

Howard, Philip. 2006. *New Media Campaigns and the Managed Citizen*. New York: Cambridge University Press.

Howe, Neil, and William Strauss. 2000. *Millennials Rising: The Next Great Generation.* New York: Vintage Books.

———. 2003. *Millennials Go to College: Strategies for a New Generation on Campus.* Washington, DC: American Association of Collegiate Registrars.

Huddy, Leonie, Stanley Feldman, Charles Taber, and Gallya Lahav. 2005. "Threat, Anxiety, and Support of Antiterrorism Policies." *American Journal of Political Science* 49: 593–608.

Huddy, Leonie, and Nadia Khatib. 2007. "American Patriotism, National Identity, and Political Involvement." *American Journal of Political Science* 51: 63–77.

Huerta, Juan Carlos, and Joseph Jozwiak. 2008. "Developing Civic Engagement in General Education Political Science." *Journal of Political Science Education* 1: 42–60.

Hunter, Susan, and Richard Brisbin. 2000. "The Impact of Service Learning on Democratic and Civic Values." *PS: Political Science and Politics* 33: 623–626.

Hurwitz, Jon, and Mark Peffley. 1990. "Public Images of the Soviet Union: The Impact on Foreign Policy Attitudes." *Journal of Politics* 52: 523–528.

ISI (Intercollegiate Studies Institute). 2006. *The Coming Crisis in Citizenship: Higher Education's Failure to Teach America's History and Institutions.* Wilmington: ISI.

Iyengar, Shanto. 1990. "Shortcuts to Political Knowledge: Selective Attention and Accessibility Bias." In *Information and Democratic Processes.* Edited by John Ferejohn and James Kuklinski. Urbana: University of Illinois Press.

Iyengar, Shanto, and Donald Kinder. 1987. *News That Matters.* Chicago: University of Chicago Press.

Jacoby, Barbara, and associates. 2009. *Civic Engagement in Higher Education: Concepts and Practices.* San Francisco: Jossey-Bass.

Jacoby, Barbara, and Elizabeth Hollander. 2009. "Securing the Future of Civic Engagement in Higher Education." In *Civic Engagement in Higher Education.* Edited by Barbara Jacoby and associates. San Francisco: Jossey-Bass, 227–248.

Jackson, Maggie. 2008. *Distracted: The Erosion of Attention and the Coming Dark Age.* Amherst, NY: Prometheus Books.

Janda, Kenneth. 1992. "Multimedia in Political Science: Sobering Lessons from a Teaching Experiment." *Journal of Educational Multimedia and Hypermedia* 1: 341–354.

Jennings, M. Kent. 1992. "Ideological Thinking Among Mass Publics and Political Elites." *Public Opinion Quarterly* 56: 419–441.

————.1993. "Education and Political Development Among Young Adults." *Politics and the Individual* 3: 1–23.

————. 1996. "Political Knowledge over Time and Across Generations." *Public Opinion Quarterly* 60: 228–252.

Jennings, M. Kent, and Richard Niemi. 1974. *The Political Character of Adolescence*. Princeton: Princeton University Press.

————. 1981. *Generations and Politics*. Princeton: Princeton University Press.

Jennings, M. Kent, and Laura Stoker. 2004. "Social Trust and Civic Engagement Across Time and Generations." *Acta Politica* 39: 342–379.

Jerit, Jennifer, Jason Barabas, and Toby Bolsen. 2006. "Citizens, Knowledge, and the Information Environment." *American Journal of Political Science* 50: 266–282.

Josyln, Mark. 2003. "The Determinants and Consequences of Recall Error About Gulf War Preferences." *American Journal of Political Science* 47: 440–452.

Kirby, Emily, and Kei Kawashima-Ginsberg. 2009. *The Youth Vote in 2008*. August. College Park, MD: CIRCLE.

Kosterman, Rick, and Seymour Feshbach. 1989. "Toward a Measure of Patriotic and Nationalistic Attitudes." *Political Psychology* 10: 257–274.

Krosnick, Jon. 1989. "Attitude Importance and Attitude Accessibility." *Personality and Social Psychology Bulletin* 15: 297–308.

Kuklinski, James, ed. 2001. *Citizens and Politics: Perspectives from Political Psychology*. Cambridge: Cambridge University Press.

Kuklinski, James, Paul J. Quirk, Jennifer Jerit, and Robert F. Rich. 2001. "The Political Environment and Citizen Competence." *American Journal of Political Science* 45: 410–424.

Kuklinski, James H., Paul J. Quirk, Jennifer Jerit, David Schwieder, and Robert F. Rich. 2000. "Misinformation and the Currency of Citizenship." *Journal of Politics* 62: 791–816.

Lakoff, George. 2008. *The Political Mind: Why You Can't Understand 21st Century American Politics with an 18th Century Brain*. New York: Penguin Group.

Lancaster, Lynne, and David Stillman. 2002. *When Generations Collide*. New York: HarperCollins.

Lavine, Howard, Milton Lodge, and Kate Freitas. 2005. "Threat, Authoritarianism, and Selective Exposure to Information." *Political Psychology* 26: 219–244.

Lehrer, Jonah. 2009. *How We Decide*. New York: Houghton Mifflin.

Levine, Peter. 2007a. *The Future of Democracy: Developing the Next Generation of American Citizens*. Boston: Tufts University Press.

————. 2007b. "A Public Voice for Youth: The Audience Problem in Digital Media and Civic Education." In *Civic Life Online: Learning How Digital Media Can Engage Youth*. Edited by W. Lance Bennett. Cambridge: MIT Press, 119–138.

Levine, Peter, and Mark Lopez. 2002. "Youth Voter Turnout Has Declined by Any Measure." Medford, MA: Center for Information and Research on Civic Learning and Engagement, Tufts University.

Lewis, Justin. 2001. *Constructing Public Opinion: How Political Elites Do What They Like and Why We Seem to Go Along with It*. New York: Columbia University Press.

Li, Qiong, and Marilynn Brewer. 2004. "What Does It Mean to Be an American? Patriotism, Nationalism, and American Identity After 9/11." *Political Psychology* 25(5): 727–739.

Lichter, Robert. 2004. "TV News Turned Sour on Bush After Iraq War Ended." *Center for Media and Public Affairs*. December 17. Washington, DC.

Loader, Brian, ed. 2007. *Young Citizens in the Digital Age: Political Engagement, Young People and New Media*. London: Routledge.

Loeb, Paul. 1994. *Generation at the Crossroads: Apathy and Action on the American Campus*. New Brunswick: Rutgers University Press.

Longo, Nicholas. 2007. *Why Community Matters: Connecting Education with Civic Life*. Albany: SUNY Press.

Longo, Nicholas, and Marguerite Shaffer. 2009. "Leadership Education and the Revitalization of Public Life." In *Civic Education in Higher Education*. Edited by Barbara Jacoby and Associates. San Francisco: Jossey-Bass, 154–173.

Lopez, Mark, and Abby Kiesa. 2009. "What We Know About Civic Engagement Among College Students." In *Civic Education in Higher Education*. Edited by Barbara Jacoby and Associates. San Francisco: Jossey-Bass, 31–48.

Lopez, Mark, and Brent Elrod. 2006. *College Attendance and Civic Engagement Among 18 to 25 Year Olds*. October. College Park, MD: CIRCLE.

Lopez, Mark, and Emily Kirby. 2007. *US Civics Instruction: Content and Teaching Strategies*. August. College Park, MD: CIRCLE.

Lopez, Mark, Peter Levine, Kenneth Dautrich, and David Yalof. 2007. *Schools, Education and the Future of the First Amendment*. College Park, MD: CIRCLE.

Luna, Carl, and Joe McKenzie. 1997. "Beyond the Chalkboard: Multimedia Sources for Instruction in Political Science." *PS: Political Science and Politics* 30: 60–68.

Lupia, Arthur, and Matthew McCubbins. 1998. *The Democratic Dilemma: Can Citizens Learn What They Need to Know*. New York: Cambridge University Press.

Lupia, Arthur, Matthew McCubbins, and Samuel Popkin, eds. 2000. *Elements of Reason: Cognition, Choice, and the Bounds of Rationality*. Cambridge: Cambridge University Press.

Lutkus, Anthony, et al. 1999. *NAEP 1998 Civics Report Card for the Nation*. Washington, DC: National Center for Education Statistics.

Macedo, Stephen, et al. 2005. *Democracy at Risk: Toward a Political Science of Citizenship*. Washington, DC: Brookings Institution Press.

Mann, Sheilah. 1999. "What the Survey of American Freshmen Tells Us About Their Interest in Politics and Political Science." *PS: Political Science and Politics* 32: 263–268.

Mannheim, Karl. 1952. *The Problem of Generations*. London: Routledge.

Marcus, George, and Michael MacKuen. 1993. "Anxiety, Enthusiasm, and the Vote: The Emotional Underpinnings of Learning and Involvement During Presidential Campaigns." *American Political Science Review* 87: 672–685.

Marcus, George, W. Russell Neuman, and Michael MacKuen. 2000. *Affective Intelligence and Political Judgment*. Chicago: University of Chicago Press.

Mattson, Kevin. 2003. *Engaging Youth: Combating the Apathy of Young Americans Toward Politics*. New York: Century Foundation Press.

Mayer, R. E. 2001. *Multimedia Learning*. New York: Cambridge University Press.

Meredith, Geoffrey, and Charles Shewe. 1994. "The Power of Cohorts." *American Demographics* 16: 22–31.

Mettler, Suzanne. 2005. *Soldiers to Citizens: The G.I. Bill and the Making of the Greatest Generation*. New York: Oxford University Press.

Milner, Henry. 2002. *Civic Literacy: How Informed Citizens make Democracy Work*. Hanover, NH: University Press of New England.

Mindich, David. 2005. *Tuned Out: Why Americans Under 40 Don't Follow the News*. Oxford: Oxford University Press.

Mondak, Jeffery. 1993. "Source Cues and Policy Approval." *American Journal of Political Science* 37: 186–212.

———. 2001. "Developing Valid Knowledge Scales." *American Journal of Political Science* 45: 224–238.

Mondak, Jeffery, and Belinda Davis. 2001. "Asked and Answered: Knowledge Levels When We Won't Take 'Don't Know' for an Answer." *Political Behavior* 23: 199–224.

Monitoring the Future. 2005. *A Continuing Study of American Youth*. February. Ann Arbor: University of Michigan, Institute for Social Research.

Montgomery, Kathryn. 2007. *Generation Digital: Politics, Commerce, and Childhood in the Age of the Internet*. Cambridge: MIT Press.

Moskalenko, Sophia, Clark McCauley, and Paul Rozin. 2006. "Group Identification Under Conditions of Threat: College Students' Attachment to Country, Family, Ethnicity, Religion, and University Before and After September 11, 2001." *Political Psychology* 27: 77–97.

Mutz, Diana, and Byron Reeves. 2005. "The New Videomalaise: Effects of Televised Incivility on Political Trust." *American Political Science Review* 99: 1–15.

NAEP (National Assessment of Educational Progress). 1998. *Nation's Report Card: Civics 1998.* Washington, DC: National Center for Education Statistics.

———. 2006. *Nation's Report Card: Civics 2006.* Washington, DC: National Center for Education Statistics.

———. 2010. *Nation's Report Card: Civics 2010.* Washington, DC: National Center for Education Statistics.

NASS (National Association of Secretaries of State). 1999. "The New Millennium Generation: A Survey of Youth Attitudes Nationwide." *National Millennium Project.* Washington, DC: National Association of Secretaries of State.

National Annenberg Election Study. 2000. Philadelphia: The Annenberg Public Policy Center of the University of Pennsylvania.

Neuman, W. Russell, Marion Just, and Ann Crigler. 1992. *Common Knowledge: News and the Construction of Political Meaning.* Chicago: University of Chicago Press.

Neuman, W. Russell, George E. Marcus, Michael MacKuen, and Ann N. Crigler, eds. 2007. *The Affect Effect: Dynamics of Emotion in Political Thinking and Behavior.* Chicago: University of Chicago Press.

Nie, Norman, and D. Sunshine Hillygus. 2001. "Education and Democratic Citizenship." In *Making Good Citizens: Education and Civic Society.* Edited by Diane Ravitch and Joseph Viteritti. New Haven: Yale University Press, 30–57.

Nie, Norman, Jane Junn, and Kenneth Stehlik-Barry. 1996. *Education and Democratic Citizenship in America.* Chicago: University of Chicago Press.

Niemi, Richard, Mary Hepburn, and Chris Chapman. 2000. "Community Service by High School Students: A Cure for Civic Ills?" *Political Behavior* 22: 45–69.

Niemi, Richard, and Jane Junn. 1998. *Civic Education: What Makes Students Learn.* New Haven: Yale University Press.

Pagano, Sabrina, and Yuen Huo. 2007. "The Role of Moral Emotions in Predicting Support for Political Actions in Post-War Iraq." *Political Psychology* 28: 227–255.

Page, Benjamin, and Robert Shapiro. 1992. *The Rational Public.* Chicago: University of Chicago Press.

Patterson, Thomas. 2002. *The Vanishing Voter: Public Involvement in an Age of Uncertainty.* New York: Knopf.

Patterson, Thomas, and Robert McClure. 1976. *The Unseeing Eye: The Myth of Television Power in National Elections.* New York: Putnam.

Pew Research Center for People and the Press. 2000. "The Tough Job of Communicating with Voters." February 5. Washington, DC.

————. 2000. "Campaign 2000 Highly Rated." November 16. Washington, DC.

————. 2001. "Terrorism Transforms News Interest." December 18. Washington, DC.

————. 2004. "Cable and Internet Loom in Fragmented Political News Universe." January 11. Washington, DC.

————. 2004. "Public Support for War Resilient." June 17. Washington, DC.

————. 2004. "Iraq Support Steady in Face of Higher Casualties." September 17. Washington, DC.

————. 2005. "More Say Iraq War Hurts Fight Against Terrorism." July 21. Washington, DC.

————. 2005. "Public Unmoved by Washington's Rhetoric on Iraq." December 14. Washington, DC.

————. 2006. "Iran a Growing Danger." February 6. Washington, DC.

————. 2007. "A Portrait of Generation Next: How Young People View Their Lives, Futures, and Politics." January 9. Washington, DC.

————. 2007. "Public Knowledge Little Changed by News and Information Revolutions: What Americans Know, 1989–2007." April 15. Washington, DC.

————. 2010. "Millennials. Confident. Connected. Open to Change." February 24. Washington, DC.

Pharr, Susan, Robert Putnam, and Russell Dalton. 2000. "A Quarter Century of Declining Confidence." *Journal of Democracy* 11: 5–25.

Plutzer, Eric. 2002. "Becoming a Habitual Voter: Inertia, Resources, and Growing in Young Adulthood." *American Political Science Review* 96: 41–56.

Pollock, Philip, and Bruce Wilson. 2002. "Evaluating the Impact of Internet Teaching: Preliminary Evidence for American National Government Classes." *PS: Political Science and Politics* 35: 61–66.

Popkin, Samuel. 1991. *The Reasoning Voter: Communication and Persuasion in Presidential Campaigns.* Chicago: University of Chicago Press.

Popkin, Samuel, and Michael Dimock. 1999. "Political Knowledge and Citizen Competence." In *Citizen Competence and Democratic Institutions.*

Edited by Stephen Elkin and Karol Soltan. University Park: Pennsylvania State University Press, 117–146.

Portney, Kent, and Lisa O'Leary. 2007. *National Survey of Civic and Political Engagement of Young People*. Medford, MA: Tufts University.

Powlick, Philip, and Andrew Katz. 1998. "Defining the American Public Opinion/Foreign Policy Nexus." *Mershon International Studies Review* 42: 29–61.

Price, Vincent, and John Zaller. 1993. "Who Gets the News? Alternative Measures of News Reception and Their Implications for Research." *Public Opinion Quarterly* 57: 133–164.

Prior, Markus. 2002. "Political Knowledge After September 11." *PS: Political Science and Politics* 3: 523–530.

———. 2005. "News v. Entertainment: How Increasing Media Choice Widens Gaps in Political Knowledge and Turnout." *American Journal of Political Science* 49: 594–609.

Prior, Markus, and Arthur Lupia. 2008. "Money, Time, and Political Knowledge: Distinguishing Quick Recall and Political Learning Skills." *American Journal of Political Science* 52: 169–183.

Putnam, Robert. 2000. *Bowling Alone: The Collapse and Revival of American Community*. New York: Simon and Schuster.

Rahn, Wendy, and Thomas Rudolph. 2001. "National Identities and the Future of Democracy." In *Mediated Politics: Communication in the Future of Democracy*. Edited by W. Lance Bennett and Robert Entman. Cambridge: Cambridge University Press.

Rahn, Wendy, and John Transue. 1998. "Social Trust and Value Change: The Decline of Social Capital in American Youth, 1976–1995." *Political Psychology* 19: 545–565.

Rankin, David. 2001. "Identities, Interests, and Imports." *Political Behavior* 23: 351–376.

Ravitch, Diane, and Joseph Viteritti, eds. 2001. *Making Good Citizens*. New Haven: Yale University Press.

Redlawsk, David, ed. 2006. *Feeling Politics: Emotion in Political Information Processing*. New York: Palgrave Macmillan.

Reeher, Grant, and Joseph Cammarano, eds. 1997. *Education for Citizenship: Ideas and Innovation in Political Learning*. Lanham, MD: Rowman and Littlefield.

Renshon, Stanley. 2005. *The 50% American: Immigration and National Identity in an Age of Terror*. Washington, DC: Georgetown University Press.

Robinson, John, Philip Shaver, and Lawrence Wrightsman, eds. 1999. *The Measure of Political Attitudes*. New York: Academic Press.

Saenz, V., S. Hurtado, N. Denson, A. Locks, and L. Oseguera. 2004. *Trends in Political Attitudes and Voting Behavior Among College Freshmen and Early Career College Graduates.* Los Angeles: Higher Education Research Institute.

Sander, Thomas, and Robert Putnam. 2010. "Still Bowling Alone? The Post-9/11 Split." *Journal of Democracy* 21: 9–16.

Schatz, Robert, Ervin Staub, and Howard Lavine. 1999. "On the Varieties of National Attachment: Blind Versus Constructive Patriotism." *Political Psychology* 20: 151–174.

Schudson, Michael. 1998. *The Good Citizen: A History of American Civil Life.* Cambridge: Harvard University Press.

Sears, David. 2001. "The Role of Affect in Symbolic Politics." In *Citizens and Politics: Perspectives from Political Psychology.* Edited by James Kuklinski. Cambridge: Cambridge University Press, 1–16.

Sears, David, and Sheri Levy. 2003. "Childhood and Adult Political Development." In *Oxford Handbook of Political Psychology.* Edited by David Sears, Leonie Huddy, and Robert Jervis. Oxford: Oxford University Press, 62–108.

Shea, Daniel, and John Green, eds. 2007. *Fountain of Youth: Strategies and Tactics for Mobilizing America's Young Voters.* Lanham, MD: Rowman and Littlefield.

Shenkman, Rick. 2008. *Just How Stupid Are We? Facing the Truth About the American Voter.* New York: Basic Books.

Sidanius, Jim, Seymour Feshbach, Shauna Levin, and Felicia Pratto. 1997. "The Interface Between Ethnic and National Attachment." *Public Opinion Quarterly* 61: 102–133.

Skocpol, Theda. 2002. "Will 9/11 and the War on Terror Revitalize American Civic Democracy?" *PS: Political Science and Politics* 35: 537–540.

Skocpol, Theda, and Morris Fiorina, eds. 1999. *Civic Engagement in American Democracy.* Washington, DC: Brookings Institution Press.

Small, Deborah, Jenn Lerner, and Baruch Fischhoff. 2006. "Emotional Priming and Spontaneous Attributions for Terrorism: Americans' Reactions in a National Field Experiment." *Political Psychology* 27: 289–298.

Smith, Stephen M., and Paul C. Woody. 2000. "Interactive Effect of Multimedia Instruction and Learning Styles." *Teaching of Psychology* 27: 220–223.

Sniderman, Paul, Richard Brody, and Philip Tetlock. 1991. *Reasoning and Choice: Explorations in Political Psychology.* New York: Cambridge University Press.

Somin, Ilya. 2006. "Knowledge About Ignorance: New Directions in the Study of Political Information." *Critical Review* 18: 255–278.

Stelter, Brian. 2008. "Finding Political News Online, the Young Pass It On." *New York Times*, March 27.

Strauss, William, and Neil Howe. 1991. *Generations: The History of America's Future, 1584–2069*. New York: Morrow.

Sturgis, Patrick, Nick Allum, and Patten Smith. 2008. "An Experiment on the Measurement of Political Knowledge in Surveys." *Public Opinion Quarterly* 72: 90–102.

Sulfaro, Valerie. 1996. "The Role of Ideology and Political Sophistication in the Structure of Foreign Policy Attitudes." *American Politics Quarterly* 24: 303–337.

Tapscott, Don. 2008. *Grown Up Digital: How the Net Generation Is Changing Your World*. New York: McGraw Hill.

Tedin, Kent, and Richard Murray. 1979. "Public Awareness of Congressional Representatives: Recall vs. Recognition." *American Politics Quarterly* 7: 509–517.

Torney-Purta, Judith. 2002. "The School's Role in Developing Civic Engagement: A Study of Adolescents in Twenty-Eight Countries." *Applied Developmental Science* 6: 203–212.

Trippi, Joe. 2004. *The Revolution Will Not Be Televised: Democracy, the Internet, and the Overthrow of Everything*. New York: HarperCollins.

Twenge, Jean. 2006. *Generation Me: Why Today's Young Americans Are More Confident, Assertive, Entitled—and More Miserable Than Ever Before*. New York: Free Press.

Verba, Sidney, Kay Schlozman, and Henry Brady. 1995. *Voice and Equality: Civic Voluntarism in American Politics*. Cambridge: Harvard University Press.

Wattenberg, Martin. 2008. *Is Voting for Young People?* New York: Longman.

Westen, Drew. 2007. *The Political Brain: The Role of Emotion in Deciding the Fate of the Nation*. New York: Public Affairs.

Wilcox, Clyde, Lara Hewitt, and Dee Alsop. 1996. "The Gender Gap in Attitudes Toward the Gulf War." *Journal of Peace Research* 33: 67–82.

Winograd, Morley, and Michael D. Hais. 2008. *Millennial Makeover: My Space, YouTube, and the Future of American Politics*. New Brunswick: Rutgers University Press.

Xenos, Michael, and Kirsten Foot. 2007. "Not Your Father's Internet: The Generation Gap in Online Politics." In *Civic Life Online: Learning How Digital Media Can Engage Youth*. Edited by W. Lance Bennett. Cambridge, MA: MIT Press, 97–118.

Yates, Miranda, and James Youniss. 1998. "Community Service and Political Identity Development in Adolescence." *Journal of Social Issues* 54: 495–512.

Youniss, James, and Peter Levine, eds. 2009. *Engaging Young People in Civic Life*. Nashville: Vanderbilt University Press.

Zaller, John. 1992. *The Nature and Origins of Mass Opinion*. Cambridge: Cambridge University Press.

———. 2003. "A New Standard of News Quality: Burglar Alarms for the Monitorial Citizen." *Political Communication* 20: 109–130.

Zukin, Cliff, Scott Keeter, Molly Andolina, Krista Jenkins, and Michael X. Delli Carpini. 2006. *A New Engagement? Political Participation, Civic Life, and the Changing American Citizen*. Oxford: Oxford University Press.

Index

About the Book

How have the momentous events of the early twenty-first century affected the Millennial Generation's political awareness and action? What accounts for the widespread youth mobilization in support of Barack Obama during the 2008 elections? How do Millennials differ from past generations in the ways that they engage in politics? Addressing these questions, David Rankin goes beyond the impact of political and cultural trends to focus on the role of higher education in connecting political interest, knowledge, and participation.

Rankin draws on rich data spanning the years 2000–2010 to offer unique insights on the Millennial cohort's civic life. He also explores the implications of those insights for political learning. His book is an invaluable contribution to our understanding of the nature and impact of generational differences in the political realm.

David Rankin is professor of political science at the State University of New York, Fredonia. He is coauthor of *Winning the White House, 2008,* and *Winning the White House, 2004,* as well as coeditor of *Transformed by Crisis: The Presidency of George W. Bush and American Politics.*